POWERPRO SERIES

HOW TO BUILD & MODIFY
CHEVROLET
SMALL-BLOCK V-8
CAMSHAFTS &
VALVETRAINS

David Vizard

Foreword by Harvey Crane, Jr.

MBI Publishing Company

Dedication

Whatever I may have achieved in my life has not been without the help and encouragement of my friends, who have not only been willing to, but without question, go the extra mile for me.

To this end, I would like to give special thanks to Roger Helgesen, without whose timely assistance this book would be unlikely to exist, Dr. Marcus Gartner, for always being there to help when needed,

and lastly my partner David Anton, for his seemingly endless patience putting up with preoccupations pertaining to my writing.

Thanks fellas, it's appreciated a great deal.

First published in 1992 by MBI Publishing Company, PO Box 1, 729 Prospect Avenue, Osceola, WI 54020-0001 USA

MBI Publishing Company books are also available at discounts in bulk quantity for industrial or sales-promotional use. For details write to Special Sales Manager at Motorbooks International Wholesalers & Distributors, 729 Prospect Avenue, PO Box 1, Osceola, WI 54020-0001 USA.

Library of Congress Cataloging-in-Publication Data

Vizard, David.
    How to build & modify Chevrolet small-block V-8 camshafts & valvetrains / David Vizard.
        p. cm.—(MBI Publishing Company powerpro series)
        Includes index.
        ISBN 0-87938-595-2
        1. Chevrolet automobile—Motors—Cylinder blocks. 2. Chevrolet automobile—Motors—Modification. I. Title. II. Series.
    TL210.V52   1992
    629.25'04—dc20   92-16732

On the front cover: Top quality camshaft and valvetrain components to help you in building a high-performance small-block Chevrolet V-8 engine. *Tom Rizzo*

Printed in the United States of America

About the Author

Author David Vizard is an experienced engine-builder, road-race and drag-race engine tuner, and engineer, having built high-performance engines for all types of cars from Camaros to dragsters to Chevrolet engines for a Lola T70 sports-prototype racer.

His workshop in California is aquipped with a 1000hp computer-controlled Superflow dyno, flow bench, and full machining and welding facilities, allowing him personally to experiment with and test the products and procedures covered in this book. Unless otherwise noted, all test results, tables, drawings and photographs in this book are by David Vizard.

The author has written more than 3,000 magazine articles and 21 books, including **How to Build & Modify Chevrolet Small-Block V-8 Cylinder Heads** and **How to Build & Modify Chevrolet Small-Block V-8 Pistons, Rods & Crankshafts**, also published in MBI Publishing Company's POWERPRO Series.

Contents

Acknowledgments and Guest Editors

I would like to thank Jack Rhoads of Rhoads Lifters Inc.; Richard and John Iskenderian of Iskenderian Racing Cams; Chase Knight and David Blye of Crane Cams Inc.; Denny Wycoff of Motor Machine & Supply; Bill "Oz" Anderson of Quadrant Scientific; Bob Benton, our Power Pro R&D engine builder; Mike Parry of Race Techniques; Allan Lockheed of Allan Lockheed & Associates; Kevin Gertgen of Performance Trends; Audie Thomas of Audie Technology; Allan Nimmo of Performance Techniques; Carl Schattilly of C&G Porting; Bill Metzger of Laser Cams; Harold Brookshire of Ultradyne Cams; Randy Brezinski of Brezinski Racing; and Brian Crower of Crower Cams.

Harvey J. Crane, Jr.

Born August 17, 1931, in Hallandale, Florida, Harvey J. Crane, Jr., was the eldest son of the family. His father was a skilled self-employed machinist and fabricator.

At the age of seventeen he found employment as a race engine and chassis builder. By the time he'd reached twenty-one, he had established his own cam company.

Some of the many milestones in his career include his election as Society of Automotive Engineers (SAE) member in 1958, and the patent of a roller cam follower design (patent #3,108,580) in 1963. He published the first 0.050in. duration cam lift numbers in 1965 (Catalog #2 Spring Edition, 1965).

In 1967 Harvey produced his first computer cam design on a time-share computer. He used a Teletype terminal through the phone lines located at ComShare Incorporated of Ann Arbor, Michigan.

Always on the search for better quality and accuracy, in 1968 he purchased a numerically controlled grinder with ten millionths inch resolution for manufacturing master cams.

With accurate masters now on hand, Harvey turned his attention to the production aspect of high-quality cams. To this end he conceived and assisted in the design of the Berco cam grinder in 1972. The Crane Corporation also purchased the first production Berco cam grinder.

In 1974 Crane Cams purchased the Universal Camshaft Company of Muskegon, Michigan, the only manufacturer of SAE 8620 steel billet roller cams.

During 1988 Harvey Crane was elected a Fellow of the Society of Automotive Engineers, and two years later he formed a new consulting company —Crane CamDesign Incorporated.

Paul "Scooter" Brothers

With his father being a mechanic, Paul "Scooter" Brothers literally started working on cars and engines as soon as he could walk. At age 15, he took up drag racing at a local level, and to support his hobby he worked as a dealership line-mechanic while in high school and college.

After receiving his associates degree in mechanical engineering, his hobby turned into a profession when he took a position with Racing Head Service (RHS) building stocker cylinder heads and working on cars at races. From 1970-1973, Scooter took a break from RHS to serve as an aircraft engine mechanic aboard a Navy aircraft carrier. When he returned to the cylinder head department, he was responsible for traveling to all National Hot Rod Association (NHRA) national events and produced heads for 60 percent of all class winners in the mid-1970s. It was during these years that Scooter raced his own Super Stocker at both local and national events.

After mastering the production of drag racing valvetrains, Scooter's efforts shifted to round-track racing— particularly in the area of large-inch carbureted short-track engines. From 1984-1989 his engines dominated dirt tracks all over the southeast.

In 1989 Scooter was appointed to his current position as research director of Competition Cams, where he and his team of engineers and technicians are constantly pursuing new technologies to perfect valvetrains for the decades to come. Some of their latest projects include an extensive study of ceramic valvetrain components and the use of a new laser process, called stereo lithography, to more accurately manufacture products.

Scooter is also highly involved in setting directions for the performance industry as a whole. He is a member of SAE. He has also been appointed to the Specialty Equipment Manufacturers' Association (SEMA) technical committee, and is a member of the NHRA sponsor council.

Dimitri "Dema" Elgin

Dema Elgin is a member of SAE. He started his automotive career in 1957, opening Elgin Machine Shop in 1960. This machine shop catered to a wide variety of machining operations, including cam grinding.

In 1985 the cam grinding was split from the rest of the machine shop, which was sold to the employees. This allowed Dema to concentrate his efforts on Elgin Cams.

During 1964 Dema met the legendary automotive engineer Ed Winfield, and began consulting with him on innovative race engine modifications.

Dema's motivation was a strong will to win. With ten years of successful drag racing, followed by fifteen years of Sports Car Club of America (SCCA) racing, he understood not only the needs of the race driver, but also the engine requirements to accomplish the task of winning.

Dema is also a lecturer at DeAnza College in Cupertino, California. This gives him a strong insight as to how best to convey a complex subject in an effective manner.

Some highlights of Dema's career include grinding the roller cams for the 209ci twin turbo Chevy for Indy in 1980. The same year he also ground the cams for the record-setting Ford Probe sports car. For Porsche of America, he designed a variety of cams for SCCA racing. In 1988, two cams Elgin designed were produced for the Buick/Olds Quad 4 engine, one being used for IMSA racing, and the other for the Production HO Quad 4 cars that went into production in 1990.

Foreword

By Harvey J. Crane, Jr.

David Vizard has made an almost life-long study of high-performance engines. Unlike some hot rodders, and even some professional race engine builders, who came up the ranks with less than a formal education, David did it the hard way.

Eight years of engineering college and university-level mechanical engineering took him into the aerospace industry, where he quickly gained a reputation for helping reduce costs of aircraft. Four years in a research laboratory staffed with some of the most highly qualified professors and Ph.D.s in the field taught him much more.

Though he emerged from this laboratory as a highly qualified engineer, there was one attribute he possessed that I feel a person must be born with rather than taught. This is ingenuity or inventiveness. That attribute has allowed David to be near the cutting edge of the technology it requires to get a race car around or down the track faster than the opposition. This has not been limited to the engine department, but also includes the development of suspension, brakes, aerodynamics, and so forth.

As deeply involved in the camshaft and valvetrain analysis and design consulting business as I am, it is refreshing to read David's material. There is a uniqueness in the knowledge contained in this book. Even though it does not cover his full range of information on the subject, it undoubtedly presents far more than other top engine builders are willing to tell you.

If you haven't personally built a Daytona 500 winner yet, then I can assure you that this book will help you achieve that lofty goal.

Harvey J. Crane, Jr.

Introduction

The principal objective of this book is to present the complexities of camshaft and valvetrain function and design in terms as understandable as possible. Amidst the smoke and fumes of hot dyno engines, I pressed brain cells long and hard for an analogy most befitting the subject. The best I could come up with relates to repeatedly packing a small gift in an ever-increasing sized box.

I'm sure you've seen this technique used to heighten anticipation: a huge box, then a smaller one, and so on, down to the gift itself. Well, learning about camshafts is a little like this with one exception—it runs in reverse! What you need to know starts off looking like a small box but as you unwrap it, what's inside proves to be bigger than the original container.

Developing a working knowledge of camshafts initially looks very simple. At some point, however, you'll make a striking revelation that there is much more to learn about camshafts than you originally perceived. After a time you'll reach another plateau, believing you fully understand the subject when, bingo, another box and another set of mental challenges appear.

Each new box holds more challenges than the last until finally, you come to the box that leaves the mind staggering. Nothing short of genius and an honors degree in mathematics will conquer this technological monster, you conclude.

We all reach this point eventually, but don't let it act as a deterrent. With the help of this book you will open many more boxes than without. It is fortunate that to be an *expert cam user*, as opposed to a cam designer, you don't need to run the cranial gray matter too near valve-float conditions. In this book I intend to highlight facts and techniques that will, without a doubt, allow you to build more power into your engine.

In most instances I will differentiate between facts and techniques that help increase power and those necessary to design camshafts. Surprisingly enough, these diverse subjects share a common goal.

To the experts who have picked up this book, I make no apologies for the fact that it starts with the most basic of concepts. Using as much tact as possible, I would like to remind those capable of specing their own camshafts that they had to start somewhere. Even the most successful engine builders among you will no doubt admit that what you've learned certainly didn't happen overnight. Who knows? Wherever you are on the ladder of expertise, possession of this book may well save you both considerable time and money to acquire the needed knowledge.

Judging by some of the early cam designs I have had the misfortune to use, some cam companies could also use a copy. I certainly wish I had had a book like this back in the fifties when I was attempting to screw together my first race engines. But such a book was unlikely to exist then and even today. Why? Because successful race engine builders are a secretive bunch. They keep to themselves any information that may give them a competitive edge (and if it doesn't, they often want to keep that a secret, too!).

A little investigating reveals that most successful engine builders or designers seem to do a lot of reading and listening and very little talking. I'm different than most race engine builders. As a consultant performance engineer I sell "speed secrets" to the highest bidder. In the past this has included race teams and manufacturers, but right now my publisher is the highest bidder.

With this book you will be "buying in" at a level I judge acceptable for someone building their first performance engine. To those who are experienced in this field, I ask your patience. Failing that, I suggest you move directly to the expert section. Wherever you start, expert or novice, I guarantee you will find within these pages information that will make the engines you build more powerful.

Camshaft and Valvetrain Basics

1

A good place to begin our discussion of camshafts is with the basic definition of the Otto four-cycle engine. In 1876, German engineer Nikolaus A. Otto defined not only the four-cycle concept for an internal-combustion engine, but also many of the mathematical formulas that predict a number of its thermodynamic properties. We're going to use this four-cycle concept as our basic building block.

Four-Stroke Theory

First, the four cycles concerned are the intake stroke, the compression stroke, the power stroke, and the exhaust stroke. In drawing A of figure 1-1 we see the piston at the top of the bore, ready to start the induction stroke. At this point the intake valve is about to open. As the crankshaft rotates, the intake valve opens, B, and an intake charge is drawn in. As the piston reaches bottom dead center (BDC) the intake valve closes and the cylinder is now sealed, ready to start the compression stroke, as shown in drawing C. Compression progresses through D until the piston reaches top dead center (TDC) at E. At this point the spark occurs and the power stroke begins.

The fuel-air charge burns, it doesn't explode. This heats up the air causing the pressure to rise, thus forcing the piston down the bore through sequences F to G. At BDC the exhaust valve is about to start opening. When things have progressed to drawing H, exhaust is starting to pass out of the exhaust port. The piston travels up the bore and on its way pushes exhaust out until it reaches TDC at A. The process then starts over again with the next induction stroke.

This all seems simple, and up to this point it is. Yet notice that in this classic Otto Cycle concept, valves open and close at top and bottom dead center. The nearby valve event diagram shows what happens in terms of crankshaft degrees (figure 1-2), and what this looks like when translated into the cam diagram (figure 1-3). Each phase takes precisely 180 degrees, which means both the intake valve and the exhaust valve are opened 180 degrees.

The compression and power stroke occupy a similar amount to each.

Such a cam timing works, but only for low engine speeds. It makes little or no concessions to momentum and resistance of airflow, nor to the forces required to accelerate the mass of the valvetrain itself. Such a concept also shows little regard for acceptable (by modern standards) cylinder filling at anything above about 800rpm, bearing in mind fundamental limitations common to all poppet-valve engine designs. The limitation alluded to here relates to valve area.

Obviously, even the most basic four-cycle design calls for a minimum of two valves per cylinder. Such being the case, neither valve can occupy more than a limited area compared to the piston area. Even under ideal circumstances a small-block Chevy's intake valve area is barely 25 percent of the piston area. If the classic Otto Cycle is

adhered to, rpm doesn't need to increase much before the intrinsic shortcomings of a two-valve design cause the piston demand to outpace the valve's flow capability.

Intake Valve Theory

Let's investigate this situation in a little more detail beginning with the intake valve. If the intake valve doesn't start to open until the piston begins its downward motion, then it becomes desirable to either open the valve rapidly or look at some other solution aimed at achieving adequate valve lift levels early enough during the induction cycle to allow good cylinder filling.

If we look at the piston motion in relation to crankshaft rotation (figure 1-4) at top and bottom dead center we see that a considerable amount of crankshaft rotation occurs for minimal piston motion. With this in mind, let's consider starting the valve opening

Ghost drawing of a Chevrolet small-block V-8 valvetrain.

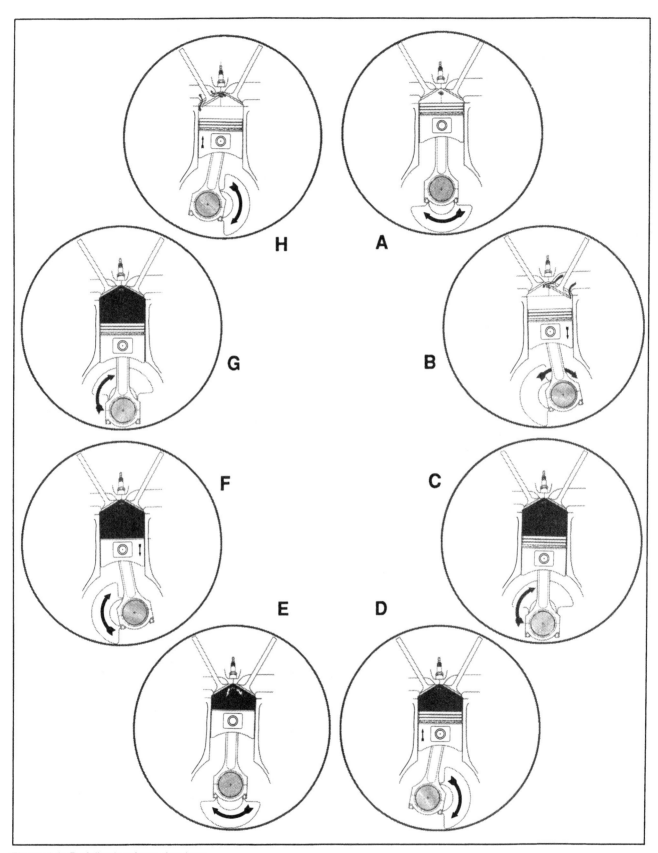

Figure 1-1: *By following these drawings, you can see how the basic Otto four-cycle engine functions.*

sequence *earlier* in the cycle. How does the situation look if intake valve opening starts when the crank is still 20 degrees before TDC?

Let's use a 350 small-block Chevy to illustrate the point.

Calculations show that at 20 degrees before TDC the piston is only 3.9 percent of the cylinder's volume short of the top of the block. In other words, if it was expelling exhaust there would be only 3.9 percent of the expendable volume of exhaust left in the cylinder. (Remember, the piston can't push out what is in the combustion chamber.) By starting the valve opening 20 degrees before TDC the intake period is

extended from 180 to 200 degrees. This represents an increase opening period of over 11 percent for only a 3.9 percent volume trade-off.

The other end of the intake opening cycle can also benefit from such techniques. It follows that if the valve can be beneficially opened earlier, it can also be closed later. We will add delayed closure to the other end of the opening phase. If we hang the intake valve open to 20 degrees after BDC the piston will have started up on its compression stroke. At low rpm it will push some of the intake charge back out. The question is, how much will it push out if the valve is closed 20

degrees late? Again, using the configuration of a 350 Chevy the amount proves to be a minimal 2.1 percent. At this point the intake timing has been stretched from 180 to 220 degrees, representing an increase of 22 percent. Yet at worst, we've lost only 6 percent of the potential displacement usage.

Ignoring all other considerations for the moment, let's see how this works out in practice. If the valves had opened and closed at the TDC points, it would be difficult to fill the cylinder in the first place and to dispose effectively of the exhaust in the second. An engine with 180 degree valve timing has a limit of 1600-1800rpm, assuming everything else is up to snuff. By extending the timing by the 22 percent just discussed, the operating range is moved up to something in excess of 3000rpm thus giving the engine almost double the rpm capability. Since an engine's power is a function of torque and rotational speed, the fact that we've been able to double the rpm means the potential for producing power has followed suit.

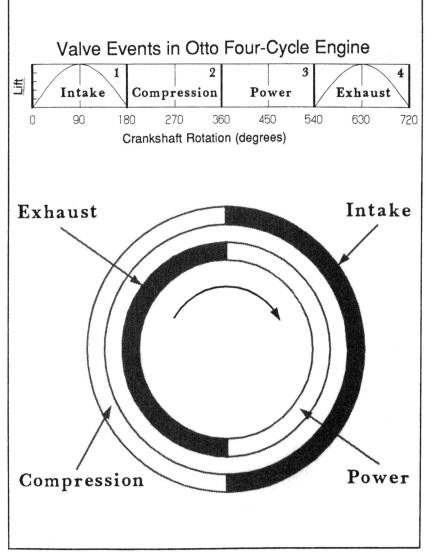

Figures 1-2 and 1-3: *In its most simplistic form, you can see that the intake valve event and the exhaust valve event both occupy 180 degrees, but it's not convenient to draw valve events for cam cards in such a manner, so the form at the top is translated to the circular form below.*

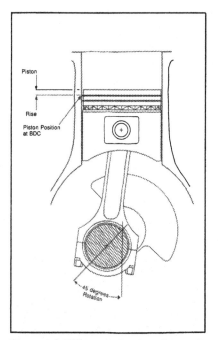

Figure 1-4: *This scale drawing of a small-block Chevy bottom end should give you some idea of the proportions involved when the intake valve closure is delayed. Here the valve closes at 45 degrees after BDC, that represents, in terms of crankshaft angle, 25 percent of the upward stroke. However, because of the rod angularity and the geometry of all the parts concerned, the piston only moves up the bore 10.8 percent of its stroke.*

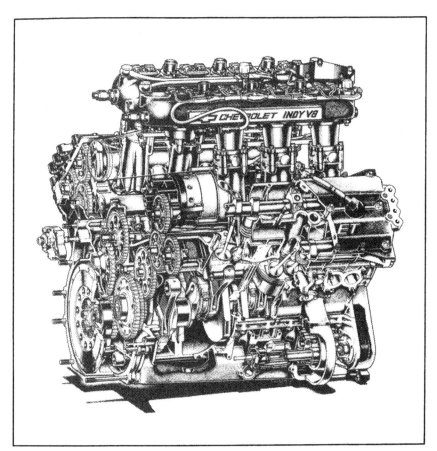

There is little that can match the breathing potential of four valves per cylinder as in this Chevy Ilmor Indy race car engine. Even though the engine and valvetrain look complex, the business of operating the valvetrain via overhead cams is less demanding than for a pushrod motor.

No matter how good your cam technology may be, if the cylinder head doesn't work, the engine won't make horsepower. So, the search for power should always start with a thorough analysis of the cylinder head on the flowbench.

Exhaust Valve Theory

Let's continue our analysis of valve events in terms of the exhaust. If the exhaust valve opens at BDC there will still be a considerable amount of pressure for it to dump. Initially, the exhaust will carry itself out because it is at a higher pressure than the outside environment. Yet as this blow-down is taking place, the piston is going to have to push against a pressure. Of course the momentum of the flywheel will carry the piston around and expel the exhaust, but forcing exhaust out under pressure absorbs energy from the flywheel. The flywheel energy used had to be obtained from the power stroke, and is now being used unnecessarily to expel the exhaust.

Let's add another phase to the Otto four-cycle concept and see where it leads us. This new addition will be a blow-down phase where the exhaust is opened significantly earlier. The sole purpose of this is to vent the cylinder down as close to atmospheric pressure as possible before the piston moves up the bore on the exhaust stroke.

For starters, assume the valve is opened 30 degrees before BDC. By doing this, how much of the power stroke will be lost? In terms of volume, the piston is only shy of sweeping down 4.8 percent of its volume. However, because of rod and crankshaft angles, the amount of power that can be extracted from the gases at the end of the stroke, even at relatively high pressure, is extremely limited. In fact, it's probably within the odd percent or so of extracting all the power possible from the gases. But by opening the exhaust valve 30 degrees before BDC, the cylinder has an opportunity to blow-down to near atmospheric pressure.

Additionally, starting the exhaust opening sequence 30 degrees earlier gives the valve a head start so when the piston has reached BDC, the valve is at appreciably higher lifts and produces a less restrictive exit passage. This earlier opening not only generates a blow-down period to clear the cylinder of the high pressure gas, but also substantially reduces pumping losses on the exhaust stroke.

Exhaust Pollution and Valve Overlap

At the other end of the exhaust cycle, a delayed closure also proves desirable. Closing the valve at TDC means that just short of this point there will be little available flow area.

As a result it will be difficult to expel the last remnants of exhaust. Because of the slow piston motion about TDC, it pays to hold the exhaust valve open past TDC and actually let it invade the induction cycle. At this point the opening and closing of both intake and exhaust have been extended. This means a period exists around TDC at the end of the exhaust stroke and beginning of the intake where both valves are open.

Initially this might look like a counterproductive step because exhaust could go out the intake and pollute the incoming charge. However, irrespective of whether back-flowing occurs or not, exhaust pollution will take place. Remember, the piston does not sweep out the whole volume contained above it as the combustion chamber volume always remains.

The piston will not clear the gases left in the combustion chamber, so if they are to be extracted it must be by some other means. If any pressure exists in the combustion chamber prior to the intake valve opening, there will always be the possibility of exhaust going out the intake, whether the exhaust valve is opened or not. On the other hand, if a low enough exhaust pressure can be produced as the piston approaches TDC, it will reduce intake charge pollution regardless of the fact both valves are open.

The phase when both valves are opened is known as the overlap period and although it initially appears to be a bad thing to do because it may inhibit smooth running of the engine, a minimal amount can actually enhance the engine's idle qualities.

Before going any further, let's take stock of the situation and consider the changes we've wrought so far on the classic Otto four-cycle events. A cam event diagram is a good tool to help simplify the process. Drawing A in figure 1-3 represents the simple 180 degree timing concept as per the basic Otto Cycle. Here, the two rotations of the engine are represented by two circles; the outer circle is the intake and compression, the inner one is the power and exhaust stroke. The additional timing discussed so far allows this cam event diagram to be redrawn to the form shown here (figure 1-5).

What is shown in the drawing is still a pretty tame cam. In reality a hot street cam can invade other phases to the extent shown by this cam event diagram without any sacrifices. The next cam event diagram shows a typical street cam (figure 1-6). You can see from the angular point of view that valve events are beginning to eat substantially into both the power and compression stroke. However, since piston motion in relation to the crank degrees is limited, little has been lost on that score, but much potential has been gained from increased valve opening.

High Speed Operation

So far we've only considered cam timing for relatively low rpm operation. Any time high output is sought, efforts will be directed toward producing or maintaining good torque at high rpm. To achieve this the engine must efficiently inhale and expel gases at high speed. Although it seems a simple enough concept, this is the biggest obstacle you're likely to face in working to achieve high output.

Again, a 350 small-block Chevy will serve as an example. This engine has a piston with an area of some 12.75sq-in. At best, the cylinder head can accommodate an intake valve a little over 2in;

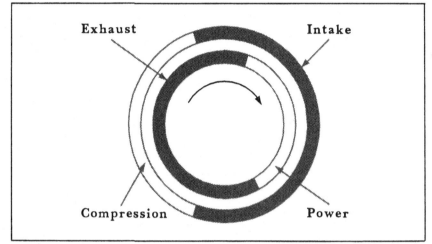

Figure 1-5: With 20-30 degrees more timing at each end of the valve event, here's what our cam event diagram will look like. Again, it appears to be eating into the power and compression strokes quite considerably, but in fact due to the geometry, it is nothing like as severe as it would suggest.

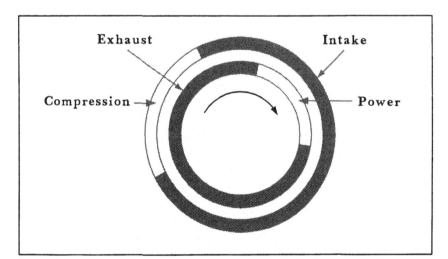

Figure 1-6: In fact, a fairly common street cam, such as the Crane 272 HMV cam, produces the cam timing event shown here. Bearing in mind that the end of the compression stroke goes right around to the beginning of the power section, then we can see that the combined time the valves are open is far greater than the time that both valves are closed.

11

this represents a maximum useful area of only 3.1sq-in. It doesn't take much in the way of math skills to figure out that the valve is less than a quarter of the area of the piston. This means if the intake valve was fully open, the gas speed through the intake valve would be more than four times the piston speed.

In this situation, as rpm increases so the piston will be able to outpace the valve's flow capability. The piston motion at high rpm is rapid enough to reach the bottom of the stroke and still leave a partial vacuum above it due to valve flow restrictions. The easiest way to visualize what is happening is to view it in terms of air pressure. A cylinder can be considered full when the air pressure above the piston at BDC is the same as atmospheric air pressure, for example, 14.7 pounds per square inch (psi), at sea level. Achieving this goal at low rpm is no problem because sufficient time exists for the event to occur to its fullest extent.

At high rpm it is an entirely different ballgame. In an engine revving at 6000rpm the piston travels up and down the bore 100 times a second. This means the downward motion of the induction stroke takes up only 5 thousandths of a second (5 milliseconds). If a 350 small-block Chevy is to completely fill its cylinders it has to move, in that time, 3.3 thousandths of an ounce (0.0033oz) of air from the intake port into the cylinder. The only force available to drive this air into the cylinder is the pressure difference between the port side and cylinder side of the valve.

Air will only flow from a high-pressure region to a low-pressure region if no other forces prevail. A pressure differential is actually needed to cause air to flow, yet the bigger the pressure differential existing at the time of the valve closure, the less the cylinder is filled.

Obviously, air needs to flow into the cylinder as easily as possible so as to require a minimum pressure differential across the valve. Unfortunately at the kind of rpm required for high output, we find that even when the piston reaches BDC a fair amount of pressure differential still exists. So the piston has arrived at the bottom of its stroke and the cylinder may, depending on how efficient the cylinder head is, be only three-quarters full. If the intake valve was closed at this point the best we can hope for is an output equal to only six of our eight cylinders, that is, three-quarters of its potential.

Next, we'll consider what could happen by deliberately hanging the intake valve open a lot longer. Right now our example is 25 percent shy of filling its cylinders. By holding the intake valve open longer, air will continue to flow in because the cylinder is still at a lower pressure. Of course by extending the opening period, two things will begin to fill the available volume; air from the port and the piston moving up the bore.

By holding the valve open until say, 50 degrees after BDC, the piston will have taken up 13.3 percent of the available space while the air will have had the opportunity to take up the difference of 11.7 percent. By holding the valve open we're giving the air a chance to better fill the cylinder.

Yet one more aspect is working for us. At 6000rpm the piston reached a speed down the bore of 62mph. Now remember, if the air has no resistance to flow it is going to reach over four times that speed at the valve. This means that unrestricted it will have reached 258mph. Because valves are not 100 percent efficient some flow and velocity will be lost, nonetheless, the incoming air can well reach a sizable proportion of that velocity.

Ram Charging

The mass of the air traveling at high speed now has momentum so not only will the air equalize the pressure in the cylinder, but also its momentum can actually cause the pressure in the cylinder to rise above that in the port. In other words, to an extent, it has ram charged the cylinder. This is an asset that would be lost if valve closure occurred at BDC. The amount of ram charging achieved is highly variable and because of other factors, sooner or later rising rpm will outpace it. Nonetheless, in developing the right cam timing this effect can enhance output over a significant portion of the rpm range.

Filling the partial vacuum and ram charging totally justify a delayed closure of the intake valve. Other factors affecting how well a cylinder can be filled are related to shock waves in the intake and exhaust system. Although we may touch on them within these pages, they are a subject for yet another book.

Valve Lift

The last point I want to cover is the necessity to get the valve clear of the valve seat as fast as possible. The reason is because of a valve's obvious low-lift flow limitations.

Mechanically, opening a valve instantaneously is impossible. Though immediate opening is not necessary, maximum outputs from a small-block Chevy require valve opening rates far faster than most mechanical restraints will allow. The way to compensate for this is to start the valve earlier in its opening phase and close it later so that when the induction or exhaust stroke does commence, the valve is at a higher lift.

If your car has to double up as a weekend warrior as well as transport to work, remember you spend more time driving it to work than racing it, and your cam selection should reflect that.

This reason alone justifies initiating early intake valve opening and late exhaust valve closing when the piston is around the TDC mark. As we've already discussed, this phase constitutes the overlap period.

Although this period has special significance as far as an engine's breathing ability is concerned, it is a subject for in-depth treatment in a later chapter. The aspect to consider here is the fact that because a very limited pressure is available to initiate flow into the cylinder, early opening of the intake is important—especially in an engine having limited valve area such as the small-block Chevrolet.

Cam Terminology

The cam card discussed earlier was the first step toward understanding some of the necessary cam jargon. But in this instance it was almost like putting the cart before the horse. Now that you understand what a camshaft must produce in the way of valve events, let's look at the lobe and some of the common terminology used to describe its attributes.

Figure 7 points out the main features of a cam profile. Arrow 1 refers to the duration period of the cam. This is the amount, in crankshaft degrees, that the cam holds the valve open. It is always expressed in crankshaft degrees rather than cam degrees. Since the cam rotates at half the engine speed, the angle the cam turns through is only half that of the crankshaft. For instance, if we have a 240 degree period cam, the valves are opened for 240 degrees of crankshaft rotation though the cam only turns 120 degrees during this time, the completion of the four cycles of course taking a total of 720 crank degrees.

The ₵ symbol refers to the lobe centerline. This is the mid position between the point at which the valve starts to open and the point at which the cam returns the valve to the seat. For most practical purposes we can assume this is also the full lift point. Area 2 is known as the tappet or clearance ramp. Because of the need to cater for expansion of the engine due to heat and adjustment for mechanical tolerances, it is necessary to have a gentle opening ramp that simply takes up the clearance between the cam follower, push rod, rocker, and valve. This portion of the rise on the cam is designed to minimize noise.

Call out 6 represents the cam lift and is the amount that the cam lobe rises

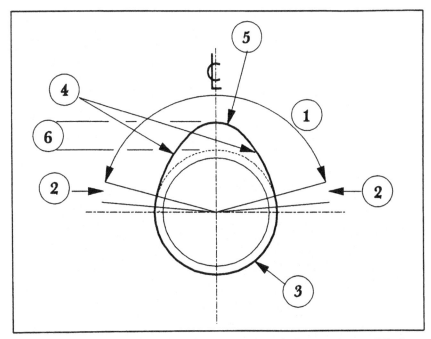

Figure 1-7: *Number 1 is a valve opening duration shown here in cam degrees but always quoted in crankshaft degrees.* Number 2 is the tappet ramp, 3 the base circle, 4 the cam lobe flanks, 5 the cam nose, and 6 the cam lift.

above 3, the base circle. Number 5 is the nose of the lobe. It is important with flat tappet cams that the instantaneous nose radius does not get too small. The tighter the radius gets, the higher the surface stresses between the follower and lobe become. This can wipe out both the cam nose and the follower.

Call out 4 indicates the flank, and to a large degree this is where all the action takes place. Approaching the optimal shape here can pay big dividends in terms of engine output.

Modern Cam Production
Cam production has moved a long way since the 1950s. At that time it took 100 hours of mathematics, plus 40 to 50 hours of machining just to come up with a workable master. These days, things are a little different.

After the basic cam characteristics have been decided on, these parameters are passed on to the profile designer, who, using an advanced profile dynamics program, will produce the figures for the master profile.

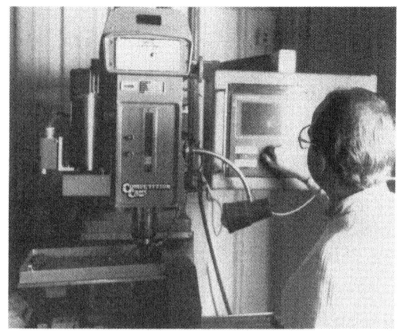

From here, the figures are passed on to a programmable precision milling machine, which machines the master cam.

Each profile is ground and then sparked out to allow the effect of any flexure in cam or machine to be nullified.

The master cam records the basic details, along with a profile number, which allows precise details of the cam form to be referenced back to the original design program.

Depending upon the type of cam, it can be heat-treated, parkerized, or given some other kind of surface treatment immediately after grinding.

The normal procedure is to polish the cam bearing journals at this stage.

Once the cam has been ground, it is checked on the type of equipment shown here. The probe and an angular displacement encoder produce electrical signals that are fed into the computer, which then analyzes the grinding accuracy of the cam.

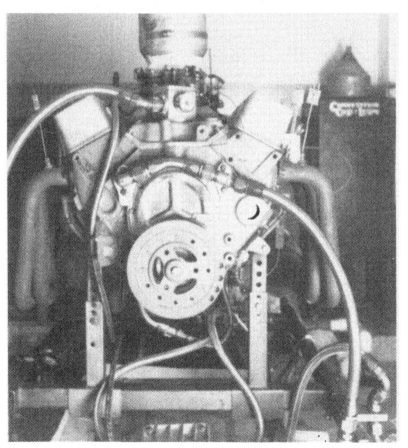

Once the cam passes this test, it's time to install it in an engine for dyno testing. Either Competition Cams runs the cam in one of their own engines, or passes it along to the engine designer to test.

Lobe Centerline Angles and Cam Advance

2

A 455hp race engine? No. This test engine was totally streetable because the cam was matched to the requirements of the special induction system, cylinder head, and exhaust. The engine's powerband started at a little over 1000rpm.

The intake manifold used can make a huge difference to the optimum cam specification required for a particular powerband.

Many automotive magazines have done cam duration features to death but have largely ignored other aspects, such as when to open and close the valves. Granted, in the quest for performance it is necessary to understand the hows and whys of duration. Fortunately, the concept of extending valve opening periods for high-rpm engines is not difficult to grasp. Yet, you don't need to look through many functional cam specifications to realize there must be more to it than simply picking a duration figure and grinding it on the cam.

Assuming you understand from chapter 1 the virtues of extended timing, then it would seem necessary only to arrive at some balance between early opening and late closing and bingo, a universally workable cam design. Such an idea may at first sound halfway reasonable. If so, how come cam timing figures look so different from engine to engine? And why is it that many top engine builders have cams specially brewed rather than using off-the-shelf ones? Worse yet, why is it that when you manage to corner one of these specially made cams it doesn't seem to perform that outstandingly in your motor?

Taken at face value, cam timing figures seem to have no attached logic. This points toward the theory that cam timing is a black art known only by a select few. Seemingly, this is what some cam manufacturers would like you to believe. Well, starting right here the lid is coming off that concept . . . so here goes!

Number Crunching

Jumping in with both feet, let's look at the cam numbers in figure 2-1. First, cam A has a 280 degree profile on both intake and exhaust and the timing figures are 30-70-70-30. That is, the intake opens 30 degrees before TDC and closes 70 degrees after BDC. The exhaust opens 70 degrees before BDC and closes 30 degrees after TDC. These numbers are nice and easy to remember and seem to have a certain symmetry to them. You may think it is a bit of a coincidence that this cam works because of the simplicity of the numbers. Such figures will produce a functional cam but whether it is optimal for the engine is questionable, as we shall see later.

On cam B, the profile is 290/290. Incidentally, profiles don't have to be the same on intake and exhaust, but assuming so simplifies explanation. Good results can be obtained with event timing of 39-71-79-31. There seems to be no apparent symmetry to the numbers; so how were they arrived at? Did they come out of thin air? Such numbers appear to be quite arbitrary.

Unfortunately the main issue here—cam timing—is clouded by an over-abundance of numbers. Therefore, it is important to find a means of simplifying the numerical description of a cam's attributes, if you will, a common denominator. Achieving this will make it easier to relate changes in cam specification in a cause-and-effect situation. At first this may appear difficult, but grasping the basics is a piece of cake. The key is that the timing numbers are the product of a few simple variables.

Lobe Centerline Angles (LCAs)

Undoubtedly the most effective tool for decoding a set of cam timing numbers into more understandable terms is the lobe centerline angle (LCA) of the cam. This concept is best appreciated in two easy steps.

First, the definition of the lobe centerline is shown in figure 2-2. If this were a 280 degree (crank) cam profile, the lobe centerline would be 140 crank degrees from the point the cam begins to open the valve. Basically pretty logical stuff. Going one step further, the lobe centerline angle as shown in figure 2-3 is the angle between the intake and exhaust lobes of one cylinder. It is, for reasons that will become apparent later, typically quoted in camshaft degrees rather than crank degrees. (Crank degrees, remember, are twice as large because of the necessary 2:1 gearing between crank and cam.)

To see where we stand with the LCA, let's go back and build an example based on cam A mentioned earlier. This particular cam is a 280/280 specification, which means the centerline of either lobe is at 140 degrees from the point of opening or closing. Using the 30-70-70-30 figures for cam A we see that if the intake opens 30 degrees before TDC (BTDC), then full lift must

occur 110 degrees after TDC (ATDC) on the induction stroke. The proof is that 30 BTDC + 110 ATDC = 140, or half the cam lobe duration figure.

Analyzing the exhaust in the same manner you can see that if the exhaust closes 30 degrees ATDC, then it was at full lift 110 degrees BTDC on the exhaust stroke. This means that the

crankshaft degrees between these two full-lift points were 220, 110 + 110.

Since crankshaft degrees are double cam degrees, the angle turned by the cam is 110 degrees. This is the lobe centerline angle.

Now for an important point: The figures also show the LCA is the same number as the full-lift angle that either

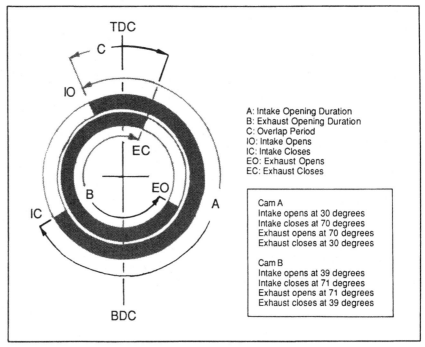

A: Intake Opening Duration
B: Exhaust Opening Duration
C: Overlap Period
IO: Intake Opens
IC: Intake Closes
EO: Exhaust Opens
EC: Exhaust Closes

Cam A
Intake opens at 30 degrees
Intake closes at 70 degrees
Exhaust opens at 70 degrees
Exhaust closes at 30 degrees

Cam B
Intake opens at 39 degrees
Intake closes at 71 degrees
Exhaust opens at 71 degrees
Exhaust closes at 39 degrees

Figure 2-1: *This diagram is the starting point toward understanding how an engine's specification alters the optimum cam timing required.*

Proof that the universal cam doesn't exist comes from many quarters. Dyno testing showed that even the rockers affect the cam's optimum timing.

17

valve reaches before or after TDC, "before" being the exhaust and "after" being the intake.

At this point we need only concern ourselves with the full-lift position of the intake valve. Our example cam is then ground on 110 degree LCA and reaches full lift 110 degrees after TDC on #1 intake. In this instance we have "split" the overlap and can say the cam is timed in "straight up." In other words, the cam is neither advanced nor retarded. To drive the point home, we can say if the full-lift position on #1 intake is the same as the LCA, no advance or retard exists. If the cam was on a 105 degree LCA and it reached full lift at 105 degrees after TDC, it would still be straight up. We have now created a datum point from which to reference the cam position.

If the valve events happen *sooner* in relation to crank rotation, that is if the intake opens more degrees *before* TDC and closes sooner after BDC, then the cam is said to be advanced. The opposite is true for a cam that is retarded. Using this system, the relative position of a cam can be quoted once the LCA is known.

Going back to the 110 degree LCA, 280 degree profile cam, if advanced 4 degrees—that is, the intake opens 4 degrees sooner and the exhaust closes 4 degrees sooner during overlap—then the cam will be timed in to reach full lift 106 degrees ATDC on #1 intake. Advancing the cam reduces the number of degrees to full lift after TDC. By retarding the cam 4 degrees, the number increases since full lift is reached later. In this instance, full lift would be at 114 degrees ATDC.

For the sake of understanding, let's take a few more examples. Assume a cam of 112 degrees LCA is timed in to give full lift at 109 degrees ATDC— $112 - 109 = 3$—so the cam is 3 degrees advanced. A cam with 102 degree LCA timed in to 98 degrees to full lift on #1 intake would be 4 degrees advanced. A cam on 108 degrees timed in to 111 degrees would be $108 - 111 = -3$ degrees retarded.

Subtracting the number of degrees ATDC to full lift from the LCA gives the advance if the answer is positive and retarded if it's negative. Thus, it is easy to see the advantage of quoting the LCA in cam degrees rather than crank degrees. Doing so makes it easy to determine whether a cam is advanced or retarded in the engine.

![Figure 2-2 diagram showing Lobe Centerline, curves A and B, Finishes Closing, and Opening Starts]

Figure 2-2: *In essence the definition of the lobe centerline is quite self-explanatory. It is half the angle between the opening and closing point.*

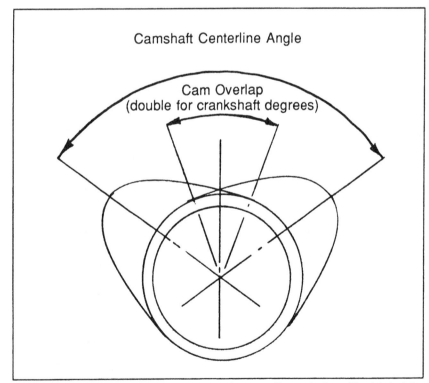

Figure 2-3: *The cam's centerline angle is the term used to define the angle in cam degrees (as opposed to crank degrees) between the centerline of the intake lobe and the centerline of the exhaust lobe.*

Calculating LCA

Not all cam grinders quote cam LCAs, so you will need to be able to figure it out for yourself from the cam timing figures.

To show how, we will use cam B discussed earlier which had a quoted timing of 39-71-79-31.

The first step is to calculate the lobe centerline of both the intake and exhaust profile. To do this we add the degrees before and after TDC, plus 180, and divide the result by 2.

For instance, our intake figure would be $39 + 71 + 180 = 290$, divided by 2, equals 145. For the exhaust it would be $79 + 31 + 180 = 290$, divided by 2, equals 145. These two figures represent the number of crank degrees turned for the cam to reach full lift from the point at which it began to open a valve.

Working only with the intake for the moment, the next step is to subtract from the half-duration figure the degrees the intake opens BTDC. In this example, it will be $145 - 39 = 106$ degrees. This has established that the intake valve reaches full lift 106 degrees ATDC.

The same exercise should now be done with the exhaust. Here the objective is to find how far away from the crank TDC is when the exhaust valve is at full lift. We find that number by subtracting 31 from 145, which equals 114. If the exhaust duration had been longer or shorter, the 145 figure would be something different. The answer of 114 is the number of degrees at which the crank is from TDC when the exhaust valve reaches full lift.

To get the LCA from these figures add them together, $114 + 106 = 220$, then divide by 2. The answer is 110, which is the cam's LCA in cam degrees.

With what has been covered so far you can determine the cam advance by subtracting the angle to full lift (cam centerline angle) from the LCA: $110 - 106 = 4$. So the cam is timed in 4 degrees advanced.

If this all makes sense, then you've already taken a big step toward removing the mystique of cam timing. From now on, you can meaningfully analyze the numerics of cam events other than simple duration. The next step is to understand the significance of the LCA, advance numbers, and how these affect the power output. To do so, we need to consider the whys and wherefores of valve overlap.

Valve Overlap

Overlap is a valve event that combines intake and exhaust opening and carries with it mixed blessings. Get it right and the payoff is big, but get it wrong and the price will be an engine that does not perform adequately. If it sounds like overlap can be trouble, it can, so it is necessary to understand exactly what effects it can have on an engine.

First, let's establish what overlap is. It is the period when both intake and exhaust valves are opened together; when the exhaust valve is closing at the end of its exhaust stroke and the intake is beginning to open prior to the intake stroke occurring. From the point of view of dynamics, it's not possible to move anything from one point to another instantly so the ex-

Built in my shop, this bracket-race 350 used a roller cam that barely fell into the race category, but because it complemented the engine's specification, the engine could reach a reliable 525hp without exorbitantly expensive bottom-end parts to hold it together.

So you can visualize the amount of valve lift that occurs, here is the position of the valve at TDC during the overlap period on a typical 280 degree street hydraulic cam.

haust valve can't be closed instantly at TDC, nor can the intake be opened instantly.

Even if we could open and close valves instantly, it is questionable whether it would be desirable to do so because overlap is not only a dynamic necessity for the valvetrain, but also a potential means of improving engine performance.

Since the intake valve is the most restrictive component within the induction system, any attempts to rectify this problem should pay off handsomely. The sole purpose of installing larger valves in a cylinder head is to improve airflow. However, a closed valve produces zero airflow and one marginally off the seat is barely any better.

Commencing intake valve opening prior to the start of the induction stroke gives the valve a head start on the ensuing demand for air it is expected to handle. Bearing in mind that even the biggest intake introduced in a small-block Chevy head is incapable of satisfying the flow requirements of a high-output engine, the higher it is lifted at any point in the induction stroke, the better.

For a valve-limited engine such as the small-block Chevy, the most important part of the induction stroke is the first half of the piston's journey down the bore. A maximum-density air column traveling into the cylinder at high speed will pay dividends by inertially ramming the cylinder later on in the cycle. A typical small-block Chevy race cam will open the intake valve some 240 thousandths (0.240in) at TDC. In other words, before the piston has begun to move down the bore the valve is already near halfway open. This proves to be beneficial to subsequent cylinder filling.

So much for the positive aspect of early intake valve opening. Now for the negative. To close the exhaust valve at TDC is impractical because the tail-end gases of the exhaust stroke won't have enough area to freely pass out. This means delayed closure of the exhaust valve and as a result it must be open at a time when the piston begins to move down the bore. That is, the exhaust valve closes during the initial part of the induction stroke.

At TDC a typical race setup may have the exhaust valve between 0.025–0.050in less lift than the intake. This means it is still an appreciable way off the seat and poses the question as to what is stopping the exhaust going out the intake valve. During low-rpm operation the answer is absolutely nothing. Therein lies the penalty of large overlap figures.

A race cam is a good example to illustrate the situation. If engine rpm is low, then as the intake valve opens exhaust will not only pass out the exhaust valve but also the intake. This will contaminate the incoming charge. Additionally, low rpm means low exhaust speed so piston motion down the bore will also draw exhaust into the cylinder from both the exhaust and the contaminated intake. This characteristic makes for the rough low-speed running associated with race cams.

Indeed, a race cam can cause the engine to completely sign off when given full throttle if rpm is too low. As rpm increases, the advantages of overlap are realized. As the speed of the outgoing exhaust increases, there is less tendency for motion to stop and reverse during the overlap period, cutting intake charge contamination.

As rpm continues to rise, the exhaust acquires sufficient velocity in the exhaust port and pipe to continue motion in the proper direction even though the piston may have started down the bore on the intake stroke.

At this point exhaust velocity is high enough to start creating a vacuum in the combustion chamber. In essence, it is now acting as a suction pump (see figure 2-4) that starts pulling the intake charge into the combustion chamber even before the piston has actually begun to go down the bore.

We have created, if you will, an exhaust-powered gas piston that operates on the induction system prior to the real piston starting its induction cycle. Initially it must seem difficult to imagine how a slug of gas can operate as an auxiliary piston initiating early induction. Yet there are ways of verifying that this is occurring. One way requires some expensive equipment

Figure 2-4: *The uppermost drawing depicts the exhaust gasses rushing out of the cylinder, down the exhaust pipe toward the end of the exhaust stroke. In essence what happens is that the mass of the gas in the pipe acts as a slug in very much the same way as the piston does in the lower drawing. Its sheer velocity causes it to draw much of the remaining exhaust out of the cylinder. If the valve closes before the cylinder can return to normal atmospheric pressure, then the only way for the chamber to reestablish its pressure is via charge drawn from the intake valve. It is by this means that combustion chamber scavenging and volumetric efficiencies over 100 percent are achieved.*

and involves monitoring pressures in the induction, exhaust, and cylinder during a typical engine cycle to see if the exhaust-intake pressures generated fall in line with what we suppose is happening. Such measurements can give near positive proof of events, but a simpler way to test our theory exists.

This entails a look at the effect nitrous oxide has on the power curve of a big-cammed engine. Nitrous oxide injection is a means of injecting a chemical containing a lot of oxygen into the engine together with the required additional fuel. In other words, a large portion of exhaust charge is being injected in liquid form. This increased charge is achieved irrespective of rpm since both nitrous and fuel enter the cylinder largely in liquid form, thus taking up minimal room. Though the intake volume hasn't increased, the presence of the nitrous does produce copious quantities of extra exhaust.

If the theory is correct, injecting nitrous oxide into a cylinder should create the exhaust output of an equivalent noninjected engine at a much higher rpm. This should remove any "camminess" from the engine. The theory is firmly born out in practice; an engine that may be off the cam at 3000rpm and just about ready to fall flat on its face will run strongly when nitrous oxide is injected. This is because the increased exhaust volume has generated greater exhaust port velocity. The net result is that the combustion chamber is scavenged and the intake charge continues to travel in the right direction instead of suffering a flow reversal.

Varying Overlap

Enough has been said about overlap to clarify the major consequences of varying it. Too much overlap kills low-end output, but is necessary for top-end horsepower. Too little overlap will cut top-end horsepower but will make the engine drivable. The bottom line is choosing overlap to suit the circumstances for which the engine will be used. Obviously, good traffic manners aren't needed if the engine spends all its time on a racetrack. By the same token, if an engine is to pull an automatic transmission or drive in heavy traffic, then it needs to have good low-end output. This means minimizing overlap.

Referring back to the lobe centerline angle, we can see that the tighter this is (the smaller the number), the more

overlap a cam will have in relation to its duration. The wider the LCA is, the less overlap it will have. For a given cam duration, choosing the right LCA will give the most functional balance between overlap and the opening period of each valve.

To sum up the basic pros and cons of varying overlap, when overlap is increased, power output can increase but the cam becomes less civilized. The vacuum at idle and cruise is decreased and there is a tendency to narrow the power band of the engine.

Along with this, the fuel consumption of the engine at less than its optimum rpm range is reduced which can significantly affect city mileage. All these factors work against big overlap numbers for a street cam. On the other hand, reducing overlap improves idle quality, fuel consumption, and idle and cruise vacuum, and widens the power band of the engine. To sum up, the cam is more civilized. The penalty paid for such civility, however, is that the engine makes less total torque and horsepower.

Another important factor in valve overlap is that it's possible to match timing numbers against engine characteristics produced. Two angular dimensions on a cam totally control the overlap period: duration and the lobe centerline angle. If the LCA is fixed, then extending the duration of intake and exhaust by 4 degrees results in 4 degrees more overlap. This is because 2 degrees of extended timing will have

gone on either end of the cam's opening and closing phase. Anytime the period of both lobes is extended, overlap increases by the same amount. Conversely, if the LCA is changed by 4 degrees it will alter overlap by 8 degrees.

Let's look at cam B again. When on 110 degree LCA with 4 degrees of advance, its timing is 39-71-79-31. The overlap this generates is $39 + 31 = 70$ degrees. These same two lobe profiles put on a camshaft at 106 degrees LCA would produce the timing of 43-67-75-35 giving an overlap of 78 degrees, an increase of 8 degrees overlap.

By holding duration constant, a change in LCA, even by a small amount, affects the cam's manners quite substantially because of its quadruple effect on overlap. An extreme example here will make the point. Consider a race profile that opens the valves for a period of 300 degrees. Normally we would assume that such a profile is far too radical for the street, and rightly so. To make maximum horsepower in say, a 350, the cam needs to be ground on 106 degree LCA. With 300 degrees on 106 degree LCA the cam comes in with a bang at about 3000rpm. Under this and it's a dead player. Given full throttle it will all but die on you. The cam then is almost unusable on the street.

So, what happens if it is now ground on 114 degree LCA? Overlap, which is the big bugaboo for flexibility and low-end power, is reduced from 82 to 70 degrees. Such a change on a typical

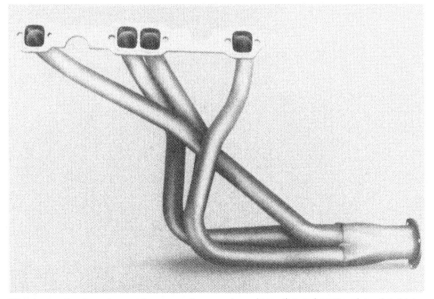

The type of exhaust used in an engine has a distinct effect on when and for *how long the exhaust valve should be opened.*

small-block Chevy will mean the engine can generate 2–4in more vacuum at idle and cruise, it will idle much smoother, it will come on the cam at least 750 and maybe 1000rpm sooner, and ultimately it will fall off the cam at the top end of the rpm range a little farther up than the tighter LCA cam did—all positive features of a wide LCA cam. The negative side is that spreading the LCA will reduce torque everywhere in the rev range, which means the price for being more civilized is reduced peak torque and horsepower.

You may be questioning the sanity of spreading the LCA if the penalty paid is reduced torque and horsepower. This need not be the case, however. Let's go one step further and look at the situation in terms of intake closure and exhaust opening. Using the same cam as an example, let's take the overlap period of our 114 degree LCA cam but close the intake after BDC and open the exhaust before BDC at the same points as for the 106 degree LCA cam. The outcome is a shorter duration for both intake and exhaust. Assuming the cam is timed in straight up, that is with no advance or retard, then changing the closure of the intake and exhaust alters timing from 36-84-84-36 to 36-76-76-36.

We now have the opening figures of the 114 degree LCA cam with the closing figures of the 106, producing a cam with some 292 degrees duration and an LCA angle of 110 degrees. So, delaying exhaust opening and advancing intake valve closure around BDC by 8 degrees has caused our LCA to tighten by 4, but the overlap area remains unaltered. As a result our new cam profile will idle, cruise, and deliver just a little more mileage and flexibility than the 300 degree cam on 114 LCA.

What, then, are the advantages of a 300 degree cam on 114 degrees LCA rather than a 292 degree cam on 110 degrees LCA? Simple. The advantage of the longer cam on 114 LCA is that its high-rpm output, say above 5000rpm, will likely be better. In other words, peak horsepower will move up as will the rpm it occurs at.

However, the 292 degree cam will produce more lower down. This is because it holds the gas pressure longer on the power stroke (due to later opening) and traps the intake charge sooner on the compression stroke (due to earlier closing). When the engine does come "on the cam," torque output will be better for the 292x110 LCA cam. The engine may make more torque, but less horsepower.

The requirement for a road cam calls for as much flexibility as possible along with whatever additional power output can be achieved without sacrificing the former. This means overlap figures need to be held as small as possible while duration figures are extended as far as possible. The result will be maximum top-end horsepower along with the necessary characteristics for a road cam.

In sum, for a street cam, which must by necessity strike many compromises, the use of wider LCAs produces more acceptable results than tight ones. Wider LCAs make it possible to use longer period cams to help out the top-end power output without necessarily penalizing drivability or decreasing low-end power.

For a race engine, no such compromises exist. A race engine is required to produce as much torque and horsepower as possible. Period!

Cam Timing Variables

3

The previous chapter started with the suggestion that striking a balance between early opening and late closing of a valve would produce a universally functional cam. Having read that chapter, the impracticalities of such a concept should be apparent. The function of this chapter is to act as a cam timing primer so that the basics are entrenched in your mind by the time dyno tests are discussed. By the time you reach the end of this chapter it shouldn't be too difficult, even for a novice, to see how the structure of cam timing falls into place.

Up to this point we've learned how engine characteristics are largely dictated by duration and overlap. In turn, the overlap is governed by the cam's lobe centerline angle, or LCA. This angular dimension proves to be the single most important attribute of a small-block Chevrolet cam. By manipulating the lobe centerline angle and, to a lesser extent, the duration, we can impart to the engine any characteristics we desire. In this chapter we will investigate how this is done along with the basic governing logic.

Internal Influences

Make no bones about it, the vagaries of cam timing are not easy to explain. Unless proven otherwise, it is not unreasonable for a novice to assume a good small-block Chevy cam will be good in *any* small-block Chevy. First, we need to effectively sow the seeds of doubt in your mind as to why this should not be and to do that, let's take two distinct configurations of small-blocks.

First, a special with a 4.155in bore and 3.250in stroke. This makes a 350ci engine but it is a short-stroke, big-bore unit compared with a stock configuration. Engine number two, on the other hand, has a 3.767in bore and 3.480in stroke as per a stock 305.

These two extremes may as well be engines from a different manufacturer. Wouldn't you think with all the variables involved it would be too much of a coincidence that they would need identical cams for optimal results? The answer is—both in theory and prac-

tice—unequivocally yes. Especially if we add to the bore and stroke differences the fact that one of these engines could be a big-valved, small-chambered engine. The other could be a small-valved, big-chambered unit. One could have headers tuned for high-rpm output, the other not. The differences go on. In fact, the only thing these two engines have in common is they both share the same name.

To see how changes in engine specification demand an appropriate change in cam spec, let's begin with a hypothetical single-pattern flat-tappet cam that gives optimum timing in a hot street engine of 350ci displacement. Assume the cam has 280 degrees of duration and the engine has an efficient high-flow intake and exhaust plus well-ported heads. Under these conditions we can expect a 280 degree cam

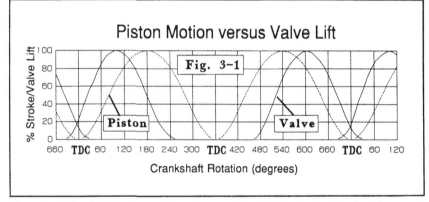

Figure 3-1: *The first step toward visualizing how piston and valve positions relate as an engine goes through its cycle is shown in this graph. From this you can see that when the piston reaches BDC the valve is typically still some 50 percent of its full lift value. On this chart the valve's motion in relation to the piston looks like it's well suited to the engine. However, what is of greater concern is the velocity of the piston in relation to the valve lift.*

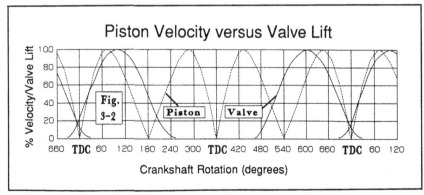

Figure 3-2: *Typically in a small-block Chevy the piston reaches maximum velocity around 74-76 degrees down the bore, yet the valve doesn't reach full lift until typically 102-110 degrees, so you can see that essentially the valve action that we are able to put into most small-block Chevys does not accelerate the valve fast enough to put full lift at peak piston demand.*

23

to produce maximum torque and horsepower when ground on 108 degree LCA and timed in at 4 degrees advance.

The first change we will make to our optimally cammed 350 is to shorten up the stroke and make the engine a 302.

Now where do we stand with the cam? What we've done is reduce the air demand per induction cycle. This means the engine has more breathing ability per cubic inch than before which, in turn, gives the engine a higher rpm potential. Also, because of the shorter stroke, gas speeds at the end of each stroke are slower at any given rpm.

The bottom line is the cam now has too tight an LCA. It doesn't need either valve open as much at TDC as before. On a 302, maximum output and the best torque curve would be produced with the LCA at about 110–111 degrees.

Conversely, if the bottom end under the same cylinder heads sported 400ci, the reverse situation would exist. A greater air demand is put on the cylinder heads and the need to have the valves open more in the earlier stages of the induction cycle is beneficial to help fill those bigger cylinders. Engine rpm potential will decrease because it now has a lesser airflow per cubic inch ratio. For the best torque and horsepower output from a 400ci motor a 104–105 degree LCA cam would be needed. Thus, by manipulating just one variable, in this case the stroke, the cam required significant changes in characteristics.

LCA Ground Rules

At this point, some ground rules relating to principal components and their effect on required cam timing would be useful. We'll start with the lobe centerline angle. To sum up the displacement examples we can say that for a given set of heads, anytime displacement is increased, the cam's LCA needs to be reduced for optimal output. Anytime displacement is decreased, the LCA needs to be increased.

The effect of cylinder heads is quite complex because an ill-conceived cylinder head design may need an off-the-wall cam. Assuming an effectively modified cylinder head, we find that as breathing efficiency increases, especially in the lower lift ranges, the required LCA spreads. If flow capability is reduced by smaller or less efficient valves, the LCA needs to be made narrower or as it's often termed, "tightened."

Stroke, of course, alters capacity but it does have its own effect on cam timing. A long-stroke engine generally needs a tighter LCA than a short-stroke engine. The reason becomes clear if we move through the logic one step at a time. As stroke length increases, then for a given capacity the bore size must decrease. Or, if the original bore size is retained, the capacity increases.

If the stroke length is increased and bore size reduced thus holding displacement constant, head breathing

Small-block Chevy engines with this kind of open chamber require about 12 degrees more opening duration to get the same power as the closed chamber heads. Unfortunately, with the longer-period cam they do not match the mid- and low-end output of a shorter-cammed, superior-headed engine.

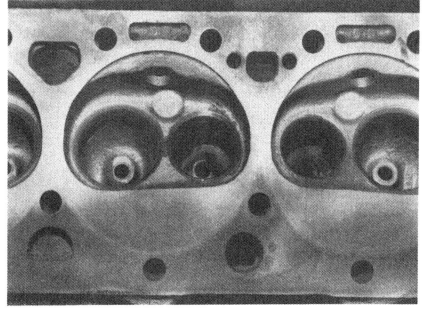

If your small-block Chevy uses factory production cylinder head castings as a basis from which to work, then this is the style of combustion chamber you should be using.

Compression Ratio Selection

One of the most useful tips for selecting compression ratio for any application of a small-block Chevy was passed on to us by Dema Elgin, of Elgin Cams.

Often those less experienced in engine building overlook matching the compression ratio to the cam profile. Since a long-period cam does not close the intake valve until the piston is well up the bore, it is necessary to employ a higher compression ratio because at low rpm that cylinder will have experienced some reverse flow, and consequently, there won't be as much air in the cylinder as expected.

In other words, the cylinder may have filled only about 75 percent of the total swept volume of the cylinder. This means that the effective or dynamic compression ratio will be far less than the calculated compression. One of Dema Elgin's observations is that most engines, when the compression ratio is maximized and matched to the cam, operate between about 8.5:1 and 9.0:1 compression, regardless of the type of engine.

Now this may seem contradictory to the high compressions used in racing, but this compression ratio is calculated not on the total swept volume of the cylinder, but on the volume left above the piston when the intake valve closes.

To give you an idea of the spread of compression ratio figures involved here, we find that with an engine using service station gasoline of typically 90-92 octanes, compression ratios based on the valve closure point of around 8.5:1 will get the job done. On the other hand, if high-octane racing gasolines are used, the compression ratio works out best nearer to 9.0:1.

Here's how to calculate the compression ratio to match a given cam. Let's assume we're going to build engines of three different specifications in the cam department. The only factor we wish to change is the compression ratio so that it optimizes the cam's potential. In each case let us assume the cam is on a 108 degree LCA and is timed to full lift at 104 degrees; i.e., the intake lobe centerline is on 104 degrees.

Let us also assume the cams give measured duration figures at the valve of 270, 280, and 290 degrees. It is important that we use the figures generated by the cam at the valve. This means that you will probably need to do a trial motor build and check to establish the crank angle at which the intake valve closes. For this I recommend one of the larger degree wheels such as the one sold by Competition Cams.

Now, let us assume the engine we are building is a typical 350 with a 30 thousandth overbore. This means that the cylinder capacity is 726cc. As a first step, let's consider how the effective compression ratio drops as the cam timing increases. For example let's freeze the compression at a conventionally measured 10.0:1. The total chamber volume required to deliver a 10.0:1 compression ratio equals cylinder volume over CR minus 1. Therefore:

$$\text{Total chamber Volume} = \frac{\text{cylinder volume}}{CR - 1} = \frac{726}{9} = 80.7$$

This means that the total chamber volume is 80.7cc.

Now let's use this chamber volume for an engine, which could have any one of the aforementioned cams at 270, 280, or 290 degrees. If the 270 cam is installed, the intake valve closes when the cylinder contains 81.5 percent of its volume. This can be ascertained by measuring, at the point of intake valve closure, how far the piston has reached down the cylinder bore. This gives a trapped capacity of 592cc in the cylinder as opposed to the theoretical 726cc.

Using 592cc as the cylinder capacity will yield a compression ratio of 8.33:1. With a 280 cam, only 78.2 percent of the charge is trapped at intake valve closure, and this yields a compression of 7.04:1. With the 290 cam, only 74.7 percent of the charge is trapped, which yields 542cc, and this produces a dynamic compression of 6.72:1.

As you can see, the engine is rapidly losing dynamic compression, and this heavily influences the large cams to drop off rapidly at low rpm

This simple burette and stand from B&B is inexpensive and a valuable aid to any serious engine builder wanting to optimize compression for the cam profile used.

When compression ratios get really high, accuracy in cylinder head volume measurement becomes very important. I use this Brezinski electronic burette.

and fail to deliver their power potential. To offset this, let us assume a dynamic compression ratio of 8.5:1 is required with whichever cam is used. To determine the static or geometric compression ratio, the combustion chamber volume required to deliver an 8.5:1 ratio based on valve closure point will need to be calculated.

Let's take the 270 cam first. The total chamber volume required will be:

$$\frac{\text{Volume at valve closure}}{CR - 1}$$

So, using this formula for the 270 cam, we have:

$$\frac{592}{7.5} = 78.9cc$$

This answer equals the chamber volume required to deliver an 8.5:1 compression ratio based on valve closure point. The static or geometric compression ratio to which this translates equals:

$$\frac{\text{Total swept volume} + \text{chamber volume}}{\text{chamber volume}}$$

which, in our case, is

$$\frac{726 + 78.9}{78.9} = 10.2:1$$

As you can see, this delivers 10.2:1, a figure I find common among excellent results for a 270 degree cam. For the 280 cam, the figures would be:

$$\frac{568}{7.5}$$

This would yield a chamber volume of 75.7cc for a valve closure-based compression ratio of 8.5:1. Inserting the chamber volumes into our conventional compression ratio calculation gives us these figures:

$$\frac{726 + 75.7}{75.5} = 10.6:1$$

For the 290 cam, the figures would be:

$$\frac{542}{7.5} = 72.6$$

for the chamber volume required. To get the static compression, we insert 72.6 into our equation:

Along with the burette, I use this stand and adaptor plate. This allows quick and easy high precision measurement of all four chambers in the cylinder head.

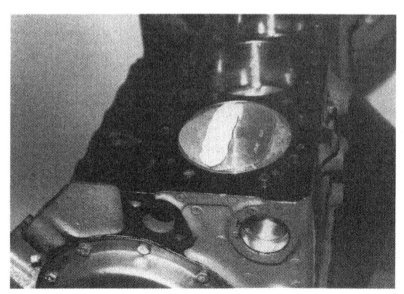

Where chamber volume is critical and valve pop-ups need to be minimized, I find it is worthwhile to measure the depth of valve pocket required by claying up the piston as seen here.

Then I use a precision piston vice to cut in a minimum depth of valve pocket required. I use this Impulse piston vice. It is versatile, precise, and allows a quick setup.

ability will have decreased because the reduced bore cannot accommodate such large valves. If stroke length is increased while bore size remains constant, engine displacement increases producing more cubic inches for the same head flow capability. Either way, the engine's breathing ability per cubic inch of displacement is reduced in relation to its stroke.

Another bottom-end factor affecting the required cam timing is the length of the connecting rods. Although we talk about cam timing in relation to the crankshaft angle, the cylinder head has no way of knowing how many degrees the crank has turned. It knows only airflow through the valve and this relates directly to piston position and velocity. Using a short rod/stroke ratio the piston hangs around BDC much longer but moves away from TDC quicker than a long rod/stroke ratio. This directly affects piston position in the bore at the time of valve opening and closing.

For instance, let's say we have a 327 engine with a 5.50in rod. If a 280 degree cam on a 110 degree LCA worked best in this motor, then to get identical cam operation in relation to piston motion, a 6.50in rodded motor would require a 279 degree cam on a 109 degree LCA. From this we can conclude that by shortening up the rod, added duration and wider LCA is needed. Lengthening the rod requires a slight reduction in cam timing and a tightening of the LCA.

Piston pin offset also affects the piston's position in the bore relative to the crank motion. Moving the pin across the piston in the direction of rotation causes the crank to be in a more advanced position for the same piston position. This means if you install pistons that have a pin offset in the direction of the crank rotation, the cam timing needs to be retarded. If the pins are offset in the reverse direction toward the thrust face, then most likely the cam needs to be more advanced.

The Chevrolet factory production head can be worth a clear 20hp and 20 lb-ft over the open style of the chamber shown here.

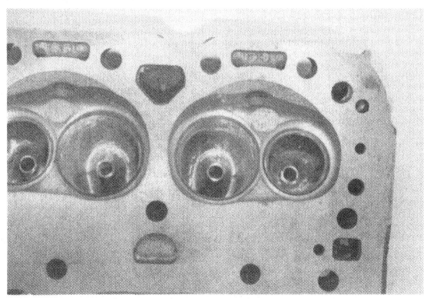

With the right porting on production cylinder heads, performance levels with a suitable cam can be impressive considering their low cost. In excess of 500hp is possible.

Valve Lift

So far we've only looked at changes in the bottom end of the engine in relation to period. But there is one factor that probably has more significance than all the timing changes put together: valve lift. With a small-block Chevy, displacements can range anywhere from the high 200ci bracket to the low 400ci range. Allowing that this large variation in capacity can be fed by virtually one cylinder head design, we find that one basic characteristic of the valvetrain needs altering more than any, this being valve lift.

With smaller capacity engines, say 260ci equipped with high-flow big-intake-valve (2.20in) heads, lifting the valve to 700 thousandths (0.700in) is almost academic.

On the other hand, high valve lifts and rapid valve acceleration rates are important for a big-cubic-inch engine. The need to get the valve into a high-flow region as soon as possible represents the best chance of supplying, with the minimum restriction, the volume of air required for a big-displacement cylinder. The ability to satisfactorily supply the demand of a small-cubic-inch cylinder with a moderate valve lift is a practicality. But making a cylinder 20 percent bigger dictates the need to open the valve to a position where it can flow 20 percent more for a corresponding position down the bore. This means opening the valve proportionally faster and higher.

Unfortunately, the flow capability of even a well-modified Chevrolet port tends to die a death at about 700 thousandths (0.700in) lift. Because this is so, attempting to lift valves to 850 thousandths (0.850in) for a big-displacement engine becomes a futile exercise.

Apart from port flow, mechanical limitations would make for an unreliable valvetrain. Nonetheless, on those big-cubic-inch engines attention paid to increasing valve accelerations returns dividends on the dynamometer and track. This necessitates selecting a cam with as rapid an opening rate as possible and a rocker ratio conducive to quicker valve opening rates. Inevitably, it means a serious look at the valvetrain as well as the cam profile.

High-Ratio Rocker Arms

Since the subject has progressed to high-ratio rockers, we may as well continue with the subject. Assume no other changes in engine spec except

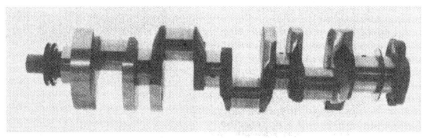

Crank and rod configuration also affects the cam timing for optimum use. A short-stroke 350 crank, such as shown here, coupled with a 4.125in bore and a long connecting rod requires a different cam specification than a more conventional 3.48in stroke motor.

Expertly modified cylinder heads aren't cheap, but these CNC machined heads from Kenny Weld are close. For a 23 degree head, airflow figures on the Weld machined heads were phenomenal, and with a suitable cam, the horsepower figures were also.

Rod length and piston crown configuration are also influential factors, but work on optimizing these rather than trying to develop a cam to offset their shortcomings.

for the installation of high-ratio rockers. In theory the seat timing remains the same, but at any point on the lift curve the valve will be farther off the seat. Although the overlap hasn't increased in terms of degrees, the overlap triangle (figure 3-1)—that is, the degrees of overlap times the mean intake and exhaust valve lift—has increased. Installing high-ratio rockers can make the engine seem slightly "cammier," and of course how much depends on the size of the cam.

Let's assume we're using the same 280 degree cam we've had all along, but with a change from 1.5:1 to 1.65:1 rocker ratios. To get the same part-throttle and low-rpm characteristics as dictated by the overlap area it will be necessary to spread the LCA slightly. A 10 percent increase in rocker ratio usually warrants a 1½ to 2 degrees wider LCA.

The same situation applies if the change is made to a long-period roller cam from an equally long-period flat-tappet cam. A typical roller cam can deliver up to about 20 percent greater valve velocity than its flat-tappet equivalent; however, the initial acceleration on a flat-tappet cam can be greater than on a roller cam. For shorter-period cams there is an opening area advantage to the flat-tappet cam, but by the time we are considering seat timing figures of 300 degrees or more, the overall advantage even in the overlap area tends to go to the roller design.

In this instance the LCA needs to be spread appropriately. Just how much depends on approximately the difference in the valve overlap triangle imparted by the roller profile as opposed to a flat-tappet profile, but typically 1 to as much as 2 degrees for 315–320 degree cams is on the right order.

External Influences

So far, we've looked at the effect that internal changes have on required cam timing in terms of the lobe centerline, but numerous external factors also influence the situation.

One of the most significant variables is the type of exhaust system employed. A zero restriction exhaust with optimal diameters and lengths to tune the induction and exhaust at rpm complementary to the cam's capabilities can have a *significant* effect on horsepower. The benefits gained mostly stem from events occurring around the TDC mark during the overlap period. The most significant aspect is the exhaust's ability to initiate the induction earlier due to its velocity in the exhaust pipe.

In simplified form, here's how it works. The momentum of the expelled exhaust in the pipe causes the pressure behind it to drop sufficiently to start intake flow, even though the piston

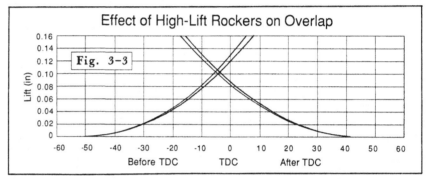

Figure 3-3: *Installing high-lift rockers does not increase the valve overlap in terms of degrees, but it does increase the area of the overlap triangle. This has the same effect as making the engine more "cammy." From this chart it can be seen that changing 1.5 rockers for 1.6s increases the effective overlap. To put a figure to it, such a change in ratio increases the overlap triangle area by some 8 percent.*

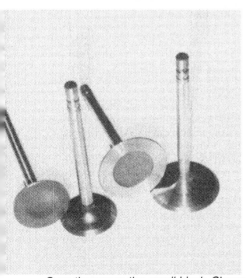

Over the years the small-block Chevy has been available with many valve sizes. This size, together with the bore and stroke, has a great influence on the cam's required timing figures.

For literally thousands of cam tests, I have used these Crane 1.5-1.6 adjustable rockers to investigate the numerous effects that ratio changes could have on the valvetrain and engine output characteristics.

may not have quite reached TDC. In this instance, both valves need to be opened sufficiently to allow the effect to take place.

If a restrictive exhaust is used, however, two things change. The exhaust gas velocities, especially near the end of the exhaust stroke, are reduced and backpressures are increased. This leads to a far greater tendency for the exhaust to pass out the intake during the overlap period. If a restrictive exhaust system is used, then it is necessary to spread the LCA of the cam to cut the overlap. In extreme cases it may also be necessary to reduce total duration.

If a highly effective exhaust system is used, tighter LCAs can be beneficial but carried too far they can result in overscavenging. In this situation the exhaust system pulls the fresh charge through the chamber into the exhaust pipe instead of leaving it in the cylinder. This may not hurt power as such, but it will adversely affect fuel consumption, which can be so important for a long-distance race motor. The obvious cure for overscavenging is to spread the LCA slightly to compensate. But another remedy exists which is often overlooked.

If volumetric efficiencies (VE) are already high—on the order of 110 percent plus—then it may be possible, depending on the VE and compression ratio combination currently used, to go

another route to extract more power from the induced charge. This requires a *reduction* of the compression ratio so the part of the fresh charge that would have flowed through the system now has space to remain in the chamber. However, this can be a delicate juggling act.

In the same vein, if the engine has a restrictive intake system due, say, to inadequate carburetor flow capacity, both intake and exhaust timing will need amending. Unfortunately, with a restrictive intake the cam timing needed at high rpm for optimal output can significantly differ from what is required at low rpm where the restriction on the intake has less effect on the engine's breathing capability. However, a grossly restricted intake is only a likely event on engines forced, by virtue of race rules, to use a two-barrel carburetor or a restrictor plate. Assuming this to be the case, we'll deal only with race cams and their interaction with a restricted intake.

First, depending upon how effective the exhaust is, there is a tendency for the required LCAs to tighten. A highly functional exhaust having good extraction effect can help create manifold vacuum to assist airflow through the restrictive induction system. On the other hand, some race regulations call for stock iron manifolds to be used. Cams for this requirement will need a slightly wider LCA. Because the re-

strictive intake causes a substantial reduction in the engine's volumetric efficiency, the volume of exhaust will be reduced.

Consequently, it is not necessary to open the exhaust valve quite as soon for an unrestricted engine. The marginally delayed exhaust opening allows a little more power to be extracted from the charge. In addition, the reduced gas volume brought about by the restricted intake means lower exhaust pumping losses than would be seen on an unrestricted motor.

The effect that a restricted induction system has on the required intake timing is quite intricate and many factors tend to counteract with each other. First, there is a need to hold the intake valve open as long as possible to allow the cylinder the best chance of filling. On the other hand, if held open a moment too long some of the intake charge may be lost back into the intake manifold because the piston has moved far enough up the bore, and cylinder pressure has equalized or exceeded the intake manifold pressure. This means that effective compression will be lost as well as some of the charge.

When the working volume of air is limited in the first place, a small percentage of change has a significant effect on power. Intake closure then becomes critical, while the timing of the intake opening point becomes exhaust system dependent.

Radical Cam Timing Changes

To clearly illustrate the point that cam events must be customized for the intended application, let's consider some applications that call for big changes; for instance, nitrous oxide (N_2O) injection and its cam requirements.

If your engine is equipped with nitrous oxide injection, then something of a dilemma exists. You have an engine that to operate optimally in either mode requires two distinctly different camshafts, one for use when the nitrous is not in operation and one for when it is.

Since this is impractical, a decision must be made as to which way to bias the choice of cam. Is it necessary to optimize power output while the engine is not in the nitrous mode, or when it is? You can strike some compromise and go halfway between, but assume here you want to bias toward the nitrous operation. How does the cam change?

My tests on a Superflow dyno revealed that one of the most influential elements furthering the negative effects of overlap was a restrictive exhaust system.

Primarily, the induction stroke and consequent cylinder filling is not as important as with a noninjected motor. When N_2O is in operation we are, in essence, pouring oxygen into the engine, mostly in liquid form. Therefore, achieving a high-density charge in the cylinder is no longer the big problem it is with a normally aspirated engine. Burning this high-density charge creates a volume of exhaust proportional to a much larger engine. This presents a problem of ridding the cylinder of the large amounts of additional exhaust created.

Solutions for the problem can take one of two forms. Ideally a cylinder head with a greatly increased exhaust valve area should be used, but a simpler fix is to open the exhaust valve sooner. Usually, opening the exhaust valve 10–15 degrees earlier gets the job done. Because timing is added only to the exhaust opening phase, the effect on the overall cam spec is to cause the required LCA to spread and advance to increase.

Using the same 280 degree single-pattern 110 degree LCA cam as previously, we'll turn it into a nitrous cam. This will entail opening the exhaust valve say, 14 degrees sooner, which results in 294 degrees of exhaust timing. If the intake phase remains as per a 280/280 cam 4 degrees advanced, the nitrous cam with its extended timing will now have a 113.5 degree LCA and 7.5 degrees of advance. Figure 3-4 shows how adding 14 degrees to the exhaust timing changes the way the cam looks on a specification chart, although intake timing remains unchanged.

The beauty of a nitrous cam is that it allows the engine to deliver a lot of additional horsepower when the nitrous is in operation because of the significantly reduced pumping losses.

The disadvantages of a nitrous cam when nitrous is not in operation are minimal. Basically, the engine drives much the same in terms of flexibility and road manners because the overlap has not changed. The only penalty is that there is a slight reduction in power in the low- and mid-range rpm, and fuel economy is slightly reduced because of the very early opening of the exhaust valve.

If you can live with this, then a cam typically speced for nitrous can bump up the power of your nitrous kit by 20–30 percent over that delivered by a typical single-pattern cam. The higher the compression ratio, the less the

negative effects of the N_2O spec can become. However, don't go overboard on the compression. (If you are intent on using N_2O effectively, read *Nitrous-Oxide Injection* by David Vizard, published by SA Design and available through Motorbooks International.)

A nitrous system, as shown here, is a great way to go for extra power, but many nitrous users don't realize that even with a street kit there can be as much as 60-70hp locked up in the camshaft unless it's speced out to suit the nitrous-injection requirements.

Supercharged Induction

In many ways, superchargers (as opposed to turbochargers) have an effect on cam requirements similar to that of nitrous oxide. Ideally, a supercharged engine needs a larger exhaust valve than its normally aspirated counter-

Many supercharged street motors have failed to deliver their true potential. Engine-builder Bob Benton built this one with the appropriate cam, and it had no problem smoking the slicks of his Z28 with its 525 lb-ft of torque on only 6lbs of boost.

part. In other words, a different intake-exhaust priority is needed to maximize output from the room available for valves. This is often an impractical solution because it can entail the need for a special cylinder head.

The next alternative is to manipulate cam timing to achieve near optimal results. For a mechanically driven supercharger, depending upon boost pressure, there's a need to open the exhaust valve a little earlier.

There is a factor countering this, however. Supercharged engines develop cylinder pressure patterns in a slightly different form to high-compression engines. Raising the compression ratio on a normally aspirated engine causes peak pressures to climb quite dramatically. The added pressure on the piston occurs mostly at the beginning of the power stroke.

A supercharged engine, on the other hand, with a lower compression and greater mass of cylinder charge tends not to reach such high peak values (unless substantial boost is used), but the pressure stays higher throughout the rest of the power stroke. This factor tends to offset the requirement for early exhaust valve opening. The reason is that a much more usable pressure still exists in the cylinder at any given time than in a normally aspirated engine. In other words, early opening of an exhaust valve on a

supercharged engine dumps far more usable cylinder pressure than does a normally aspirated engine. Therefore, there's a need to carefully consider the exhaust valve opening point for a blown engine as it is often a critical factor.

There is also a need to minimize exhaust stroke pumping losses which on most supercharged small-blocks are likely to be high due to the almost inevitable lack of exhaust valve area. Additionally, it is desirable to keep the exhaust valve closed as long as possible to get the most from the available cylinder pressure without incurring excessive pumping losses.

This means a high lift on the exhaust valve of a supercharged engine is often beneficial, whereas a normally aspirated engine is far more sensitive to exhaust duration than it is to lift or acceleration. Exhaust valve closure needs to be similar to what is expected in a normally aspirated engine. However, the need to open the intake valve as early as a normally aspirated engine is not present because the engine is operating under a positive pressure differential. Thus, the boost pressure is going to scavenge the combustion chamber.

Since we're typically dealing with 5 or more pounds per square inch, the amount of scavenge pressure differential available is higher than would be

expected from a tuned extractor exhaust used on a normally aspirated engine. Because of the pressure differentials involved, the intake valve should not be opened as soon, otherwise some of the incoming charge will pass out the exhaust. Since horsepower was used to compress this charge, it doesn't make sense to throw away it and the fuel it contains.

Thus for a supercharged engine the intake valve should be opened later than for a normally aspirated engine. A hot street cam would require the LCA to be spread 3–4 degrees and the cam timed in with 1–2 degrees less advance.

Turbo Cams

Selecting a cam for a turbocharger can be difficult. The main reason is because turbo kits commonly available vary so much as far as installed airflow characteristics are concerned, that they impose a great variation on the cams required. As of 1992, it's necessary to customize a cam to suit a particular turbocharger installation. Realistically, it won't do much good to order a custom cam for a turbo installation unless you know the precise parameters of the engine. The best you can do is guess at the requirements.

Probably the most important consideration for optimal turbo motor cam timing is the amount of exhaust backpressure existing in the system in relation to the induction pressure. Remember, in spite of what turbo proponents claim, the engine doesn't get the boost for free. It's developed by extracting heat and pressure energy from the exhaust, which is derived from the pressure difference across the exhaust turbine. The turbine extracts energy via the pressure drop across it. If the intake boost pressure and the exhaust backpressures are similar, then cam overlap figures can likewise be similar to those for a normally aspirated engine.

However, small-block Chevys with turbo setups having approximately a 1:1 pressure ratio across them are rare. It takes an efficient turbo setup and effectively modified cylinder heads to generate anything approaching this situation. Most have a considerable pressure differential across them, typically in the range of 1.5:1 to as high as 2:1. In other words, 10psi of boost typically equates to 15–20psi of exhaust backpressure. The engine sees this backpressure as a restrictive exhaust system.

The cams required for turbo motors are radically different from those for normally aspirated engines. Even within the framework of what is required, the characteristics of the turbo have a profound effect on the timing figures needed. A lot of the turbo motor's characteristics must be known before a cam match can be achieved.

Opening the intake valve while the exhaust is appreciably off its seat achieves nothing except to dump exhaust out through the intake valve. This has numerous adverse effects on the intake charge. It causes the charge, which is already at a high temperature, to become even hotter. It also contaminates the charge with pre-burned exhaust. This cuts the burn effectiveness, requires a slightly richer mixture ratio to ignite it effectively, and adds to the ignition advance requirement for optimum cylinder pressures. In addition, it makes the engine more prone to detonation.

As you can imagine, none of these factors are conducive to either reliability or output. The key to designing successful cam timing for a turbo motor with high exhaust backpressures is to have little or no overlap and often run the situation where there is negative overlap; early exhaust valve closure around the TDC mark; later exhaust valve opening for good low-end and mileage; and moderate intake valve closure ABDC.

Summing up a turbo cam, it requires an intake typically 20–30 degrees shorter than the exhaust. It also needs a wide LCA such as 120 degrees or more and requires installing retarded with 2–10 degrees often being of the right order. If you are contemplating building a serious turbo motor, then I suggest you study the requirements of a turbo cam as detailed in chapter 6.

Street versus Race

So far, the criteria by which we've determined cam selection have been based on maximizing power and torque for a given intake period. Unfortunately these factors can carry certain unacceptable penalties, especially if the cam is to be used in a street engine. For a street cam, another set of criteria may influence the selected cam timing figures. Such things as drivability and engine vacuum to operate essentials such as vacuum brakes, heater-air conditioning controls, and so on, must be taken into account. Also, enough cruise vacuum should exist so that any onboard engine management computer can correctly interpret such things as required ignition timing and fuel flow.

Under such circumstances, it may be necessary to design a cam that closely replicates the original vacuum characteristics. In this case it is necessary to choose timing figures that produce the best power consistent with vacuum rather than the best power for a given intake period.

Following this path inevitably leads to limiting overlap and extending timing at the other end of the opening period on both intake and exhaust. This produces a cam with a wide LCA, much wider than would be the case if power alone was the criterion. Indeed, the dictates of adequate vacuum, both at idle and cruise, may demand LCAs 4–8 degrees wider than would normally be the case.

Summing Up

At this point, you should realize that the universal cam or a cam choice based on the fact that it worked in somebody else's motor cannot be effective if your engine is significantly different. To be effective a cam should suit the characteristics of *your* engine. Does this mean that every cam should be customized? Not necessarily. Cam manufacturers tend to produce specs based on criteria most applicable to the marketplace, which in turn is related to what they see as the typical engine.

For instance, most small-block Chevrolet street cams are designed for a 350 with a four-barrel carb and headers. A look through a cam catalog will reveal the equipment recommendations required to make the most of a particular type of cam. There are straight replacement cams that will produce better results than a stock cam with no other changes required. At the other end of the scale there are race cams that certainly won't do anything significant for your engine unless the engine is appropriately prepared in every other area.

Aside from technical considerations, marketing influences also help shape the specification of a cam you may buy. For instance, some cam manufacturers see idle quality and cruise economy as having a slightly greater importance than all-out torque and horsepower. Granted, such cams produce a lot more power than the stock items, but they trade off a little of the power increase for more civilized manners. Alternatively, other cam companies may have produced their cams with a greater bias toward torque and horsepower, with idle quality taking a back seat. It all depends on how each company views its market segment.

Understanding how a cam's specification can shape an engine's characteristics can help you make a more educated choice. Also, if you have an engine that is significantly different from the norm, understanding the facts will help you customize a suitable cam spec just like the pros. Let's say you have gone to great lengths to build a maximum-inch motor. Under these circumstances you can reasonably expect an off-the-shelf cam to be less than ideal. Knowing what effect each change in engine specification has on the required cam spec can pay off.

Figure 3-4: Comparison of Nitrous Cams

	280/280	280/294
Intake opens	34	34
Intake closes	66	66
Exhaust opens	74	88
Exhaust closes	26	26
LCA	110	113.5
Advance	4	7.5
Intake centerline	106	106
Exhaust centerline	114	121
Overlap	60	60

Figure 3-4: *The use of nitrous requires an earlier opening of the exhaust valve while other factors such as the intake remain unchanged. The following chart shows how this effects the cam spec on what starts off as a hot street single-* *pattern 280 degree cam on 110 degree LCA. All the numbers that change are the consequence of adding the extra timing to the opening side of the exhaust profile only. See how doing so causes the LCA and advance figures to change.*

Comparing Camshafts

4

As stated previously, half the battle in understanding camshafts involves working with and correctly interpreting numbers. It's easy to mistakenly assume that once you understand what cam specification the engine needs you are home free. You can look through catalogs until you find a cam with the required number of degrees duration, lift, and timing; with the thousands of different cams available, there almost certainly will be something close to what the engine needs. But deciphering exactly what it is you are getting from the cam manufacturer may be a different thing altogether.

Comparing Cam Lift

Choosing a cam on this basis should be simple, but in reality there is far more to it. Because the motion imparted to the lifter by the cam lobe must begin smoothly, it is difficult to define the exact point at which it begins. To get around this the Society of Automobile Engineers (SAE) has adopted some standards as guidelines for the industry (SAE J-604/501). These relate to the amount of follower lift that occurs at the cam in relation to its timing.

For a hydraulic camshaft, timing figures are those produced when the valve has lifted 6 thousandths (0.006in) from the seat (figure 4-1). Because the stock rocker ratio is 1.5:1, 6 thousandths (0.006in) at the valve equates to 4 thousandths (0.004in) at the cam. For a mechanical cam the SAE standard calls for the quoted timing to be at

6 thousandths valve lift plus the specified valve lash. This means a typical mechanical cam of say 22 thousandths (0.022in) lash should have its duration quoted when 28 thousandths (0.028in) rocker tip motion has occurred.

So much for SAE standards. The question is, does the cam industry adhere to these standards? For hydraulic cams the answer is yes, many do, but there are some notable exceptions, such as Isky and Competition Cams. For mechanical cams the reverse is most certainly true. In checking catalogs it seems each cam manufacturer goes for its own valve lift timing point. For instance, a 20 thousandths (0.020in) tappet lift for a solid lifter cam is not uncommon.

While making comparisons among one group of cams, the differing measurements are not much of a problem. The real dilemma arises when a comparison is made between one type of cam and another. For example, let's say a comparison is needed between a 280 degree hydraulic cam and a 280 degree solid lifter cam. The catalog informs us that for the same seat timing, the solid lifter cam lifts some 30 thousandths (0.030in) higher. All things being equal, we could reasonably assume that additional valve lift means better top-end output without necessarily losing any bottom-end output.

Unfortunately most things are far more equal. First, almost all lift figures are gross values. This assumes the effective lift begins from the base circle of the cam and the valve lift delivered is the total cam lift multiplied by whatever rocker ratio exists. For a hydraulic cam it typically takes 4-6 thousandths (0.004–0.006in) tappet lift to counteract the valve train deflection before the valve actually moves. Timing figures quoted at 4 thousandths (0.004in) tappet lift produce valve opening figures of similar magnitude. But for a solid lifter the situation is more than just a little different.

Many cam manufacturers quote solid lifter timing figures at 15 thousandths (0.015in) tappet lift, but may run a valve lash clearance at 26 thousandths (0.026in). So if the camshaft selected generates 280 degrees of duration at 15 thousandths (0.015in) follower lift the timing at the valves will be less because the resulting 26 thousandths (0.026in) timing lash at the valve is bigger than the required timing lash. If the tappet clearance required is 26 thousandths (0.026in) then this supposedly 280 degree cam is only going to deliver about 275 degrees of seat-to-seat timing. Additionally, the extra lift you thought the solid lifter cam had diminishes somewhat when the lash is subtracted.

Cam Timing

Comparing cam profiles to cam timing figures is not as easy as it looks, but timing cams based on seat timing figures is almost impossible. For this reason other methods for determining "installed" cam timing are used. Because the tappet moves so slowly during the initial cam lift phase it is difficult to measure with any degree of accuracy how many degrees of rotation have taken place for a given lift. Not only is this technique a poor approach in itself, but any inaccuracies of the position in the block can add significant errors. (For more information, see *How To Build & Modify Chevrolet Small-Block V8 Pistons, Rods & Crankshafts*, also by David Vizard in the Motorbooks International PowerPro Series.)

To see how measuring errors can accumulate, let's look at an example. For instance, it is easy to be 2 or 3 degrees out on a hydraulic cam when

Figure 4-1: Comparison of 280 Degree Hydraulic and 282 Solid Cam

	Advertised duration	Advertised duration @ 0.050in	Measured duration @ 0.050in minus lash	Advertised lift	Measured lift with 1.5 rocker
Hydraulic	280	230	231.4	480	471
Solid	282	236	229.6	495	472.5

Figure 4-1: *Because figures are taken at a different standard, making cam comparisons proves more than checking out numbers. From the advertised figures the 282 solid-lifter cam looks to be mea-* surably "bigger." When comparisons are made on a like-for-like basis, we find that the hydraulic cam is close to the solid, though the advertised figures don't reflect that.

trying to determine when 4 thousandths (0.004in) *tappet* (0.006in valve) lift has taken place because the slope of the lift in relation to rotation is relatively gentle. To obviate this problem the 50 thousandths (0.050in) tappet lift checking point was devised. The story goes Chevrolet engineers working on solid lifter cams for the off-road program noted that the valve lift and follower lift coincided when 50 thousandths follower rise had occurred. By using a 50 thousandths follower rise as a checking point, the velocity of the tappet in relation to the crank rotation was much higher so it was much easier to accurately define that point on the camshaft.

Valve Opening Rates

By introducing the 50 thousandths (0.050in) lift point into day-to-day cam specifications, it became possible to partially define another aspect of a camshaft that is, to a large extent, not revealed by any numbers other than possibly lift. An important aspect of any cam is how fast it opens the valves and the most important place to have fast opening rates in the lift curve is right from the seat.

Just knowing a cam's duration and lift tells little about its opening rate. Obviously, if it has a lot of lift for a given duration it must be opening the valve fast. But it is still possible to have a cam with fast initial opening rates while not necessarily having a noticeably higher lift.

Putting it another way, a high lift implies, but does not guarantee, fast initial opening rates but a low lift does not necessarily preclude them. However, by knowing the 50 thousandths tappet lift figures, a comparison can be made between the seat (or so-called advertised) timing and the 50 thousandths timing.

A look at stock Chevrolet cam profiles used back in the 1960s (which some of the larger but less-forward-thinking parts houses are, as of 1991, still copying and selling) will reveal relatively lazy opening rates. These cams tend to have a long duration, but are a little shy on lift. The slow opening rates show up especially when a comparison is made between the seat and 50 thousandths timing figures.

Subtracting the 50 thousandths figures from the seat figures often results in a difference of some 70 plus degrees. In other words, with these cams it takes 35-37 degrees of rotation for the tappet to move from 4 thousandths

(0.004in) to 50 thousandths (0.050in) rise. Lazy acceleration rates such as this may produce a quiet camshaft and valvetrain but is not necessarily good for producing power.

In an undervalved engine such as the small-block Chevy rapid valve opening rates, especially on the intake, can have a dramatic effect on power output. More modern cam profiles—such as those produced by Isky, Competition Cams, Ultradyne, and Crane, to mention just a few—open valves much quicker. A comparison of the seat to 50 thousandths timing shows a typical difference of 50-56 degrees. The implication here is that it takes 25 or so degrees for the follower to move from the 4 thousandths (0.004in) to 50 thousandths (0.050in) lift point. This is about 30 percent less time than the old Chevrolet profiles.

Harvey Crane coined a term for the difference between these two figures, and called it the hydraulic intensity. Once explained it does, to an extent, describe what is happening. This is especially true when one considers that Crane dubbed a new range of fast opening rate cams, High Intensity Cams. The implication was that they had a high hydraulic intensity.

Valve Flow

Apart from helping to establish cam timing and getting an idea of the rate of opening produced, the 50 thousandths figure has another important significance and it relates to flow at the valve. Obviously at low valve lift flow is minimal, especially on the intake. If

potential power gains are viewed in relation to seat timing and 50 thousandths timing, we find that for the most part the engine's output is affected more significantly by extended 50 thousandths tappet lift timing than seat timing.

Some figures produced during an extended cam test session should illustrate the point (figure 4-3). The numbers should be viewed as a guide rather than an absolute because of the difficulty in controlling all the parameters concerned, unless special profiles were designed specifically to prove the point. In this particular test three cams were used. Cam 1 was 212 degrees duration at 50 thousandths (0.050in) and 276 degrees at 4 thousandths (0.004in) and was considered the baseline cam. Cam 2 had a higher hydraulic intensity with 220 degrees timing at 50 thousandths and the same 276 degrees on the seat. The last cam was a low intensity item with a somewhat outdated profile producing 212 degrees timing at 50 thousandths and a much longer 284 degrees timing at 4 thousandths (0.004in).

On the face of it this test may look totally valid but the problem is the maximum valve lift varied slightly between these cams. Measured at the valve, the high intensity cam was 8 thousandths (0.008in) higher than the baseline cam and the low intensity cam was 10 thousandths (0.010in) shy of the baseline cam. This amounts to some 18 thousandths (0.018in) difference in valve lift between the highest and lowest and thus needs to be accounted for.

Figure 4-2: Comparing Hydraulic Cam Intensity Ratings

Cam	Seat Duration	0.050in Duration	Intensity
Comp Cams 268H	268	222	46
Comp Cams 280H	280	232	48
Crane HMV-272-2 NC	272	216	56
Crane HIT 280 NC	280	224	56
Isky Mega 270	270	216	54
Isky Mega 280	280	232	48
Wolverine WG 1103	270	204	66
Wolverine WG 1137	280	214	66

Figure 4-2: *Looking at the intensity of these various cams in the 270-280 range, one would assume that the Competition Cams profiles are easily the fastest opening of the group. Not an unreasonable assumption, until you take into account that each has their own measuring standard. For instance, Competition Cams uses 6 thousandths (0.006in) to quote the advertised seat*

duration, whereas Crane uses 4 thousandths (0.004in). This alone makes the Crane cams look slower opening, regardless of whether they were or not. To top it off, Isky uses 0.006in on the opening side and 0.009in on the closing side, and to compound the confusion further, I haven't a clue as to what Wolverine uses to compute their advertised duration. So making comparisons is, at best, dodgy.

Figure 4-3: Effect of Opening Rate on Output for Typical Street Spec Engine

Engine: 350 Small-Block Chevy

RPM	Cam 1 Torque	HP	Cam 2 Torque	HP	Cam 3 Torque	HP
2500	358	170	353	168	350	167
3000	354	203	352	202	344	196
3500	357	238	362	242	351	234
4000	347	264	353	269	344	262
4500	336	288	340	291	333	285
5000	319	304	322	307	320	305
5500	301	315	304	318	302	316
6000	279	319	287	327	282	322

Cam 1: Seat timing: 32-64-72-24
      Seat duration: 276-276
      0.050 timing: 0-32-40-8
      0.050 duration: 212-212
      Seat duration, 0.050 duration: 64 degrees
Cam 2: Seat timing: 32-64-72-24
      Seat duration: 276-276
      0.050 timing: 4-34-44-4
      0.050 duration: 220-220
      Seat duration, 0.050 duration: 56 degrees
Cam 3: Seat timing: 36-68-76-28
      Seat duration: 284-284
      0.050 timing: 0-32-40-8
      0.050 duration: 212-212
      Seat duration, 0.050 duration: 72 degrees

Note: All test cams were hydraulic. Lifters were refaced and re-used in same lifter bore for each cam.

Figure 4-3: *There may be a lot of numbers here to digest, but they all point to one thing—namely that quicker opening rates to produce longer 50 thousandths (0.050in) timing figures pay off more than extending total seat timing.*

When checking out cam events, it is necessary to establish TDC accurately. On pistons with a large-bore clearance, piston rock can be a problem, so it is necessary to take measurements from the center of the piston, not the edge.

The test shown in figure 4-4 relates the difference in power achieved when a small rocker ratio change was made that resulted in an average of 21 thousandths (0.021in) more lift per valve on the same engine but with a cam of a different spec to those used in the previous valve acceleration test. Using a cam of a different spec was not intended to confuse the issue, it's just that at the time, rockers were being tested and not camshafts.

From the rocker tests we can see that the higher lift didn't really help power until up in the high rpm range. This effect needs to be superimposed on the differences revealed by the valve acceleration test (figure 4-3). The high-intensity cam with 10 degrees more timing at 50 thousandths produced an increase in peak torque of 5lb-ft while peak horsepower went up by 8.

Conversely, the low intensity cam with 8 degrees more seat timing produced 3lb-ft *less* in peak torque though at the top end a 3hp increase was seen. These maximums are significant, but the main point to note is that the low-intensity cam with its longer seat duration produced noticeably less bottom end.

So, cams with rapid opening rates look good but there can be some relatively serious negative side effects. Obviously increased opening rates come about because higher velocities are achieved.

Edge Riding

Ultimately, the velocity that can be put into a tappet is limited by the diameter of the follower itself. Past a certain point the follower will "edge ride" on the cam which will almost instantly wipe out the cam lobe. Building in too much follower velocity is not something cam manufacturers unwittingly do; it is simple to calculate how much velocity can safely be used for a given size of follower. However, a problem does arise in that the cam follower bores aren't always machined in the correct place.

This means if a cam follower bore is displaced, and they can be by anything up to 20 thousandths (0.020in), there is a possibility that a high velocity cam can edge ride in your particular block. This being the case, the cam manufacturers must make allowances while still approaching the limit as closely as possible. On occasion, a badly machined block will consistently "eat" cams. When this occurs it usually involves the same lobe every time. Cams with lower lifter velocities tend to avoid this problem.

Cam Lobe Wear

Cam lobe wear due to misplaced followers is a realistic possibility but there are also metallurgical constraints. Higher lifter accelerations and velocities mean more loads and the need for higher spring forces. This means that even if everything was precise in the engine, the surface loading on the cam and follower is greater. As a result, reliability can diminish. In most cases it is the cam that fails but as previous power tests show, rapid opening rates are very desirable in terms of horsepower. So it can often pay to take precautions against rapid cam wear by having the cam surface-hardened.

There are several processes that can be used for this, two being coldcasing and ion-nitriding. If heat treatment is not readily convenient, some other options are open to you. For instance, a set of low-ratio rockers, such as those sold by Competition Cams, reduce the surface load produced at the cam and follower interface, thus easing break-in. Alternatively, you can break in the cam with lower poundage springs. Running at 2000-3000rpm for half an hour can considerably enhance cam profile life. After the critical break-in phase is over with, the correct springs and rockers can be installed.

Valvetrain Noise

The last point concerning rapid-opening-rate cams is that they can be noisier than their slower-opening counterparts. The faster the valve opens, the more critical the profile becomes in terms of suppressing noise.

For the most part, valvetrain noise is not a big issue. The point is made because there are occasions when good output is required from an engine that needs to sound like it was meant to power a limousine. Under these circumstances you should lean toward cams with more moderate opening rates and use this as part of a quiet-engine-build program. This would include such things as closer fitting pis-tons and crankshaft clearance, and so on. But for the most part, when building a high-performance engine any increase in valvetrain noise is drowned out by the noise produced by other high-performance parts.

Solid Lifter Cams

Utilizing the 4 and 50 thousandths (0.004 and 0.050in) tappet rise figures to determine the rate at which a valve opens or the intensity of a camshaft doesn't present any problems with a hydraulic cam. However, the same technique applied to solid lifter cams

Figure 4-4: Valve Lift Test

Engine: 350 Small-Block Chevy

| RPM | 0.420in Lift | | | 0.441in Lift | |
	Torque	HP		Torque	HP
2500	337	160		336	160
3000	340	195		340	195
3500	346	231		346	231
4000	347	264		348	265
4500	341	292		342	293
5000	328	312		331	315
5500	310	324		311	326
6000	289	330		291	332

Figure 4-4: *The figures quoted here show how valve lift can affect power output. Because these numbers are really close it was necessary to take averages of as many as half a dozen runs to be able to come up with a trend. Even so, with an average of 21 thousandths (0.021in) lift change, mostly around peak valve lift, the engine's output increased by approximately 1 percent, and that is a borderline accuracy figure for any dyno and engine combination to record.*

Breaking in a radical flat-tappet race cam is an important procedure if the cam is to live. Probably the simplest way is to use these 1.2 ratio rockers from Competition Cams, as they considerably ease the load on the cam follower interface.

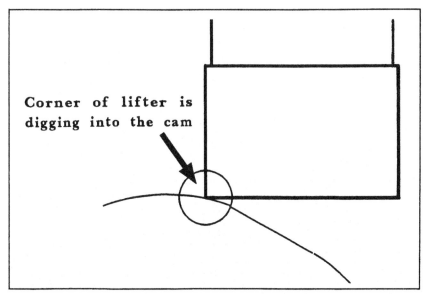

Corner of lifter is digging into the cam

Figure 4-5: *Lifter diameter is important. Trying to put too much velocity into a flat tappet lifter results in edge riding. In technical terms you can say that any time the eccentricity of the contact point from the center of the cam exceeds the radius of the follower, edge riding will occur and the system will wipe itself out in short order.*

can easily produce some misleading answers. The only consistency from one solid lifter cam to another and between one manufacturer and another is the 50 thousandths figure.

Some manufacturers quote the seat or advertised timing at 15 thousandths (0.015in), some at 20 thousandths (0.020in), some at 22 thousandths (0.022in), and some manufacturers aren't even consistent in their own catalog. This means comparing seat timing figures on solid lifter cams is of strictly limited value. But the problem doesn't end there.

The "quoted" seat timing figures are rarely those produced in practice because the valve lash is usually different than the value the seat timing was quoted at. In effect, this makes the seat timing figure only valid for comparison when all cams concerned are measured at a similar follower or valve lift rise.

At first it might seem that the 50 thousandths figure could be used to make valid comparisons with other cams, even a hydraulic, but even this proves not to be the case. At about 4 thousandths (0.004in) tappet lift the hydraulic cam is just about to open the valve, meaning by the time the tappet rise has reached 50 thousandths, typically some 28 degrees later, 46 thousandths (0.046in) of tappet rise has been transmitted to the valve via whatever rocker ratio exists. For a small-block Chevy this is typically 1.5:1. As a result 69 thousandths (0.069in) of lift will have been produced at the valve after about 28 degrees of crank rotation.

Let's assume the same rate of rise for a mechanical cam and say it takes 28 degrees to get from 4 to 50 thousandths tappet rise. If the lash is 24 thousandths (0.024in), by the time the tappet reaches 50 thousandths lift, at best only 26 thousandths (0.026in) has been transmitted to the valve. This results in a valve lift of 39 thousandths (0.039in). This is almost half of what the hydraulic cam is at that point in spite of the fact that a solid cam could appear to have similar specifications.

Let's get back to the 50 thousandths timing and consider how valid this is for a comparison. Because the tappet of a solid lifter cam is put into motion much earlier than a hydraulic cam, it tends to reach the 50 thousandths tappet lift figure earlier in relation to the real seat timing figure. This makes a solid lifter cam appear to have more valve acceleration and velocity than a hydraulic cam, though in reality this is rarely the case. When considering such a comparison, always remember that 15–20 thousandths (0.015–0.020in) lift on a mechanical cam is there for the sole purpose of producing the desired valve lash.

For what it's worth, when comparing mechanical and hydraulic cams, a first approximation can be had by taking 5 degrees off the timing and subtracting all but 6 thousandths of the valve lash from the gross valve lift of the mechanical cam. Though by no means precise, using this technique does give a clearer picture, and applies to mechanical roller and flat tappet cams versus flat tappet hydraulic cams. Hydraulic rollers adhere to the 4 thousandths lift figure, so a comparison between them and a regular flat tappet hydraulic cam is easy to make. Likewise, assuming the lash figures and checking clearances are similar, a comparison can be made between flat-tappet mechanical and roller cams.

If you're going to put enough money into a small-block Chevy to build a 550hp blower motor like this, it makes sense to study every aspect of the procedure in order to maximize your investment. Understanding your cam timing figures comes high on the list.

An accurate dial gauge, a suitably modified pair of lifters, and a big protractor are all you will need to do a reasonably accurate check of the cam timing figures that your camshaft will deliver once installed. Remember, for various reasons, these figures could differ substantially from those printed on the timing card.

Duration, Lift, and Power

5

Up to this point, lots of camshaft technicalities have been discussed but only a minimal amount has been said about the desired end product, namely, the increase in engine output. It may seem as if we've taken a long time to get around to the subject, but if elementary aspects of cam timing aren't understood first, there will be little chance of making optimal choices.

Test Engine Specifications

To demonstrate the effects of duration, increased lift, changes in lobe centerline angle (LCA), and so forth, a relatively basic 350 cam test engine was built in my shop.

Although the term basic might be offhandedly used here, much thought went into building this cam test engine. To get meaningful results it was necessary to put together an engine sensitive only to cam changes. This meant building an engine where all other components would reasonably satisfy both low- and high-rpm requirements so as not to affect the engine's power output in their own right. For instance, it was necessary to select an intake manifold that would be just as happy running at 2000rpm as it would be at 7000rpm.

The exhaust system was another area of concern. Obviously, a small-cammed motor tends to favor smaller pipes and a big-cammed motor, bigger pipes. Thus it was necessary to use an exhaust system that would be relatively neutral throughout the tests. Although achievement of all these goals is not practical, it is possible, with experience, to assemble an engine that tends to satisfy such requirements within reasonably close limits.

The cam test engine utilized a set of 186 pocket-ported head castings, which, in conjunction with a little head milling and high-compression pistons, delivered a 10.5:1 compression ratio. The intake manifold used was an Edelbrock Victor Jr. with nothing but minor reworking to port-match it to the heads. Carburetion was via an electronic 650 Holley which had a little massaging done to it to increase its airflow to about 700 cubic feet per minute (cfm). These modifications in-

The K&N Stubstack proved effective at cleaning up the airflow into a Holley carburetor, thus making the typical carburetor run better at the bottom end as well as at the top end. This was a great asset for cam testing, as it made the tests less dependent on carburetor capacity. On one test, the K&N Stubstack actually showed a 22hp increase.

Any time exhaust flows the wrong way, it seriously impedes the production of power, especially in the lower rpm ranges. Some substantial gains in low-end output and a reduction in camminess of the motor can be achieved using this style of header.

cluded thinning the butterfly shafts down to a minimum, removing the choke plate, and installing a K&N Stub Stack. All these modifications contributed to the increased flow.

Dealing with the exhaust system and its effect on power output in relation to its size was probably the most critical part of the test, but this was effectively taken care of by using a 1^7/$_8$in diameter antireversion-type exhaust system. Tests indicated that this system could virtually duplicate the low-end output of a conventional 1^5/$_8$in pipe while still enjoying the free-flowing attributes of the larger pipes.

Last, there was the ignition system to deal with: obviously, changing cams alters ignition system requirements. For this a programmable unit was used which allowed a timing curve to be built without moving from the console of my Superflow dynamometer. An adjustable belt drive made by Jessel Engineering was used to simplify cam and cam timing changes. The main asset of this belt drive is that advancing or retarding the cam could be done in seconds and without the hassle of tearing down the front of the engine.

Once in operation, the test engine underwent several thousand cam tests. It went through a number of rebuilds and reconfigurations to explore the many facets of cam and valve opera-tion. But in spite of its specialized nature, the data must be viewed as a means of showing trends rather than concrete results. Granted, the trends displayed were positive, but they are trends nonetheless. This point is being emphasized because of the difficulty of isolating any single cam characteristic that would account solely for any power change.

Let's begin with the premise that a relatively short-period cam having near-optimal timing on both intake and exhaust has been installed and is delivering positive results. If the intent is to explore the effect of delaying intake valve closure, then we must consider what else this may affect.

For instance, it is likely that delaying the intake valve closure point will cause an increase in the engine's ability to breathe at high rpm. However, a significant improvement in top-end output may not follow from the improved breathing because the additional exhaust volume produced will cause a rise in backpressure. The greater exhaust restriction caused by the increased quantity of gases involved is cutting into the potential power gain.

This shows that changing one aspect of the cam design may upset the delicate balance of proportions elsewhere in the engine spec. The net result is that the potential to achieve something positive on any single change made may, to an extent, be offset because other design areas may be adversely affected. But this is something we have to put up with so bearing this in mind, let's see what effect various design parameters have on the power output of our small-block Chevy.

Duration

There are three ways that duration can be increased on a camshaft. First, we'll deal with the intake side as it is usually the more influential. The effect of increased duration can be explored by extending it on the opening side, the closing side, or dividing it between

Figure 5-1: Cam Intake Duration Test Engine: 355 Small-Block Chevy

| | Cam 1 | | Cam 2 | | Cam 3 | | Cam 4 | |
RPM	Torque	HP	Torque	HP	Torque	HP	Torque	HP
2500	350	167	348	166	338	161	343	163
3000	348	199	350	200	338	193	349	199
3500	351	234	352	235	342	228	354	236
4000	347	264	347	264	342	260	352	268
4500	334	286	342	293	341	292	349	299
5000	328	312	330	314	333	317	334	318
5500	281	294	286	300	287	301	289	303

Cam Hydraulic Timing Specs

Cam	Intake	Timing	Intake duration	LCA	Advance
1	20	60	260	110	0
2	28	60	268	108	-2
3	20	68	268	112	$+2$
4	24	64	268	110	0

Figure 5-1: *Study these numbers. Basically they reveal the relative importance of extending timing on the leading and trailing edges. However, when considering these results bear in mind the magnitude of the changes in power also depend on original timing figures used as a starting point. The results of the tests will be more meaningful and easier to understand after studying the effects cam advance and LCA can have. Such effects need to be superimposed upon these results.*

both. Such a test was done on the cam test engine, but before looking at any results we should review the test conditions and their possible effect on the outcome.

First, the camshafts used had exhaust durations longer than normal to ensure a reasonably adequate exhaust flow for whatever induction flow was achieved. Second, the baseline cam was on 110 degree LCA. This is relevant since experience with the cam test engine, as with most high-performance 350s, indicated that an LCA of 106–108 works best. Thus, extending the timing in the forward direction could be more favorable because the wider lobe centerline has already retarded the opening point beyond ideal conditions.

Bearing these two points in mind, let's look at the test results in figure 5-1. These numbers demonstrate the relative importance of adding leading- and trailing-edge valve timing. As can be seen, both contributed to horsepower, but the addition of leading-edge valve timing delivered lower-mid and midrange torque increases while still helping the top end to some extent.

The very low end suffered a little probably because of the increased overlap and increased exhaust contamination it would have brought about. On the other hand, the trailing-edge timing cut low-end power and didn't make any appreciable difference until 4500rpm, where it began to improve.

Looking at this in terms of volumetric efficiency (see figure 5-2) we see the same kind of trend so there are no big surprises. In essence, everything is operating as expected.

One point to note since it would change the results of the test is that this particular test engine had no measurable backpressure from the exhaust system. Opening the intake valve earlier allowed it to be open farther at any point in the first half of the induction cycle. Bearing in mind that a 350 small-block Chevy is valve limited, we can see that opening the intake valve earlier allows the engine to breathe and fill the cylinder better during the first half of the induction cycle. Remember, peak piston speed occurs at about 74 degrees ATDC so the greatest demand on cylinder filling is made quite a ways prior to the halfway point of the opening cycle.

During the second phase of the induction cycle from the position of peak piston speed to valve closure, there is usually some 70 percent more time available for filling. This makes

the opening area not quite as critical but don't write off its significance because when rpm is high, every bit of breathing area counts and the catch-up game becomes important.

Before getting into precisely what the catch-up game is, let's continue with the early valve opening and its implications. Because the valve was opened earlier, a greater charge was drawn into the cylinder. This heavier charge was largely retained because of the earlier *closing* of the intake valve. An early closing favors a higher trapping efficiency, that is, the amount of the charge trapped in the cylinder before the intake valve closes. By opening the valve earlier and retaining the original closing point, the trapping efficiency has not significantly changed.

On a typical small-block Chevy the intake valve with a 268 degree cam on 110 degree LCA—timed 4 degrees advanced and utilizing a 5.700in rod—closes the valve 26 percent up the bore. Early intake closure usually leads to a good low-end torque output simply because a minimal amount of charge is pushed back out of the intake. Yet there is a price paid for this in the form of reduced power potential at the high end of the rpm range.

This brings us to the second phase of testing where intake valve closure is delayed but the intake is opened at the same moment. In this situation, at low rpm there is less charge trapped in the cylinder, hence a reduction in low-end torque. However, as rpm increases there is more time for the pressure within the cylinder, which will be below that of the port, to equalize with that in the port. In other words, the vacuum created in the cylinder that draws the charge in is better satisfied

at high rpm because there is more time for it to catch up.

At this point we will ignore any inertial ramming effect because, for the most part, cylinder ramming at the end of the induction cycle on a typical street engine is minimal. To do so, the engine has to be equipped with good cylinder heads, a well-matched intake system, and a camshaft that will allow the engine to run to the kind of rpm where port velocities are sufficient to generate ram effect. For the cam test engine, though, cylinder and port pressures were not measured to establish the fact for sure, but it is unlikely any significant ramming effect at the end of the intake cycle was occurring. Changes in power were most likely the result of port-to-cylinder pressure differentials being given additional time to balance out, as far as possible, prior to valve closure. As can be seen from the chart, the delayed intake closure reduced low-end horsepower on the test engine, midrange was about the same, and top-end power increased slightly.

Having found what happens with extremes, the next and most obvious move is to split the additional timing evenly between opening and closing sides of the inlet profiles. These are the figures produced in column 4 of figure 5-1. Note that the finer benefits of both are not realized everywhere in the rev range. For instance, the negative effect of late closure cancels out much of the positive effect early opening had when it was the sole cam profile change.

Basically what happens is that the combined early opening and late closure allows the engine to run to higher rpm, thus producing more top-end power. This is because the early opening allows better cylinder filling in the

Figure 5-2: Intake Duration Test: Effect of Intake Timing on Volumetric Efficiency

RPM	Cam 1	Cam 2	Cam 3	Cam 4
2500	80.9	81.1	79.6	80.8
3000	81.0	82.1	79.6	81.7
3500	82.9	83.3	81.6	83.1
4000	83.0	84.1	83.3	83.3
4500	81.0	81.8	81.7	82.0
5000	78.1	79.0	79.0	79.2
5500	74.2	75.1	75.3	75.3

Figure 5-2: *As these figures show, relatively large changes in timing figures may only have a moderate effect on the volumetric efficiency. This being the case, we can only conclude that the* greater power differences produced by these minor changes in volumetric efficiency are seemingly the result of the more efficient use of the air.

first phase, therefore the late closing doesn't need to catch up so much at high rpm. The net result is an increase in top-end power.

Exhaust Timing

The cam test engine was used in the same way to look at the effects of exhaust timing. A different base cam was chosen, however, one with the same intake and exhaust timing. The decision to use a single-pattern cam as a baseline was decided upon because, for the most part, it is standard practice with many high-performance cams. Additionally, the cylinder head flow characteristics of intake to exhaust were fairly well balanced at the normally accepted level of 75 percent flow on the exhaust as compared with the intake.

In other words, by accepted standards, the exhaust side of the engine wasn't in any dire need of additional exhaust flow. Therefore, extended timing would not be curing any acute problem in this area.

Again, as per the intake, 110 degree LCA was used and the engine was equipped with an exhaust system having virtually zero backpressure. In fact, the exhaust is efficient enough to cause a limited amount of extraction in the same way an all-out race engine does.

With these factors in mind, let's check the results in figure 5-3. Column 1 shows the baseline figures and column 2 represents the power curve with the exhaust valve opened 15 degrees earlier. This means it cuts the length of the power stroke by 15 degrees. On this particular test cam it represents a reduction in the length of the power stroke by 13.3 percent. The figures reveal that the power dropped, but not by anything like the same percentage. The reason is that the farther down the stroke the piston is, the less gas pressure there is on it.

Extracting the last lb-ft of energy from the high-pressure gases in the cylinder is difficult because they have dropped to a relatively low pressure compared to their peak values. Also, the crank and rod angle is heading rapidly toward the least favorable position for extracting those last remnants of power.

Figure 5-3: Exhaust Duration Test Engine: 355 Small-Block Chevy

RPM	Cam 1 Torque	HP	Cam 2 Torque	HP	Cam 3 Torque	HP	Cam 4 Torque	HP
2500	358	170	357	170	342	163	357	170
3000	356	203	358	204	346	198	360	206
3500	358	239	361	241	349	233	362	241
4000	344	262	350	267	337	257	350	267
4500	330	283	334	286	321	275	338	290
5000	311	296	317	302	302	287	321	306
5500	278	291	283	296	276	289	284	297

Cam Hydraulic Timing Specs

Cam	Exhaust timing	Exhaust duration	LCA	Advance
1	60-20	260	110	0
2	75-20	275	114	4
3	60-35	275	106	-4
4	68-27	275	110	0

Figure 5-3: *From the test shown here the relative importance of adding extra timing can be seen. Additional duration to the exhaust opening side, closing side, and splitting it evenly between the two. For these tests the intake timing was held constant. A point that's worth bringing up here is the fact that these results pertain to an engine having an efficient exhaust system and effective headers. If more backpressure had existed, then best results may have been achieved with the timing figures of Test 2, rather than Test 4.*

As rpm increases, so we see the loss in power over the baseline cam being recouped until at the top end of the rev range, the longer timing is actually producing more horsepower. The reasons for this appear twofold.

First, at high rpm there is less time for the cylinder to effectively blow-down. Opening the exhaust valve earlier extends the blow-down time prior to BDC and cuts pumping losses because cylinder pressures drop much nearer to atmospheric levels *before* the piston starts the exhaust stroke for real. Indeed, if blow-down occurs rapidly and effectively enough, an extraction effect can be generated even prior to the piston starting back up the bore. If this extraction occurs the cylinder pressure at BDC can actually drop below that of atmospheric. However, this is not likely to be the case with the test engine used here because of the relatively low rpm and the class of cam profile involved.

Extending the exhaust timing into the power stroke, then, looks good for mid- and top-end output, but not so good for the real low-end torque. Also, such extended exhaust timing cuts the fuel efficiency of the engine at part throttle.

Yet all factors should be weighed and balanced. If you are looking for a certain amount of power increase from your engine, remember it can be

Figure 5-4: Exhaust Duration Test: Effect of Exhaust Timing on Volumetric Efficiency

RPM	Cam 1	Cam 2	Cam 3	Cam 4
2500	80.2	80.3	78.2	80.3
3000	80.9	80.9	78.4	81.0
3500	83.0	82.9	78.8	83.3
4000	83.1	83.2	79.6	83.8
4500	81.9	82.0	79.2	82.6
5000	78.4	78.3	77.4	78.9
5500	74.7	74.5	74.6	74.6

Figure 5-4: *Here the volumetric efficiency produced by the cams and cam specs in the chart Figure 5-3 is shown. Notice the volumetric efficiency figures of column 4, with the cam having greater overlap, shows the greatest increase. The indications are that the extra power is brought about through the production of a small header-induced scavenge effect in the combustion chamber, rather than from the earlier opening of the exhaust valve to achieve a greater blow-down effect.*

achieved by a combination of changes. For instance, extending the exhaust timing 15 degrees and the intake 10 may prove to be more beneficial than extending both intake and exhaust by 12.5 degrees. Although extended exhaust timing may not look good for fuel economy, by using slightly shorter intake timing than would normally be the case it is possible to pick up mileage due to reduced overlap.

Column 3 of figure 5-3 is the result of extended exhaust timing added to the closing side of the exhaust event. The exhaust valve is now closing much farther into the intake opening phase and by doing so increases overlap by 15 degrees. This change of cam spec caused a noticeable loss of vacuum at low rpm and idle as well as producing a lopey engine. In addition, it was necessary to enrich the air-fuel mixture for smooth idling.

As far as output was concerned, low-end power was down, but as rpm rose, the amount of power lost compared with cam 1 lessened until at 5500rpm it was only off by 2lb-ft. The closing of the two curves probably came about because engine rpm had reached a point at which the exhaust pipes were able to deliver a degree of extraction effect on the cylinder, thus starting the new intake charge on its way in a little earlier.

In the last column of figure 5-3 the effect of splitting the additional timing between the leading and trailing edge of the exhaust valve event is shown. This produces the best results yet. Note that the power increase starts from about 3000rpm and progresses on up the rev range. Again, though not shown on the chart, the early opening and later closure has some negative effects at part throttle. Though not nearly as discernible as in previous tests, less vacuum was seen at idle as well as a slight reduction in part-throttle fuel economy.

Just as a matter of reference, it is possible to see the increased scavenging effect produced by the delayed closure of the intake valve by checking the volumetric efficiency figures from the Superflow dyno. Figure 5-4 charts the volumetric efficiency produced by the four test cams. These figures show that early opening of the exhaust valve did not measurably change volumetric efficiency, whereas late closing of the exhaust valve while cutting volumetric efficiency at low rpm tended to improve it at higher rpm. This shows that the way exhaust is handled can affect both pumping losses and the volumetric efficiency of an engine.

Additionally, early opening of the exhaust potentially reduces pumping losses. But as long as the effect of reduced pumping losses outweighs the decrease caused by reducing the effective power stroke, the engine will make more power.

Column 4 of figure 5-4 shows the effect of splitting the additional overlap evenly between the leading and trailing edge of the cam lobe. Though this gives the best results, it is not necessarily the best way to go.

How exhaust valve timing is handled during overlap largely dictates how well the cylinder is scavenged. A valuable point to understand here is that scavenging can only take place if the exhaust is free-flowing. If exhaust backpressure exists, late closing of the

Figure 5-5: Exhaust Duration Test With System Backpressure
Engine: 355 Small-Block Chevy

RPM	Cam 1 Torque	Cam 1 HP	Cam 2 Torque	Cam 2 HP	Cam 3 Torque	Cam 3 HP	Cam 4 Torque	Cam 4 HP
2500	338	161	336	160	318	151	330	157
3000	336	192	335	191	312	178	333	190
3500	332	221	335	223	306	204	335	223
4000	314	239	317	241	281	214	316	240
4500	296	253	304	260	253	216	299	256
5000	250	278	256	243	—	—	253	241

Cam Timing Specs

Cam	Exhaust timing	Exhaust duration	LCA	Advance
1	60-20	260	110	0
2	75-20	275	114	4
3	60-35	275	106	−4
4	68-27	275	110	0

Figure 5-5: *There isn't a lot that needs to be said about this chart. If you study the numbers you will see that exhaust backpressure of any sort is bad news on a high-performance engine. Basically the bottom line is that backpressure is counterproductive to all of your tuning efforts in whatever area it may be.*

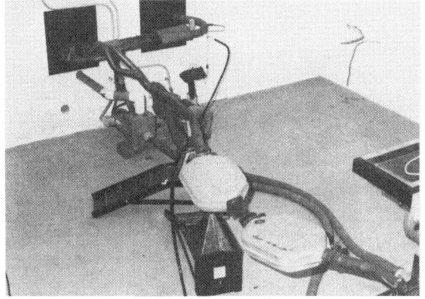

Exhaust back pressure significantly affects the required optimal cam timing.

This test started with two pellet-type catalytic converters.

exhaust valve can be extremely detrimental to power.

By re-testing the cams in column 2 and 3 with a restrictive muffler system, the effect of backpressure on power can be seen in figure 5-5. The baseline power is significantly down over that in the previous figure. This is due to the backpressure affecting the entire running of the engine. Interestingly, with this being a relatively short cam the increase in backpressure did not have a measurable effect on the volumetric efficiency. Therefore the loss in power is due solely to increased pumping losses on the exhaust stroke.

By opening the valve earlier as in column 2, the same trend of reduced low-end power was seen. At the top end the early opening of the exhaust again added extra power. In column 3 we see the effect of closing the exhaust valve later. Here, such a move was almost catastrophic. The low-end power took a considerable dive and the power figures never reached the output produced by the baseline cam in column 1. From this we can see that late closing of the exhaust valve with an exhaust system of significant backpressure is harmful to horsepower.

In more meaningful terms as far as applications are concerned, we can say that cams with big overlap are at a severe disadvantage if used with an exhaust system with high backpressure. In other words, it would be possible to install a cam and lose far more low-end power than would normally be the case unless attention was paid to the exhaust system. This could be one of the reasons some of the bigger cam manufacturers such as Crane Cams tend to produce their off-the-shelf aftermarket cams on wide lobe centerline angles. The wider LCAs can keep overlap to a minimum, thus making the engine less sensitive to inadequate exhausts.

Extending Intake and Exhaust Duration

We've reached a point where we can put the best of various aspects of both intake and exhaust cam timing together to make the most effective cam possible on a given LCA. In this section we will look at the effect of extending the timing of both intake and exhaust in two stages over a baseline cam.

In this particular test, a relatively wide LCA was chosen for the baseline cam because fairly long timing periods were to be used and we needed to avoid the negative effects of excessive overlap. The baseline cam was 270 degrees on the intake and 282 on the exhaust. The first cam change made utilized 285 degrees on the intake and 296 on the exhaust. The last cam was 300 degrees intake and 312 exhaust. Basically, we can say each cam was stepped up 15 degrees from the predecessor.

Running these cams through the cam test engine produced the power figures shown in figure 5-6. There are several points to be made here. First, the shape of the curves are similar with the bigger cam moving everything up the rpm range.

Second, peak torque produced by each cam was not significantly different. Whatever torque occurred did so farther up the rpm range.

And last, peak volumetric efficiency values also did not change by much, although there was a trend for them to marginally increase with the bigger cams. This was probably due to more effective exhaust extraction of the bigger cams.

As expected, progressively increasing the duration caused the vacuum at idle and cruise to progressively decrease. This is an important factor to consider when making a cam choice for a vehicle with vacuum accessories and brakes. As shown by the graph, adding 30 degrees of timing from the baseline cam with no significant increase in lift was worth some 32hp. On the test engine this represented about a 15 percent increase. That's the good news.

On the debit side, it moved the rpm band at which 90 percent of peak torque was available from 1500 to 4500rpm for the baseline cam to 3250 to 5500rpm for the 300/312 cam. This puts the long-duration cam well out of the streetable category if a stock or near-stock torque converter is to be retained for an automatic transmission. Of course, with a manual transmission a cam of this size could be used on the street, although with little bottom-end output to the engine, it would make the car somewhat tiresome to drive.

Like everything else, adding duration to the camshaft has its place in the quest for extra power from your small-block Chevy, but the amount used must always be tempered by the application you have in mind for the engine.

Figure 5-6: Effect of Extended Intake and Exhaust Timing on Power Engine: 355 Small-Block Chevy

RPM	Cam 1		Cam 2		Cam 3	
	Torque	HP	Torque	HP	Torque	HP
2500	333	159	312	149	—	—
3000	350	200	342	195	342	195
3500	360	249	355	237	352	235
4000	372	283	370	282	364	277
4500	358	307	368	315	373	320
5000	344	327	350	333	360	343
5500	285	299	326	341	343	359
6000	—	—	282	322	303	346
6500	—	—	—	—	276	341

Cam Specs

Cam	Duration	LCA	Lift*	Advance
1	270/282	112	0.442/0.448	4
2	285/296	112	0.447/0.448	4
3	300/312	112	0.450/0.450	4

Measured on number 1 cylinder. Due to rocker and pushrod geometry variations, there was about 0.006-0.008in variation in lift on the rest of the valves.

Figure 5-6: *These numbers tell a basic story. It's so simple it hardly seems worth repeating, but from these figures we can see that the bigger the cam, the more top-end horsepower and the less lower end there is. There's no 2500rpm figure for the biggest cam (3) simply because it wouldn't run at full throttle at these rpm. However, at less than full throttle it would produce some power, but it was way off* that produced by the shorter cams. The full potential of cam 3 for the top-end power though, was not achieved simply because the engine didn't have sufficient compression. If you intend installing a cam of this size in your engine you need to read and thoroughly understand what we say about compression and its effect on big cam function.

Low Lift Flow—Just How Important Is It?

Many cylinder head specialists do not consider low valve lift flow important on high-performance and racing cylinder heads. Their reasoning is that since the valve is 200-250 thousandths (0.200-0.250in) off the seat before the piston actually starts on the intake stroke, the flow capability below this point is academic. However, for a high-performance street or race engine, this is not true.

Theoretically low lift flow should help the engine builder find more horsepower. But, theory is one thing, practice is another. My tests strongly indicate that a valve's low flow performance is critical to the production of power, and here's the reasoning behind it.

The first important factor is that the piston cannot "see" how far a valve has opened. At any given point during the rotation of the engine, the piston "sees" only how freely gasses may pass into or out of the cylinder.

The second factor concerns the well-known fact that the faster an intake valve is opened, and for that matter, closed at the other end of the induction cycle, the more torque and horsepower the engine is likely to make. This is especially relevant on a small-block Chevy, which at best is under-valved. Also the nature of its pushrod/rocker-type valvetrain means limited valve opening rates.

The bottom line here is that any improvement in flow, either by bigger valves, improved valve efficiency, or faster opening rates, improves power output. If the low lift flow capability of a valve is improved, the engine reacts exactly the same as it would to faster valve acceleration rates.

Of course, there may be instances when substantially improved low lift flow rates can actually hurt the power of an engine, but only because the cam specification now no longer applies to that cylinder head.

Remember, the cam specification must match the characteristics of the cylinder head. If the low lift flow is improved dramatically, back-pumping can occur earlier on in the closing phases at the end of the induction stroke. This will make it necessary to close the intake valve slightly sooner.

If you're back-to-back testing a low flow at low valve lift head versus high flow at low valve lift, the engine will "think" the cam is longer on the

By simply grinding a 30 degree back-cut on the valve, low lift flow can be dramatically increased.

The lip just inside the seat area of this intake valve causes a marked reduction in flow at low lift.

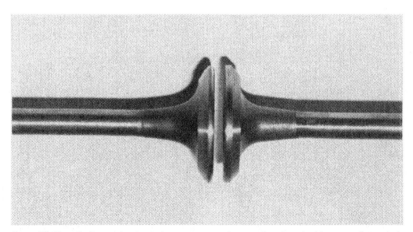

Low lift flow is important on the exhaust to aid cylinder blow-down. Here you see the difference between a stock valve and one modified to improve blow-down. Notice the stock valve has a square margin and no 30 degree back-cut, whereas the modified valve has a 30 degree back-cut and a generous radius on the front-face-to-margin area. The low lift flow on the modified valve is up to 18 percent better.

closing phase. It will also think the overlap triangle is greater, which could lead to excess scavenging of the chamber during overlap and result in high fuel consumption.

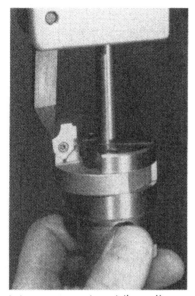

It is necessary to set the cutter as accurately as possible in the tool holder. This normally requires a high-powered magnifying glass, and under such circumstances, sizes can be set to 0.002-0.003in.

The area leading into an exhaust seat can be important, especially where the chamber follows the form of the cylinder wall. This part of the valve circumference is said to be shrouded.

So, to obviate these problems, if a big difference is made in the flow capabilities of a cylinder head at low lift, the cam timing may need to be shortened up. The result will be better fuel economy and more low- and mid-range torque. In other words, the engine will make a better power spread.

To minimize the effect of the shrouded area as much as possible, a form, such as that shown on the tool here, can be applied to the top side of the valve seat.

Valve heights are also important to avoid over-scavenging the combustion chamber or excessive camminess. This is the setup I use to control intake to exhaust valve heights. It allows precision within one or two thousandths.

As far as the exhaust is concerned, low lift flow is important. One of the most important phases of the exhaust stroke is the blow-down period prior to BDC. If substantial gains can be made in the low lift flow capability, it means that the exhaust valve could be held closed longer.

Whereas this may not be a prime requirement for a racing engine running at high rpm, it could be for a street motor. By holding the exhaust valve closed longer, better fuel economy can be obtained. Also, better low-end power can result.

At high rpm, the difference will be minimal because early opening of the exhaust valve does not, on a high compression engine, eat into the power output of the engine as much as you would imagine. Most of the horsepower developed on the power stroke takes place before the piston is halfway down the bore—this is more so the higher the engine compression.

A late exhaust opening only takes on greater importance when the engine is operating at part throttle and the effective or dynamic compression ratio of the engine is much reduced. For instance, on a street motor cruising down the street, the existing dynamic compression ratio may be as little as 2:1 or 3:1. In these instances, a later opening of the exhaust valve is better, and the effect of a rapid blow-down can pay off by allowing a later opening of the exhaust for economy and yet still allow the engine to make good top-end power.

When it comes to getting from A to B quickly, more top-end power is not always the answer. But more *usable power* is always the answer and the key to this is selecting adequate duration for the job.

For the most part, hot rodders usually go overboard on the amount of duration used for their motors. But the effect of duration actually lessens once duration over about 310 degrees is considered. At about 330 degrees duration there is virtually nothing to be gained in the way of extra horsepower. Thus it is important that the amount of timing used in both intake and exhaust be considered along with the lift and lobe centerline of the cam.

Effect of Valve Lift

For the next series of tests, which concerns the effect of valve lift, it was not possible to totally isolate lift—this would have required a unique test situation. Indeed, it's not certain that this would have been the best way to run the test even if it had been practical.

To get an idea of how lift affected output, sets of selected rockers were made up. These rockers had a ratio of 1.42:1, 1.50:1, and 1.61:1 and on a baseline hydraulic cam of 280 degrees by 0.300in lift produced gross valve lifts of 426, 450, and 483 thousandths (0.426, 0.450, and 0.483in) respectively.

At first it may seem as if only the valve lift is changing here, but this is not the case. Although seat timing remains virtually constant, the use of a high-lift rocker means valve accelerations have increased, therefore extra lift occurs everywhere in the lift envelope.

If the 50 thousandths (0.050in) valve lift period produced by the 1.42 rockers is measured, we find that when 1.6s are installed, the period produced at 50 thousandths valve lift will be longer. In essence, using the high-lift rockers has also extended, to a limited degree, the amount of effective cam timing. Nonetheless, the effect produced by higher lift rockers on the power curve is interesting.

Apart from testing with different rocker assemblies, the cam test engine spec had changed slightly for this test. In an effort to show up the differences that might occur, the engine had been equipped with a 3.750in stroke crankshaft, bringing the displacement to 383ci. Along with this a set of ported Dart II iron heads was installed. The idea was to increase both the air demand of the engine and its airflow

capability, with the notion that any differences caused by valve lift should show up as bigger power differences.

In the chart (figure 5-7), you can see the effect of changing the intake rocker ratio only. Notice that the higher lift rocker has a slight effect on reducing low-end horsepower. It is acting as if the cam has more duration, which is exactly the situation described earlier.

Because the valve is opening faster, the effect of duration has partially increased and the end result is that low-end horsepower has started to

drop. However, the gains at the top end of the rpm range are well worthwhile.

If the test cam had been shorter, say 260 degrees, the loss of low-end power would not have been as much. Indeed, with short cams (about 260 degrees or less) a power increase can be seen throughout the rpm range when lift is increased.

Increased lift for the intake, then, is good for a small-block Chevy and it almost always shows up as an increase in volumetric efficiency. Obviously part of this will be due to the more rapid acceleration of the valve, and

Figure 5-7: Effect of High-Lift Rockers on Intake Engine: 383 (3.750in stroke, 4.030in bore)

RPM	1.5 RR		1.6 RR		Gain	
	Torque	HP	Torque	HP	Torque	HP
2500	363	173	359	171	−4	−2
3000	376	215	371	212	−4	−3
3500	390	260	393	262	+3	+3
4000	397	302	402	306	+5	+5
4500	398	341	403	345	+5	+4
5000	393	374	401	382	+8	+8
5500	361	378	372	390	+11	+12
5750	340	372	355	389	+15	+17
6000	314	359	328	375	+14	+16
6250	281	334	303	360	+22	+26

Figure 5-7: These figures demonstrate typical power increases when changing from a 1.5 to 1.6 rocker ratio on the intake only. Crane adjustable rockers were used for this test, and the appropriate change in ratio was seen. The test cam was a dual pattern cam. In practice most gains will be greater than this if a change from the stock rocker to a 1.6 rocker is made. Most stock rockers are considerably less than 1.5, whereas most aftermarket rockers are about the ratio claimed. This test showed upper rpm increases of 12-16hp. Our tests by replacing stock rockers with a 1.6 intake has yielded figures typically in the 15-20hp range for a mildly modified 350.

Figure 5-8: Effect of High-Lift Rockers on Exhaust Engine: 383 (3.750in stroke, 4.030in bore)

RPM	1.5 RR		1.6 RR		Gain	
	Torque	HP	Torque	HP	Torque	HP
2500	363	173	355	169	−8	−4
3000	376	215	368	210	−8	−4
3500	390	260	387	258	−3	−2
4000	397	302	395	301	−2	−1
4500	398	341	399	342	+1	+1
5000	393	374	391	372	−2	−2
5500	361	378	362	379	+1	+1
5750	340	372	340	372	0	0
6000	314	359	316	361	+2	+2
6250	281	334	282	336	+1	+2

Figure 5-8: From these numbers you can see that the higher rocker ratio on the exhaust served very little purpose. Low end output was definitely adversely affected, while top end power made minimal gains. This cam—a dual-pattern design—had 10 degrees longer exhaust timing than intake. On a short single pattern cam more positive results are obtainable when used on the exhaust, but regardless, the greatest dividends are seen on the intake.

part will be due to the increase in total lift. Separating the cause and effect of both these factors is impractical, but a fair guess would be that each contributes about 50 percent to the overall increase in power.

The same type of test on the exhaust did not produce such conclusive results. For the most part, the gains in power from the exhaust were small and hardly out of the bounds of experimental error. Though power may be affected by valve accelerations and total lift, it is more dependent on duration. The escaping exhaust gases prefer time rather than area from which to escape the cylinder. Adequate valve lift and accelerations are obviously required, but past a given point adding more of these characteristics appears to achieve little on the exhaust side.

On occasions, dyno tests have shown that it is possible in some instances to actually *lose* power by increasing exhaust valve accelerations and total lift. From this point of view it seems that softer exhaust profiles, especially on race engines, tend to do a better job.

Figure 5-9 shows the effect of combining both high lift on the intake and the exhaust. As can be seen in column 3, the best combination turned out to be the 1.61 rockers on the intake with the 1.5 rockers on the exhaust. The reason the 1.6-1.6 combination worked slightly better at the top end was probably because the volumetric efficiency produced by the 1.61 intake rockers demanded more exhaust flow at high rpm to cut pumping losses on the exhaust stroke. Apparently, in this case at least, the greater valve opening area supplied by the 1.6 exhaust rockers gave the necessary minimal increase.

Now that duration and lift have been analyzed, the question arises of just how to apportion it. Since we're dealing with the small-block Chevrolet it is possible to be reasonably specific, though different combinations of intake and exhaust can dramatically alter what is required. It seems that an optimal cam between say, 260–310 degrees duration in flat-tappet or hydraulic designs produces best results by employing a higher ratio rocker on the intake than the exhaust and slightly extended exhaust timing. More exhaust timing is required as the rpm increases.

Figure 5-9: Effect of High-Lift Rockers on Intake and Exhaust Engine: 383 (3.750in stroke, 4.030in bore)

| RPM | 1.5 RR | | 1.6 RR | | Gain | |
	Torque	HP	Torque	HP	Torque	HP
2500	363	173	353	168	− 10	− 5
3000	376	215	369	211	− 7	− 4
3500	390	260	384	256	− 6	− 4
4000	397	302	394	300	− 3	− 2
4500	398	341	397	340	− 1	− 1
5000	393	374	400	381	+ 7	+ 7
5500	361	378	374	392	+ 13	+ 14
5750	340	372	356	390	+ 16	+ 18
6000	314	359	330	377	+ 16	+ 18
6250	281	334	303	361	+ 22	+ 27

Figure 5-9: *Combining high-lift rockers on both intake and exhaust helps top end marginally over the results produced by a high ratio on the intake only, but low-end output suffered measurably. Again the situation is marginally exaggerated by virtue of the dual pattern cam used. Loss of low-end output would have been reduced or eliminated if a single-pattern profile had been used.*

Lobe Centerline Angles

While investigating the effect of additional timing on the leading or trailing end of a lobe and freezing the position of the other lobe, it is important to remember that apart from changing the duration of one or the other we are also, by virtue of such changes, altering the lobe centerline angle, or LCA.

For instance, opening the exhaust valve 8 degrees earlier is, in effect, spreading the LCA by 2 degrees. Yet this is not the only parameter that changes.

If the position of the intake valve is frozen but timing is added to the opening side of the exhaust, not only have we widened the LCA but we have also changed the cam advance. Remember, the measure of a cam's advance or retard in the engine is referenced from the lobe centerline. A 110 degree lobe centerline cam put in at 110 degrees to full lift on number one is timed in straight up, that is, no advance or retard.

Let's say we add 8 degrees to the exhaust timing and in so doing make the cam 112 degrees. Then if the intake is reaching full lift at 110 as in its original position, it is now 2 degrees advance. From this you can see that the two factors—lobe centerline angles

To optimize cam timing for each test and circumstance, 98 percent of my cam tests are done with an adjustable belt-drive system, such as the one shown here. Ignition and fuel are also optimized for each test.

and the cam's timing into the engine—are interlocked.

At this point we will look at the lobe centerline angle and its effect on engine output. However, any changes in LCA are also accompanied by a cam-timing optimizing procedure. Because a particular lobe was frozen during previous tests in this chapter, optimizing timing was something not done until now. Relatively wide LCAs have been used simply because they tend to make the engine more flexible. The reason is that wide angles produce less overlap for a given amount of opening duration than tight ones. This was covered earlier, but it won't hurt to mention it again.

As the lobe centerline angle is tightened, so the amount of overlap is increased. The more overlap a cam has, the greater tendency it has to run badly at low rpm, and produce low vacuum and bad idling characteristics. On the other hand, the early opening of the intake valve is conducive to good cylinder filling and the early closing is good for trapping efficiency. On the surface this should mean good results in terms of torque output. So much for theory. Let's look at some tests.

Again, these were done in our cam test engine and a relatively mild Iskenderian 270 Mega cam was employed. A single-pattern cam was used to simplify the viewing of the results. The graph, figure 5-10, shows the results of testing cams at 111, 108, and 105 degrees on the lobe centerline angle. Just for good measure the power curve for a stock 929 cam has been thrown in. As it comes from Isky, a Mega cam is normally ground on 108 degree LCA so a comparison between the stock 108 LCA cam shows just how much this cam can increase horsepower in a typical warmed-over small-block Chevy.

The changes made by the LCA are significant. Notice that going from 108 to 105 didn't make that much difference in the engine's output, but not shown on the power curve is the effect that the change of LCA had on the engine's idling characteristics. With a 105 degree LCA the engine loped much more at idle with idle vacuum being down considerably, and the engine had a tendency to run much rougher until it came up on the cam.

Of course, a relatively short cam like this coming up on the cam occurred at a comparatively low rpm. But going to 108 degrees cured much of the bad side effects and still produced good power.

Yet spreading the LCA another 3 degrees had quite a dramatic effect on the power output.

On the negative side, both power and torque dropped. On the positive side, the engine idled much more smoothly, produced much better vacuum, and generally was a more civilized engine. Why? Because the overlap triangle was reduced quite markedly.

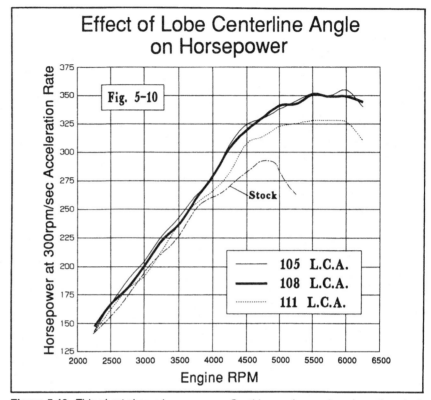

Figure 5-10: *This chart shows how cam LCA can change an engine's output. Basically the LCA has more effect on torque than any other single change in cam spec. The particular cam used in this test was an Isky 270 Megacam. For each test the cam timing was optimized.*

On this graph we also show the stock cam which is usually timed into most small-block Chevys 4 degrees retarded from optimum. The fitment of most 270 degree cams, be it Crane, Competition Cams, or Isky, will, if they're ground on the same LCA produce similar results to this.

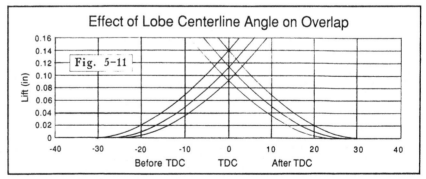

Figure 5-11: *What you see here is the effect that changing the LCA has on the overlap triangle. The largest overlap triangle is produced by the tightest LCA, and to give you some sort of idea as to how much this changes, calculations show that changing from 111 degree LCA*

to 108 increases the overlap triangle area by 40 percent. Going from 111 degrees to 105 increases it by 86 percent. As you can see, relatively small changes in the LCA produce substantial changes in the overlap triangle—that is why most engines can be so sensitive to the LCA.

Figure 5-11 shows the proportions of the effective overlap triangle for the three LCAs concerned. As significant as the actual number of degrees involved is, the area of the triangle and a graphic representation allow the kinds of proportions we're dealing with to be more easily visualized than just numbers.

From these tests, then, it can be seen that for a 350 small-block Chevy the optimum LCA appears to be between 105 and 108 degrees. The question is, how variable is that optimum LCA? Is it something that is basic to the entire range of Chevrolet engines, or does it change as engine spec changes?

In practice the lobe centerline angle for optimum torque and power output proves one of the least variable cam spec numbers, but it is by no means fixed and it will come as no surprise that numerous factors affect its optimization.

The key to understanding how the optimum LCA changes is to visualize your engine in terms of cylinder breathing capability versus bottom-end displacement. In its simplest form we can say that as cylinder head flow per cubic inch drops, the LCA will need to be tightened. If it improves, it will need to be wider. From this it is evident there are two main variables: cylinder head flow and engine displacement.

Assume for a moment a fixed design of cylinder head. If such heads were

used on say, a 300, 350, and a 400ci engine we would find that typically the optimum LCAs would tighten up about 3 degrees per 50ci. From these figures we could expect the 300ci engine to produce the best results about 110 LCA, the 350 around 107, and the 400 engine around 104. If a marked improvement was made in the cylinder heads, those lobe centerline angles could spread.

For instance, we could find that the 300ci engine now operated best on 112 LCA, the 350 on 109, and the 400 engine on 106. To be optimal, these last figures would have to be extremely good cylinder heads. Realistically, most engines require LCAs a degree or two tighter than these. For instance, a good 406ci circle-track or off-road engine typically runs best with about 104 degrees LCA, for a 350 about 107 degrees, and for a 300ci motor 110–111 appears to get the job done.

All these LCA figures relate to race cams that produce a moderately good power band. But when monstrous long-period cams such as those used in all-out drag-race engines are considered, the indications are that the engine will only accept a certain amount of overlap before any additional overlap serves no useful purpose.

For a typical 23 degree valve cylinder head it is not uncommon for the engine to draw the line at overlap figures much greater than 106–108 degrees or so. This doesn't mean there isn't more

power to be had by further extensions to cam timing. But to make it work it is necessary to tack the additional timing on to the end of the intake cycle and the beginning of the exhaust. This has the effect of spreading the lobe centerline angle. You are probably beginning to appreciate that the cam numbers are all so interrelated that it is not possible to separate any one number from another.

Though cylinder head design and cubic-inch displacement are the two main factors affecting the lobe centerline angle required of an engine, several assumptions have been made. They all hinge on the fact that the numbers quoted are for maximum torque and power from an engine that has no artificial restrictions such as those that could exist on the exhaust and induction systems. Other factors such as drivability, fuel economy, and so on, exert an influence as well. Such factors will affect the cam LCA chosen.

Take, for instance, a restrictive exhaust. Too much backpressure in the exhaust causes the optimal LCA to spread because restrictive exhaust systems do not take kindly to cams generating a high degree of overlap. Excessive overlap allows the exhaust to back-flow into the intake. The cure is to spread the LCA if the restrictive exhaust cannot be eliminated.

If you are camming an engine for economy, overlap is not good so if a reasonable amount of power is sought, then consider a wider LCA as this tends to deliver better mileage and fuel efficiency during part-throttle operation. Again, for many street applications it is necessary to have good engine vacuum, and too much overlap destroys this. Too much overlap can be brought about by too tight an LCA. So again, for a street cam wider LCAs are favored.

Figure 5-12 shows the rate of vacuum drop-off with overlap. Vacuum is lost far faster by increasing timing in the overlap area than it is by increasing timing at either end of the two cycles; that is, the closing side of the intake and the opening side of the exhaust. Indeed, it is possible to open the exhaust early and have virtually no ill-effect on manifold vacuum. On the other hand, closing the exhaust late and opening the intake early can have a dramatic effect on vacuum reduction.

Let's consider the effect of the intake system on the lobe centerline of a cam. The tests done in figure 5-10 were for a single four-barrel motor which is the most common type of specification. If

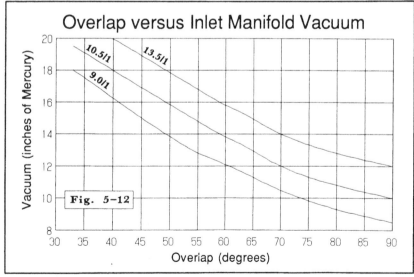

Figure 5-12: *This graph gives a good guide as to how much vacuum your engine is likely to have assuming that it's built well and uses a 10.5:1 compression. As you can see from this chart, reducing* *the compression reduces the vacuum seen everywhere, irrespective of the length of cam used, and increasing the compression improves the vacuum.*

the cam is required for a two-barrel-class race motor or an engine with a tunnel ram or IR (isolated or independent runner) type system such as a set of downdraft Weber carbs or the like, then this can affect the optimum LCA required. Also, should fuel injection figure into the equation, then there are some idiosyncrasies you should be aware of.

But let's deal with the restricted motors first. Anytime the induction side of an engine is restricted it brings about a number of rearranged priorities within the engine. The first of these is the fact that it becomes important to ensure that as much charge as possible is trapped in the cylinder at the intake closure point so compression pressure prior to ignition is as high as possible.

In other words, earlier closing of the intake is necessary to promote as high and effective compression ratio as possible. A higher than normal measured or "static" compression ratio is also needed because a restricted engine is unlikely to have a volumetric efficiency much higher than about 80 percent.

A key to developing more power from a restricted motor than your rival's is knowing precisely when to close the intake valve. This means closing the intake valve the moment the pressure in the cylinder equals the pressure in the port. Of course this factor applies to any engine, but it becomes more important with a restricted engine because the higher the rpm goes, the less the absolute air pressure in the intake manifold becomes. The lower air pressure reduces the effective compression ratio and increased rpm means more power lost to internal friction. Only so much air can pass through the carburetor, so developing power becomes an exercise of air management.

A cam for a restricted motor with an earlier closing on the intake will move the intake lobe centerline around so that it closes up the LCA. Also, where the valve is opened is a point worthy of consideration. If the exhaust system is functioning well and developing a good extraction effect, then the intake valve can be opened moderately early to start the intake charge on its way into the cylinder as early as possible.

However, it's important not to open the intake valve too early because the extraction effect could pull the fresh charge straight through the intake and allow some to go out the exhaust. Some regulations for restricted motors call for stock iron manifolds to be used. Unless well ported, these can develop a little backpressure due to their lesser flow capability and they also tend to have a lesser extraction proficiency. For such manifolds the optimum lobe centerline angle tends to spread somewhat, or to be more precise, the amount of overlap the engine can tolerate tends to be reduced.

As far as intake closure point is concerned, this can change significantly if a restrictive exhaust is used. A two-barrel engine with a restrictive exhaust, or indeed almost any engine with restrictive exhaust, tolerates less total intake timing with most, if not all, of the reduction taking place in and around the overlap period. If regulations call for a restrictive exhaust it pays to give the cylinder a little more time to blow-down. Opening the exhaust valve about 5 degrees earlier seems to marginally help the situation.

Since IR induction systems are becoming popular, it is worthwhile to look at the effects such an intake system has on optimum cam timing.

With an IR system there is a greater potential for cylinder ramming, both from inertia and the shock-wave tuning that can be generated. It helps to understand that an IR system tends to promote low-end output as compared with a single four-barrel setup. The reason is that the effect of induction pulse softening as experienced with a single four-barrel plenum-type manifold is reduced or eliminated.

For instance, if a set of Webers is used, then when the intake valve opens the intake pulse generated by the piston is communicated directly and with minimal damping to the booster of the carburetor. There is no shared plenum to soften it and this results in better atomization of fuel. For an injection

Seats that produce high flow figures and seal up effectively are essential to a high-performance engine; therefore, precision seatwork in the cylinder head is a must. All my head work is done on a state-of-the-art Serdi seat and guide machine. For test engines only, the nearest to perfection is good enough, otherwise test results can be distorted.

When high compressions are needed on a small-inch small-block Chevy, there is always a trade-off between valve cut-out depth, dome height, and combustion-chamber configuration. When compression ratios above 13:1 are required, valve-pocket configurations become critical.

system, we can see that induction pulse softening has no effect on fuel atomization since it is solely handled by the fuel-injection pressures involved. Either way, both aspects help build bottom-end power.

Though not necessarily true with big cams, tests have shown, initially at least, that an engine equipped with an IR system can tolerate having the intake open and close earlier than its single four-barrel counterpart. Thus, an IR system runs better with a slightly tighter lobe centerline angle. However, if the engine is fuel injected there can be some outside influences that temper this.

For instance, when using a Bosch fuel injection with a flap-valve air metering system, induction pulses reflected up the intake system can affect the flap valve and cause metering difficulties. The only way around this is to spread the lobe centerline angle to compensate.

The same situation, though to a lesser extent, can apply to hot-wire mass flow sensors and the like. A large amount of overlap from a tight lobe centerline angle can, because of momentary reversions at the sensor, make the system think it is passing more air than it actually is. When this happens an excess of fuel is delivered to the engine.

Cam Advance

Earlier, this chapter dealt with the effect of freezing the cam timing on the intake or exhaust and making changes to the other cam lobe by extending its timing one way or another. This looks like a simple enough way to optimize first exhaust timing and then intake, but it proves not to be the case. There is so much interaction between intake and exhaust, which obviously must occur during the overlap period, that if the intake timing were optimal with a given exhaust lobe, changing the exhaust lobe almost inevitably changes the optimal position of the intake lobe.

As previously mentioned, freezing one lobe on a camshaft and altering the other changes the overall cam spec by more than just the duration of the altered lobe. Not only does such a move affect the LCA, but it also changes the cam advance. For example, a 270 degree single-pattern cam on 110 LCA timed straight up would have a timing of 25-65-65-25.

In an earlier chapter the lobe centerline and cam advance were discussed as two useful facets in isolating the cam timing requirements. Here is where this can be put to use.

In most instances such as in a carbureted, free-flowing exhaust, normally aspirated small-block Chevy, the engine runs best with about 4 degrees of cam advance. This number seems to work for a wide range of cam duration figures and lobe centerlines, so let's apply it to the example cam. Advancing it 4 degrees produces the timing 29-61-66-21. Is there anything special about the 29-61 intake timing? No, there isn't;

it only applies with the particular exhaust used.

If we change the exhaust lobe by adding 8 degrees onto the opening side, this creates a dual-pattern cam of 270/278 degrees. Tacking on 8 degrees to the opening side of the exhaust changes the LCA from 110 to 112 degrees. Assuming that the intake is frozen in the *previous* 4 degree advance position, adding the extra exhaust timing now means the cam is 6 degrees advanced.

In other words, it delivers full valve lift at 106 degrees after TDC as per the 29-61 timing, but the lobes are now on a 112 degree LCA instead of the previous 110. However, the engine ran best with the intake timing at 29-61 when it was a single-pattern cam on 110 degree LCA. Would this timing hold true with the exhaust extended into the power stroke?

The answer to that question is almost inevitably no. Even though the exhaust has been changed only on the opening side, the optimum intake timing will most certainly have been affected. As it happens, in most cases the engine will still benefit from 4 degrees of cam advance. To hold 4 degrees of advance, the intake timing will change the intake opening from 29 to 27 degrees for the opening point and 63 degrees for the closing point. This is 2 degrees later than the previous case and illustrates the interaction between the exhaust and intake. Although the overlap has remained the same with both cams at 50 degrees, the position of the overlap in relation to piston motion has moved. Spreading the LCA has caused the optimum overlap position to be slightly retarded.

This example should bring home why cam timing figures become so much more simplified by looking at them in terms of advance relative to the lobe centerline angle. The bottom line is that if you have a cam with unspecified timing, then if the LCA is known and the cam is put in with 4 degrees advance, chances are it will be close to optimum whether it's a single- or dual-pattern cam. There are exceptions to the 4 degree advance rule, but it holds true over a wide range of normally aspirated engines. Engines equipped with a superchargers or turbochargers and nitrous oxide injection tend to require substantially different advance figures to normally aspirated carbureted engines, but this will be dealt with as a separate issue in the next chapter.

The larger the cam, the more critical the carburetion. Fully race-prepared Holley carburetors, such as this Braswell item, are certainly not cheap, but they make finding the horsepower a lot easier.

Cams for Nitrous, Superchargers, and Turbos

6

This chapter deals in greater detail with the cam timing figures necessary to make the most from nitrous-oxide-injected, supercharged, and turbocharged engines. All these applications have their own idiosyncrasies that set them apart from more common normally aspirated engines. Let's begin with a serious look at cams for nitrous-oxide-injected engines since this form of power augmentation has become popular.

Nitrous-Injected Engines

When considering cam timing for a nitrous-injected engine it is necessary to identify which aspects of engine operation should benefit most from possible changes. Granted, more horsepower is what is required, but a decision must be made as to whether horsepower should be improved with the nitrous *off* or *on.*

The characteristics of an engine are so different in these two situations that they warrant separate treatment. Also, because the requirements are so divergent, improving the power with the nitrous off may not significantly affect the amount of power gain with the nitrous on. Conversely, if a cam is designed to work with the nitrous on, your engine may even lose power over what can be had with the nitrous off. If this sounds a little perplexing, read on.

When nitrous oxide is injected into the engine, along with the relevant quantity of additional fuel, a substantial amount of extra cylinder pressure is developed and this is where the extra power comes from. Along the way to producing this extra power, a large volume of additional exhaust is also produced. If no measures are taken toward suitable handling of this additional exhaust it will cause pumping losses to climb astronomically. Thus, if an engine were to be designed from scratch to make maximum use of nitrous oxide injection, it would utilize an exhaust valve of much larger diameter than is normally the case for a noninjected engine. This will make sense if you consider that the engine's intake requirements won't change much.

When injected, a lot of nitrous enters the engine in liquid form and as such, doesn't take up an appreciable amount of room in the intake tract. Also, the way the nitrous is injected into the intake tract can sometimes enhance the airflow into the engine.

Of course, a balance of temperatures is taking place as some of the liquid nitrous will turn to a gas by virtue of the heat absorbed from the intake tract. Depending upon the type of nitrous system used, the volumetric efficiency as far as the normally aspirated operation is concerned will normally drop by 10–15 percent. In other words, if an engine had 100 percent VE while running without the nitrous oxide, injecting the nitrous can drop this to 85–90 percent. In this context, nitrous nozzles situated relatively close to the intake valves have less effect at reducing the engine's volumetric efficiency on air.

On the other hand, plate systems mounted between the carburetor and intake tend to have a greater effect at reducing the engine's air volumetric efficiency simply because there is more time and greater opportunity for the nitrous to pick up heat from the intake tract and thus expand.

Regardless of the heating, cooling, or displacement effects that are going on in the intake tract, optimum intake timing for a nitrous engine remains substantially the same whether the injection is in operation or not. Indeed, because the engine is literally having oxygen poured into it the intake becomes a very uncritical phase when the nitrous is in use. For instance, although high-lift cams help power, their percentage effect on power output is substantially reduced when nitrous figures in the picture. It is hardly worth bothering to develop the valvetrain for maximum lift with its usual attendant reduction in reliability in a nitrous engine. It is far better to try and squeeze in a little more nitrous as this is inevitably more reliable.

The development of a cylinder head for a supercharged engine is not the same as that for a normally aspirated engine. Substantially different parameters apply. One of the few experts in this area is Carl Schattilly of C&G Porting in Tucson, Arizona. After appropriately developing the cylinder head, a cam could be used that more closely approaches the theoretical optimum, rather than the usual Band-Aid mismatch.

Intake timing figures are also not critical unless so much nitrous oxide is being injected that a long intake timing is used solely to try and cut low-end torque. Believe it or not, a heavily injected nitrous engine in a lightweight vehicle can produce low-end torque figures that can often cause embarrassing situations for the chassis designer. Apart from this, the big torque numbers could also produce mechanical problems for the engine. Remember, a high-torque output is the direct result of high cylinder pressures.

With a constant-flow nitrous oxide system, cylinder pressures increase as rpm comes down. Utilizing a long intake period, which has the effect of cutting the volumetric efficiency of the air part of the induced charge, can help drop the low-end torque and consequently cut the cylinder pressures to more manageable levels in terms of engine reliability.

Although this peripheral information on cylinder pressures may be interesting, it doesn't alter the fact that the intake timing, as stated previously, does not need to be in a significantly different position with a nitrous engine than with a normally aspirated engine.

Without a doubt, the single most important problem to address is what to do with the exhaust and how to cut the substantial pumping losses that can occur as the quantity of nitrous injected is stepped up. Ideally, the problem is one of cylinder head design rather than cam design. The greater the proportion of power developed by nitrous oxide, the greater the proportion of space used in the cylinder head should be devoted to the exhaust valve. An engine developing 40–50 percent of its output by virtue of nitrous oxide should have an exhaust valve at least as big as the intake and maybe bigger. If this were the case, the exhaust timing required could remain very similar to that of a normally aspirated engine.

Specialty cylinder heads designed to be optimal when nitrous is in use do not exist at the time (1991) and therefore it is necessary to come up with a Band-Aid fix. The fix is to open the exhaust valve early and allow a greater time for blow-down to occur. Granted, the earlier opening eats into the power stroke and one that has a considerable amount of cylinder pressure late on in the cycle to boot. But the payoff is there because the power lost to pumping losses can be so much greater than that of the loss caused by an early exhaust valve opening.

To give an idea of the differences between intake and exhaust timing, our own cams have successfully utilized 20–25 degrees of additional exhaust timing, most of which is needed on the opening side of the exhaust profile. Let's consider the implications of this.

If the exhaust is opened earlier by virtue of having timing tacked on to the opening side, then we are also spreading the lobe centerline angle as well as increasing the period of the exhaust. However, tests have shown that for the most part the intake timing needs to stay where it would have been for a regular normally aspirated engine.

Normally, if the LCA is spread from 108 to 114, and best power is produced with 4 degrees of advance, it would be necessary to pull the intake timing back from 104 to 110 degrees. In this particular case, however, holding the intake as it was and spreading the LCA is what gets the job done. This means the cam is now in a very advanced position in relation to its lobe centerline and proves to be exactly what is required for a nitrous engine.

Depending upon the amount of nitrous oxide injected, a small-block Chevy usually responds well by having a cam with 20–25 degrees more exhaust timing, an LCA 2–4 degrees wider, and the cam set in the motor with 6–8 degrees of advance. What these moves can be worth in terms of power can easily be seen in the nearby chart (figure 6-1). By camming the engine correctly, gains of 30–60hp are relatively common, depending upon the amount of nitrous oxide used.

Although horsepower is its major asset, there are some advantages to a nitrous-orientated cam that are not apparent from the power figures of a graph. The first concerns reliability for a given output. The additional power generated by a nitrous cam comes about not by virtue of increased cylinder pressure so much as by making better use of the existing cylinder pressures. Remember that any additional power realized already existed in the cylinders and has been unlocked by the earlier exhaust valve opening. The additional power would normally be lost because a late-opening exhaust valve causes such high pumping losses.

A second point is that if nitrous is used to boost a street engine, at first it seems obvious to use as big a cam as possible and suffer whatever deficiencies it may have in terms of civility. But consider this: A nitrous cam utilizes a wide LCA cam and it doesn't need a lot of intake duration. These two parameters dictate that even a big nitrous cam

Here's a shot of the porting on the head for a supercharged engine. Take a look at the size of the exhaust valves; you'll see they're much nearer the size of the intake valves. The extra exhaust flow gives good cylinder blow-down without the usual unwanted necessity of opening the exhaust valve early.

will be streetable, which proves to be the case and in practice a near race nitrous cam in a street motor still produces a very drivable vehicle.

The only negative aspect of a nitrous cam for normal operation is that the early exhaust opening cuts mileage. If you can live with that, then even a race nitrous cam makes a good, streetable piece. This allows you to enjoy the benefits of flexibility while the nitrous is not in use, along with the awesome power that nitrous can deliver when it is in use.

Supercharged Engines

To avoid confusion lets define exactly what is meant by a supercharged engine. For the purposes of this chapter it will mean an engine with a mechanically driven supercharger, irrespective of type, which is used in conjunction with a zero to low backpressure exhaust system. When we discuss cams for turbocharged engines it will become evident that exhaust backpressure is a significant factor affecting the choice of cam timing figures.

Having made the distinction between super and turbochargers, we will go one step further and differentiate between the two types of mechanically driven superchargers. These include positive-displacement superchargers and those that are not.

For those who are unfamiliar with the difference, take a look at figure 6-2. Two types of superchargers are shown. Unit A is the classic gear-type supercharger. It can have either straight intermeshing rotors or, as shown, spiral-type intermeshing rotors. The particular style shown is the spiral screw intermeshing rotor type developed by Fleming Thermo-Dynamics and manufactured by Sprintex. As the intermeshing rotors turn, air is literally forced into the engine in the same fashion as with a piston. Leakage aside, turning the supercharger one revolution pumps a certain amount of air into the engine irrespective of any other criteria. Restricting the outlet will cause the boost to climb to whatever level it takes to overcome the restriction.

On the other hand, type B is the kind of supercharger that relies on kinetic energy imparted to the air to develop the supercharge pressure. Boost is related to the square of the turbine speed, and airflow is directly related to the amount of pressure downstream of the supercharger. At any given rpm there will be a "stalled"

pressure above which the supercharger will not go. It will do nothing more than hold this pressure. Conversely, a rotor or piston pump, ignoring leakages, will continue to raise the pressure until mechanical limitations call a halt to the proceedings.

The positive-displacement blower has the ability to supply boost right off idle. So if the supercharger has 50 percent more capacity than the engine, it should supply ½ an atmosphere of boost irrespective of the rpm so long as the engine can handle the boost.

Nevertheless, a turbine-type supercharger such as the Latham axial supercharger shown will only produce when the rpm of the turbine reaches a

speed where sufficient kinetic energy can be put into the air to develop the boost. With this type of supercharger the faster it spins, the greater the boost becomes. At low rpm it provides virtually zero boost, but at higher rpm it can furnish a great deal of boost.

At first it may seem that the positive-displacement blower must be the way to go. If low-end power is what you require, then it most certainly is. But its pumping efficiency is usually significantly less than turbine-type superchargers. Turbine superchargers tend to heat the air less than positive-displacement superchargers and as a result they can develop more power per pound of boost when the boost

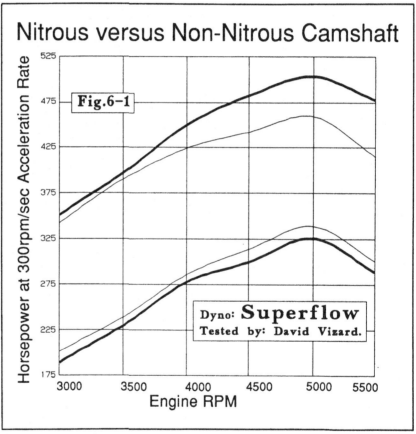

Figure 6-1: *The benefits of a cam specifically for nitrous use are obvious from this test. The bold line is the power output produced by a nitrous cam with and without nitrous oxide injection. Notice that when the nitrous oxide is not being used, the cam produces slightly less power than an optimized non-nitrous cam. On the other hand, when the nitrous is in operation, a cam specifically matched to its requirements produces much greater top-end power. The principle reason is that such a cam takes care* *of the exhaust side flow in a much more appropriate manner. The vast increase in exhaust volume brought about when nitrous is in operation, has to be dealt with in an appropriate manner, otherwise pumping losses will considerably reduce flywheel power. A typical nitrous system without an appropriate nitrous cam can be losing 40-60hp, and remember, this is power that already exists in the cylinders, it's just not getting to the flywheel because it is re-absorbed as a pumping loss on the exhaust stroke.*

does come on. So it's really a case of deciding where the power is required before making a supercharger choice.

Understandably, all these different characteristics between superchargers can mean that different cam characteristics are required. Let's take the positive-displacement supercharger first and see what it needs in the way of cam timing. Supercharging, like nitrous oxide injection, creates much more exhaust. The difference, though, is that all the oxygen that passes the intake valve in a supercharged engine will do so in the form of gas as opposed to liquid.

On the other hand, all that additional charge weight creates more exhaust and this tends to demand a different ratio of intake-to-exhaust-valve sizing.

Though a larger exhaust valve is required for a supercharged engine at the expense of some intake diameter, the requirement is not as radical as with nitrous oxide. This is because the supercharger still needs to push the charge past an intake valve and the freer flowing the intake valve is, the better.

So much for cylinder head technology. But let's see what is required in the way of a cam starting with the intake valve opening. On a supercharged engine the intake pressure should be significantly higher than the exhaust backpressure. The only time this would not be the case is when a very poor exhaust was used. With the intake pressure higher than the exhaust we find that if the overlap is too great, the intake charge will flow through, scavenge the chamber, and then continue to flow out the exhaust.

Consequently, part of a valuable charge of fuel and air is now being lost down the exhaust system and serving no practical use other than polluting the atmosphere and possibly heating up the exhaust to a greater extent than necessary. Unless very high rpm is involved, a supercharged engine needs less overlap than a normally aspirated engine and this inevitably means a cam with lobe centers a little wider than is normally required.

If we're talking in terms of 5psi of boost or more, then the LCA for a supercharger cam needs to be 4–6 degrees wider than the optimum cam for a normally aspirated engine. Applied to a 350ci engine we find that the typical 108 degrees used for maximum torque and horsepower needs to be widened to 112–114 for best results on a blower motor. If engine displacement increases or decreases, then the lobe centerline angle will need to be adjusted accordingly.

At the other end of its cycle, the intake valve action doesn't need to be

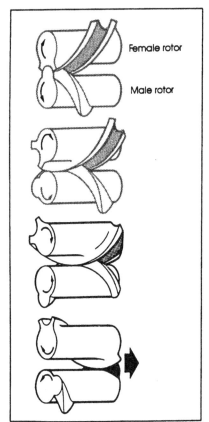

Figure 6-2: *The blower depicted in A is an example of a positive-displacement blower. What I've done here is show only one scroll on each rotor so as to simplify the drawing. With this type of supercharger, rotating the engine forces the air into the manifold. The less air that comes out of the manifold at the other end, the higher the boost gets. In theory, if there's no leakage this type of compressor could compress the air to thousands of psi.* Whipple Industries

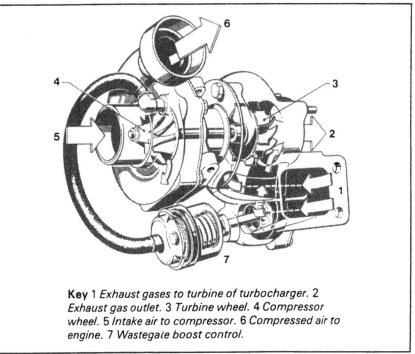

Key 1 *Exhaust gases to turbine of turbocharger.* 2 *Exhaust gas outlet.* 3 *Turbine wheel.* 4 *Compressor wheel.* 5 *Intake air to compressor.* 6 *Compressed air to engine.* 7 *Wastegate boost control.*

Figure 6-2B: *Here we see the typical working parts of a turbocharger. This is a type of supercharger that relies on kinetic energy to build air pressure in the manifold. In other words, it is not a positive-displacement-type supercharger. The basic function is as follows. Air is drawn in at 5 by the spinning turbine (4) then centrifuged out at high velocity. It then leaves the scroll at 6. Due to a combination of flow resistance by the engine and the speed and volume of the* air being pumped, the pressure in the manifold will build accordingly. This type of supercharger can be driven either by an exhaust-driven turbine, as shown here, in which case it's known as a turbocharger, or the exhaust turbine side can be deleted, and it can be belt driven. Vortec and Paxton Superchargers are of this type. The advantage of a belt-driven supercharger is that there is no boost lag due to the time necessary for the exhaust to accelerate the turbine up to speed.

too dissimilar from that of a normally aspirated engine. If high rpm is involved, then a certain amount of delayed closure will be necessary so there is time for the pressure in the manifold to equalize with the pressure in the cylinder. The amount of closure delay after BDC is usually less than for a normally aspirated engine. If the engine is required for low-rpm output, a relatively short cam duration will get the job done. However, to an extent there is a factor taking place that works in our favor.

Obviously as engine rpm increases, the amount of air that can flow into the cylinder during the intake cycle decreases because of valve restriction. What this does in most cases is cause the boost pressure to climb and although it doesn't completely compensate for the fact that the cam timing needs to be longer, it does, in part, help the motor to keep on running up the rpm range when it would otherwise have ceased to do so.

A point worth noting here is that you can, by juggling with cam timing figures, get a supercharger to show higher boost figures in operation. But it pays to remember that the object is not developing boost, but developing horsepower and the two are not always synonymous. The highest boost figure you will ever achieve from a Roots-type supercharger is when the supercharger is driven flat out and the intake valves are welded shut. This will provide maximum boost but absolutely no horsepower and it hopefully emphasizes the intended point.

Let's move on to the exhaust. Here we have something of a dilemma. A supercharged engine tends to make its horsepower a little differently in the cylinders than does a normally aspirated engine. To illustrate this point, take a look at a typical pressure diagram in figure 6-3. This graph shows the pressure traced for a normally aspirated engine versus a supercharged engine. Note that with the supercharged engine the loop it makes is much fatter, although peak pressure in many cases is not as high. Translated into a real world situation this means a normally aspirated engine makes about 80 percent of its power in the first 20 percent of the stroke. At the tail end of the stroke little additional power can be extracted from the gases. Proof of this is the fact that early opening of the exhaust valve does not actually cut the power much at low rpm.

A supercharged engine, on the other hand, has much higher cylinder pressures at the point of valve opening. This means the potential exists to throw away much more usable energy from the high-pressure gases in the cylinders. But the fact that there is a greater volume of gases indicates that an early exhaust valve opening to cut pumping losses would be wise. The two requirements are contradictory, so a dilemma exists. Should the exhaust valve be opened early to cut pumping losses, or should the valve be held on the seat longer to take advantage of the high-pressure gases?

To better view the situation, let's assume a single-pattern cam has been installed in the engine. Such a cam will give good results when put on the correct lobe centerline angle for a typical supercharged installation. It may not produce the best torque and horsepower toward the mid and top end of the rpm range, but it will work well low down. Also, it would tend to be

good for fuel economy, at least for a supercharged engine.

If the exhaust valve timing is extended into the power stroke so as to cut pumping losses, then it is possible for the engine to generate more horsepower in the mid and top end of the rpm range but the price to be paid will be a reduction in the low-end output. This is because at low rpm there is time to get rid of the exhaust gases, and opening the valve earlier wastes pressure energy that could have been constructively used.

But let's look at the reverse situation. What if the exhaust timing is shortened up in an attempt to make use of the exhaust gases for that much longer? Well, at low rpm this certainly helps the output of the engine. It also helps fuel consumption at part throttle. But the problem then arises as to how to adequately rid the cylinder of exhaust as rpm increases. At face value a short cam doesn't look like such a good idea and it isn't if the ratio of exhaust to

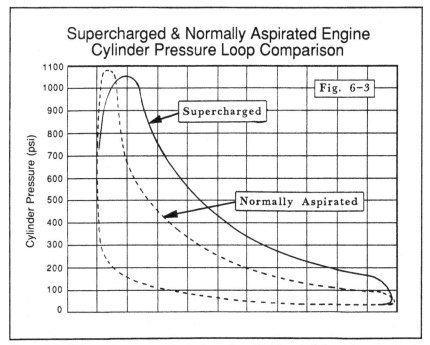

Figure 6-3: This graph compares typical cylinder pressure loops produced by normally aspirated and supercharged engines. Note that the supercharged engine does not necessarily produce any higher peak pressures in the cylinder. However, due to the differing expansion ratio of a low-compression engine, the pressures stay high longer. This means opening the exhaust valve earlier has greater detriment to power and fuel efficiency, especially at part throttle. On the other hand, if the exhaust valve is kept closed too long, the cylinder will not adequately rid itself of exhaust prior to the start of the exhaust stroke. The correct way to deal with this is to alter the ratio of intake and exhaust valve sizes to more adequately deal with the exhaust. This subsequently allows the use of a cam with more appropriate timing to make nearer optimal use of the greater cylinder pressures.

intake flow is typically that of a normally aspirated engine. Yet anytime the exhaust-to-intake ratio can be made nearer unity the short exhaust timing cam begins to look better.

Putting a 1.65in diameter exhaust valve into a typical small-block Chevrolet head and retaining the 1.94in intake valve can work quite well if the exhaust port is subsequently developed to flow well. If your budget stretches to a custom set of heads, then there is a great deal of extra latitude as to what can be done.

I've had experience with heads having exhaust valves up to 1.80in diameter, while still retaining as much as 2.02in diameter intake. Under these circumstances a single-pattern cam, or even a dual-pattern cam with a shorter exhaust timing, can work well.

Another point worth noting here is that because we are often talking about short-period cams, the exhaust valve acceleration becomes a little more important than with a normally aspirated engine. In an earlier chapter we discussed the effect of exhaust valve acceleration. The tests done indicated that greater valve acceleration rates on the exhaust had little effect on power.

On the other hand, more exhaust timing had a substantially greater effect on output from a normally aspirated engine than the rate at which the valve was opened. With a supercharged engine the exhaust valve opening rate begins to have a measurable effect.

If the budget will accommodate it, a roller cam that can put a lot of lift into the valve from just before BDC to about 25 percent into the exhaust stroke seems to pay off in a supercharged engine. Fortunately, this is an area where a roller profile excels. As a result, they allow the engine to develop all the bottom-end power that you would expect from a positive-displacement supercharged engine along with a noticeable gain in mid- and top-end output.

The graph in figure 6-4 shows the output of a street 350 small-block with a Magnuson Magnacharger pumping some 6psi into the engine. Though not a very high boost, the engine produced some extremely respectable figures in terms of torque and horsepower. Along with this went a glass-smooth idle at 500rpm, so the engine was quite civilized. The cam used was a roller profile having some 500 thousandths (0.500in) lift with 265 degrees of timing on the intake and a lesser timing of 260 degrees on the exhaust. The heads used on this engine had a bigger than normal exhaust valve at 1.65in diameter and a highly developed seat and port for the requisite flow characteristics.

If the cylinder heads had been reworked in a more normal fashion, the longer exhaust timing cam spec just may have paid off. For instance, the cams that B&M Automotive Products sell to go along with their street supercharger kit inevitably have 8–10 degrees more exhaust timing than intake. Since most engines that these blowers will be used with have heads designed for normally aspirated use, the idea of using more exhaust timing makes sense. Figure 6-5 shows what happens to the power on a B&M blown motor when the stock cam is replaced with one of their blower cams.

Now consider a turbine type of supercharger as opposed to the more common positive-displacement type just discussed. Again, as in any other cam situation, a choice must be made between low-, mid-, or high-end horsepower. Most superchargers dealt with here that fall into this category have low boost capability at low rpm.

On the other hand, most of them have good or exceptional boost capability at high rpm. Remember, specing a cam is really all about juggling

A big blower on a small-block, such as the Mega Blower from B&M, means that a small-block can produce the kind of torque figures expected of a big-block.

However, too much cam in the engine will kill this, as boost will go out the exhaust valve.

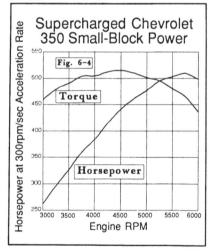

Figure 6-4: Here is the output of a 350ci small-block Chevy using a Magnacharger delivering 6lb of boost. This engine utilized a short cam, 9.0:1 compression, and was endowed with as many attributes as possible to make it a totally civilized street motor. A 600rpm idle and relatively good mileage were included on the agenda. This engine pushed a 3,400lb street Z28 to trap speeds of 116mph, with street gearing and a tight torque converter, which was chosen to give good mileage.

numbers so the end result produces the kind of power band best suited to your requirement.

If the engine in question is a race unit, then low-end output is of no great concern so long as it's enough to get the car out of pit road and onto the track.

For a street motor, however, it is necessary to consider the entire spectrum of an engine's output. This isn't by any means a new revelation, but the point needs to be reinforced because it concerns turbine-type superchargers more than the positive-displacement type. With turbine superchargers the engine is inevitably going to deliver a lower torque output in the low-rpm range because of the limited boost available. It is relatively safe to assume that at low rpm such an engine-supercharger combination will react to camming more like a normally aspirated engine. Thus, the opportunity exists to cam the engine to better low-end output and let the usually high capability of a turbine-type supercharger boost take care of the top end.

For a street motor this is a good philosophy to adopt. As such it means selecting a cam with a *tighter* LCA than would normally be used with a positive-displacement-type supercharger. This, in effect, results in an earlier opening and closing of the intake valve compared to that given by a cam designed for use with a positive-displacement supercharger.

The earlier opening and closing will allow the engine to breathe more effectively at low rpm, trapping more charge weight to enhance low-end output. Expected timing would be similar to a short-period cam timed in as for a normally aspirated engine. The amount of overlap required would also

These oxygen sensors in the exhaust were connected up to K&N Mixture Analyzers. This test established that the lean limit of combustion became richer as the valve overlap was extended. This means more overlap, more fuel consumption, whether the engine was normally aspirated or supercharged.

The characteristics of the turbine supercharger, such as this Vortec item, are completely different from that of a positive-displacement Roots blower. Cam requirements vary accordingly if this type of system is to be compatibly matched.

Shown here are the rotor and stater vanes of a Lathan axial-flow supercharger. In essence, this is similar to the compressor stage of a gas-turbine aircraft engine. It delivers boost efficiently at high speed. Boost at low speed is negligible, and therefore, for an effective street motor, the engine needs to be equipped with the right design of cylinder head and then cammed accordingly.

be fairly similar to that used for a short-cammed, normally aspirated engine.

The only major differing factor is the opening point of the exhaust valve. The necessity to generate the best low-end output consistent with good mileage at cruise demands opening the exhaust as late as possible in the power stroke. However, for the sacrifice of a little low-end horsepower, substantial gains can be made at the top end.

For the circumstances we are dealing with here it pays to consider the context of such gains. Remember, a turbine-type supercharger is capable of delivering a lot of boost at the top end and it could be that in spite of the late opening of the exhaust valve, there is enough boost to deliver all the top-end horsepower required of your engine and then some.

It is not impractical to build an engine that with 12–15psi of boost can generate 600hp upstairs. This may well increase to 625hp if an extra 10 degrees of exhaust timing is added to the opening side of the exhaust cam. However, it pays to ask if that 25hp is more

important than the 15–18lb-ft of additional torque to be had from the short-period cam at around 1500–2000rpm. Because of the rapidly escalating boost with rpm, such a motor is already going to have a steeply climbing torque curve in relation to rpm.

So long as you're not a total power freak, the shorter exhaust timing produces a nicer, more streetable power curve than the one having the additional exhaust timing. If you take into account that an engine for a blower application is a low-compression engine and therefore tends to deliver less torque for any given absolute manifold pressure than its normally aspirated counterpart, then you can see that pepping up the low end makes sense.

Getting the benefits of both ends may appear impossible, but not so. For a little more expense and the use of rapid leakdown lifters, you can get much of what's potentially available at both ends of the rev range. We'll go into more detail on rapid leakdown lifters in a later chapter. But the main point here is that rapid leakdown lifters cut duration mostly from the closing side

of the cam. If you relate that to what has been said about early and later closure of the exhaust, you can see that installing such lifters on the exhaust side will help reshape the power curve to a more desirable form.

Let's review the situation for a moment. So far, recommendations indicate choosing a cam more along the lines of that for a normally aspirated engine. However, as rpm increases, the boost will also increase and all the arguments against using timing similar to a normally aspirated cam appear to apply.

The key is not to use too much overlap. Though the preferred lobe centerline angles are more akin to those for a normally aspirated application, overlap periods used should not be excessive. Typically, overlap periods should be good for output in the 1500–2500rpm range where turbine-type superchargers are traditionally doing little or nothing. By the time the engine reaches 3000rpm there is hopefully a reasonable amount of boost onboard. But 3000rpm is a significant enough engine speed to begin to give whatever boost is occurring too little time to blow through the chamber and out through the exhaust.

Here's the scenario: With a turbine supercharger the boost increases with rpm. The choice of a moderate overlap period for low rpm means that as the time for scavenging the chamber shortens up, it is compensated for by an increase in boost. As a result, chamber scavenging remains relatively effective over a fairly wide rpm range.

The end result will be a power curve that climbs steadily with increasing rpm and the potential exists to produce a greater top-end output than would be expected from a positive-displacement-type supercharger. Of course, we must consider that the amount of boost that can be used will be limited by the detonation level of the engine. It would appear that either way, be it positive-displacement or turbine supercharger, the same limitation is going to apply. However, a turbine supercharger inevitably puts *less heat* into the air so, for a given compression ratio, more boost can be used before detonation occurs.

Looking at the power output of a given engine limited by detonation reveals that, in general, a turbine-type supercharger is good for 2–4psi more boost than its positive-displacement counterpart. By thoughtfully specing out the cam it is possible, to an extent,

A Vortec supercharger on a typical tuned-port-injected 350 is worth 100-120hp, even with the stock cam, but more is available at both ends of the rev range with a cam with more appropriate timing.

to compensate for the low-end output deficiencies of a turbine-type supercharger. Granted, this means shortening up the cam, but any disadvantages of the shorter timing are offset by the greater efficiency of the turbine supercharger at high rpm.

Inevitably there will be applications where a race-only situation exists, in which case the cam timing for a turbine supercharger begins to take the form more consistent with that expected of a supercharged application. Not surprisingly, the final form is, of course, cylinder head dependent. If the engine is built from the outset to be supercharged and has a larger exhaust flow capacity than normal, then something nearer a single-pattern cam is going to do the job. Failing this, however, exhaust timing extended into the power stroke will be required. Again, not wanting boost to escape out through the exhaust valve, the amount of overlap used must be limited.

As a starting point it is not a bad idea to consider your engine as a normally aspirated small-block.

If at this point you figure out the rpm and just how much cam it would need to run normally aspirated to produce peak power at the chosen rpm, then calculate about 1 to 1.5 degrees less for each pound of boost put through the engine. For instance, if peak power were anticipated at about 7500rpm a flat-tappet cam for normally aspirated application would require an overlap of 90–95 degrees. If 20psi of boost is expected at 7500rpm from the supercharger, then use a cam with about 20 degrees less overlap.

Turbocharged Engines

My experience with turbocharged engines dates back to the early 1970s when commissioned by Chrysler UK's competition department to develop a turbocharged engine for one of their then-popular four-cylinder Sedans. The intention was to produce a high-performance version of this vehicle to market in competition with the Ford Lotus Cortina. The project proved successful, with the vehicle passing European emission standards while producing 0–60mph in 5.5 seconds. For a 90ci car this was good for 1973 and even better for 1990. However, the beginnings of the oil crisis put to rest plans to build 1,000 of these cars as fuel consumption became a greater priority in the minds of the public than outright performance.

Though successful at the time, it now seems that as far as cam requirements for this engine go, it was largely a case of stabbing in the dark. With the knowledge subsequently gained for cams in turbocharged engines it seems, as of 1990 at least, that most cam and turbocharger companies are still stabbing in the dark. To be honest, outside of Honda Formula 1 turbo engines, most of our current technology on camming turbocharged small-block Chevrolets comes from one man: Alan Nimmo.

In years of dealing with hot rodders to professional engineers, Nimmo has proven himself time and again to be one of the most thought-provoking and ingenious turbo engine experts. Nimmo concerns himself greatly with the cam timing requirements of a turbocharged engine and it was while working with him on turboed small-block Chevys that one important aspect of cam design for a turbocharged engine came to light. It can be summed up in one simple rule: *Forget the dynamics, just look at the pressures.*

This has been dubbed the Nimmo axiom, and adopting it in various degrees has allowed great strides in terms of camming turbocharged en-

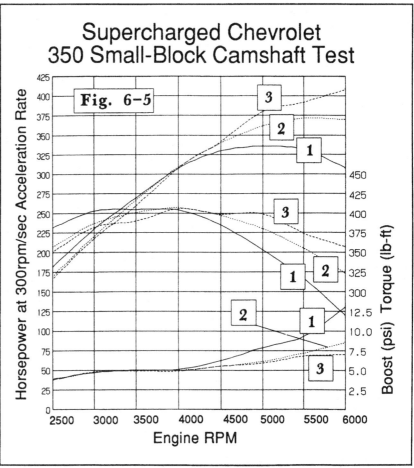

Figure 6-5: *If your budget doesn't run to modified cylinder heads specifically for the use of a supercharger, here's what you can achieve with simple cam-timing changes. The figures shown here were supplied to us by B&M from tests done on supercharged engines having the minimal amount of work on the long lock. Curve 1 is a stock 929 Chevrolet cam. Curve 2 is a moderate street cam having 262 degree intake timing with 272 exhaust. Cam 3 had 282 degrees of intake seat timing with 292 degrees on the exhaust. The figures produced here were achieved with stock heads utilizing 1.94in intake and 1.50in exhaust valves. As you can see from the figures, extending the timing did not make a significant difference to the peak torque output, but it did move the torque curve up the rpm range, giving the engine more top-end power, but suffering the traditional loss in low end.*

gines, especially for the street. To see how the Nimmo axiom works, let's look at the pressures existing during operation of a typical turbocharged small-block Chevy.

The first step toward visualizing the pressures involved in a turbo small-block is understanding that *Chevrolet never intended it to be turbocharged.* Turbocharging a small-block Chevy basically means adding a turbo to an engine designed explicitly as a normally aspirated unit.

Second, most camshafts used with turbo kits—the quality of whose design ranges from good to questionable —will also have been intended for normally aspirated use. Whatever turbo kit you have chosen out of this range is immaterial at this point. The object of the exercise is to make the most of it, and for this it will be necessary to know what kind of intake boost and exhaust backpressures are being dealt with.

If you intend to purchase a kit, then any reputable manufacturer should have the information on hand. The information required will be a curve of intake boost and exhaust backpressure versus rpm. If the manufacturer

doesn't have these figures or isn't prepared to divulge them, then seriously consider whether you are dealing with the right company.

If you already have a turbocharger installation on your engine, this information is not difficult to acquire. Anyone capable of installing a turbo kit in the first place should be more than capable of measuring the significant pressures produced without too much trouble.

Establishing the intake pressure-rpm curve is no problem as the boost gauge and tach delivers this information. A plot of these achieves half our requirement. To get the exhaust back-pressure, tap into the exhaust manifold between the cylinder head and the turbo and install a long copper tube to absorb the heat and connect it to a pressure gauge. For most street kits, there is going to be about a 2:1 pressure differential across the engine. This can vary, though, depending upon the type of installation, how race orientated it is, and how effective the cylinder heads are. Once the two pressure curves have been acquired you're in business.

Applying the Nimmo axiom to a turbo engine essentially means pro-

ducing the most effective exhaust management possible. To see how, take a typical situation where, under full-throttle conditions, exhaust back-pressure is twice the intake pressure. If the cam used has overlap typical of most cams, we find that when the intake valve opens the boost pressure is only half of the pressure existing in the cylinder. Consequently, a fresh charge will not enter the cylinder but exhaust will take the easier path through the intake valve and into the intake system.

This undesirable event does two things. First, the hot exhaust charge dumps considerable heat into the intake charge, and second, it pollutes it with burnt noncombustible gases. Both are serious detriments to the power output of an engine.

The first step toward reducing this problem to a minimum is to close the exhaust valve at whatever point the cylinder contains the least amount of exhaust gases. Experience indicates that something very close to TDC gets the job done and this means using cams that close the valve at or certainly no farther past TDC than about 10 degrees. If we consider the pressure existing in the chamber when the piston is at TDC it will be obvious that dynamic effects aside, the pressure will be equal at least to the pressure in the exhaust manifold.

For a turbo engine boosted at 10psi, the exhaust pressure when that much boost exists is going to be about 20psi. If the intake valve opens at the moment the exhaust valve closes there is still going to be 10psi more pressure in the combustion chamber than in the intake manifold. So no inward flow will take place, in which case there is no point opening the intake valve yet.

As the piston goes over TDC and begins down the bore, the pressure in the combustion chamber will drop. If the piston is allowed to travel down the bore far enough for the pressure in the cylinder to drop to that of the intake manifold, then no back-flowing into the intake manifold will take place. Accommodating this situation usually means delaying the opening of the intake valve to some 20–35 degrees after TDC.

Such a cam timing can be said to have negative overlap. If the exhaust valve closes at or around TDC and the intake valve opens 35 degrees after, there is a 35 degree period where *neither* valve is open. When the intake valve does open, the pressure in the

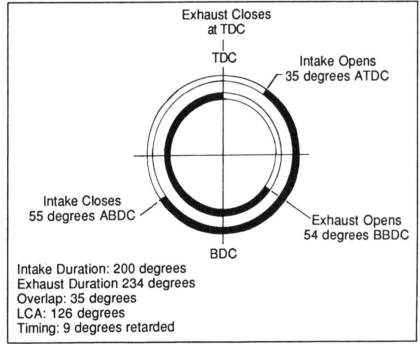

Intake Duration: 200 degrees
Exhaust Duration 234 degrees
Overlap: 35 degrees
LCA: 126 degrees
Timing: 9 degrees retarded

Figure 6-6: *A cam with this timing was successfully used in a turbo small-block Chevy that had about a 2:1 pressure ratio differential between intake and exhaust. The engine produced somewhere in the region of 1000hp with 28lb of boost put into it. Torque output was in excess of 1000 lb-ft. Idle and throttle response with this cam timing proved good, and the performance in a 3,300lb car was nothing short of awesome.*

cylinder is rapidly dropping so charge flows from the intake manifold into the cylinder. No back-flowing occurs.

Conducting events in this fashion around TDC proves effective in many ways. First, the intake manifold charge picks up less heat from the exhaust so more boost can be used. Second, the new charge is less polluted because more exhaust was forced to go out the exhaust valve rather than being allowed to escape out through the intake valve. Although intake charge contamination still occurs by virtue of the exhaust contained in the combustion chamber, it is considerably less than had the exhaust valve been open during the intake phase.

Handling the exhaust-intake situation around TDC by considering the relative pressure balance is 90 percent of the way toward making a successful turbo cam. The closing of the intake valve and the opening of the exhaust valve are far less critical to the operation of a turbo engine than events around TDC. The late opening of the intake valve does mean that if the intake valve is closed at a relatively normal point, then the amount of intake duration that can be used is very limited. For instance, assume a valve closure at 55 degrees after BDC. If it wasn't opened until 35 degrees after TDC, then the intake duration total will be only 200 degrees.

Few cam manufacturers have profiles this short and because it is a short profile there won't be much lift on the profile itself. Thus to make the most of the situation, a high-lift rocker becomes more important, though not essential. Getting the camshaft right, even with stock 1.5 ratio rockers, produces some excellent results and may produce as much horsepower from your turbo engine as you require.

The amount of power produced from the engine that the cam experimentation was done on did not involve anything ultra exotic in the valvetrain. However, with a suitable intercooler the cams chosen did allow as much as 28psi of boost to be put through a small-block Chevy which ultimately produced around 1,000hp at 5000rpm. To put that into perspective, that's 1,100lb-ft of torque which is about what a 750ci Pro Stock-style engine would put out if such a thing existed.

To finalize the point on valve lift, 1.5in rockers will function well, but better results can be achieved by refining the valvetrain. This would entail using high-ratio rockers.

Now for the exhaust. For low-rpm applications, good mileage, flexibility, and response from a no-boost condition, a late opening of the exhaust valve is desirable. As rpm rises, an earlier opening of the exhaust will pay off. It is necessary to consider your priorities here. Up to outputs of 500–600hp at least, a late opening of the exhaust valve is perfectly acceptable.

So how late is late? Well, 50 degrees before BDC is an acceptable value of exhaust valve opening for a typical turbo street application, especially for a truck where towing and low-end capability are important. If higher rpm applications are in mind, then up to 70 degrees before BDC still works.

Up to now we've looked at opening and closing points as independent entities. Let's put them on a cam and see what we have in terms of duration, lobe centerline, and advance. Figure 6-6 represents a typical successful cam timing diagram for a turbocharged engine having a pressure differential across it of 2:1. With an intake duration of 200 and exhaust of 234, the LCA works out at 126 degrees and the cam set into the engine at 9 degrees retard. In an engine boosted at 20psi this cam produced excellent mileage at cruise, a glass-smooth 450rpm idle, and good throttle response.

Apart from the most obvious assets of making the engine run smoother, there are many more benefits to selecting suitable timing for a turbo motor. This is especially important on a turbo motor with a lot of backpressure. Curing the ills of the reverse-flowing exhaust gases tidies up the entire operation of the engine. Apart from being better mannered, it runs cooler, the engine can accept more boost because it is less sensitive to detonation, and so on.

Let's talk about its sensitivity to detonation for a moment. One would think that if exhaust gases pollute the intake charge, then since its combustibility has dropped it is less likely to detonate. This is true. However, it seems that the heat put into the intake charge by the exhaust promotes detonation more than the exhaust dilution reduces it. As a result, late opening of the intake and early closing of the exhaust for negative overlap is beneficial because it allows more boost.

If a decision on the boost level has already been made it can allow the compression ratio to be raised. This, of course, has the benefit of pepping up the low-end power which, on a turbo

motor, is always sadly lacking unless a great deal of work is done to rectify the situation. The added compression not only helps the bottom-end but also improves part-throttle cruise mileage and boost response of the turbo.

With the kind of cam timing proposed here, it becomes practical to utilize compression ratios as high as 9:1 and still use 12–15psi of boost without detonation. Of course, good spark and fuel management is required to do this, along with a respectable intercooler.

Turbo Race Cams

Balancing pressures and ignoring dynamic effects seems to work pretty well with cams for engines operating with a lot of backpressure. However, the more sophisticated the turbocharger installation systems get, the less reliance it seems can be put on the pressure balance technique to design the camshaft.

As the base engine and turbo system become more compatible with a view to more output as a prime objective, if competently designed there is likely to be a lower pressure differential across the engine. An effective design competition system should see absolutely no more than 50 percent greater backpressure in the exhaust than boost pressure in the intake.

It is possible with enough development to get the intake-to-exhaust pressure ratios near unity or even cross over. The closer you get to this situation, the more the cam spec needed will approach that required by a normally aspirated engine.

With the essentials of cam timing for a competition-oriented engine covered, let's look at refining the system so the valvetrain delivers its best. So far, everything dealt with has been in terms of a flat-tappet hydraulic cam, the most basic system for the small-block Chevy.

The question now posed is whether or not it is beneficial to go to a roller cam as used on normally aspirated engines. The answer is yes, there are advantages to it, but there are a few things to consider.

First, intake valve accelerations seem to be, within reason, less critical than on a normally aspirated engine but still influential. If you have a turbo engine delivering adequate power for the job (a difficult condition to conceive of with some speed freaks), then it is possible, by shortening up the cam timing and using the greater velocities

The delivered valve spring forces are important if seat bounce is to be avoided. Because of boost pressure and, in a turbo engine, exhaust back pressure, delivered seat forces may need to be increased. Tight control of spring specifications with a spring tester, such as this precision Jennings unit, is essential.

normally expected of a roller cam, to pep up the bottom-end and still retain top-end horsepower.

On the exhaust side, valve accelerations seem less critical. Having said this, experience indicates there is a little contradictory evidence here. Tests show that a bigger exhaust valve than normal enhances the power curve by bringing the boost on slightly earlier and improving the response to the throttle pedal. A bigger exhaust valve obviously presents a bigger breathing area to the cylinder quicker and one would think the same effect could be achieved with a valvetrain that opened the existing size of valve faster. For the most part, this proves not to be the case.

Rapid opening rates on the exhaust valve seem to return very little in terms of dividends. Nor for that matter does high lift on the exhaust valve produce any worthwhile gains. Thus, we have a situation where the engine seems responsive to a larger valve, but not to increased exhaust valve accelerations.

From this one can conclude that the effect of the larger exhaust valve takes place in the first few degrees of open-ing where the increased flow is directly proportional to the increased exhaust area available due to its bigger diameter. On the other hand, what the cam has in the way of profile to open the valve quicker may not produce the same effect in the first 3 or 4 degrees of opening because of valvetrain flexure, the rate the tappet ramp generates lift, and so on. So although it looks as if the effect of a big valve can be duplicated with rapid opening rates on the cam, in reality it proves not to be the case. This doesn't mean that high-velocity rapid opening profiles are a waste of time. It means their assets in terms of additional power apply mostly to the intake.

However, there is a source of power increase from a roller, as opposed to a flat-tappet cam, that occurs irrespective of the valve opening rate produced. Roller cams have less friction than flat-tappet cams so internal engine friction is cut and a gain in output results. Removing friction from the cam to follower interface can be a very valuable asset, especially on a highly boosted engine as we will now discuss.

Boost and Valve Springs

One aspect of supercharged or turbocharged engines that is easily overlooked is the substantially different valve spring requirements compared to a normally aspirated engine. Even if the engine is only going to run at moderate rpm, it is necessary to reevaluate the valve spring seat force to determine its adequacy.

For instance, take a supercharged engine with 15psi boost and a moderate rpm expectancy of 5500. Under such circumstances a normally aspirated engine would require no more than 85–90psi of spring force to keep the valve seated. But let's put 15psi of boost into our small-block Chevy and see what happens to the valve seat force applied by the spring.

The intake valve on a small-block Chevy is typically a little over 3sq-in. Therefore, 15psi of boost pressure on each square inch of valve means there is 45lb trying to open the valve. This is operative mostly prior to the overlap period when exhaust backpressure is low. Thus the force available by the spring to prevent seat bounce has been cut by 50 percent.

Unless this is compensated for, problems controlling the valvetrain will almost inevitably occur. One might assume that the spring force would have to be increased on a pro rata basis to keep pace with the amount backed off by the boost, but not so.

The situation of pressure balances existing at the valve during the closing phase, which is the most important toward controlling seat bounce, is somewhat complex. The least control of the valvetrain and the worst situation exists at high rpm and a transition from no throttle to full throttle. However, some compensation for the boost pressure is always needed in any supercharged engine and if not taken into account, sooner or later an intake valvetrain control problem will rear its ugly head.

Since too much valve spring force is always harmful, as harmful as too little, it is necessary to reach a realistic compromise as to how much extra spring force is needed when the valves are on the seat. As a rule of thumb we calculate how much is backed off by boost pressure (area of valve multiplied by boost pressure), then add $2/3$ of that figure to the amount the cam profile needs for use in a normally aspirated engine.

For the exhaust valve in a mechanically supercharged engine the valve spring seating force need only be at the level expected from a normally aspirated engine. But for a turbo engine, backpressure in the exhaust manifold is going to attempt, during the intake stroke, to open the exhaust valve in much the same way boost on the intake does. Some additional spring force will be necessary to keep the valve seated. Of course anytime a combination of increased spring loads and a flat-tappet cam exists, there is a likelihood of premature wear on both the cam profile and the lifter.

With a supercharged engine exhaust lobe profile wear can be aggravated by the fact that on those engines boosted at relatively high-boost pressures, the cylinder pressure seen at the time of exhaust valve opening is considerably higher than in a normally aspirated engine. Consequently, the amount of force trying to keep the exhaust valve closed is higher, so the initial loads at the exhaust valve opening point are higher. This, coupled with the higher spring forces needed for a blown engine, often means an increased wear rate on a flat-tappet cam. Though not a problem at moderate boost levels, it can become a problem when boost figures exceed about one atmosphere and for this reason it pays to give serious consideration to a roller profile for a high-boost engine.

Cam Profiles

7

The almost universal use of the poppet valve has come about largely due to its inherent reliability and ease of manufacture. However, the valvetrain that operates it probably has to contend with more compromises than any other aspect of engine design. To understand why, consider what the valvetrain must do for a valve to perform its intended function as efficiently as possible.

Valvetrain Operation

To begin with, the valvetrain must open the valve as fast and as far as possible to allow the cylinder to breathe effectively through the cylinder head ports. For a given opening period, generating maximum valve lift means maximizing velocity and acceleration. Achieving success here allows higher engine rpm, consequently, the valvetrain must also operate at a higher speed. To control the valve motion at these higher speeds, valve springs need to be stronger. To minimize deflection with a stronger valve spring, the valvetrain needs to be stiffer, leading to an increase in weight which in turn needs yet more valve spring to control it. It's easy to see that the circumstances are going to lead to some difficult compromises.

The bottom line is that camshaft profile design is important. Without sufficient attention to the design of what is commonly known as its dynamics, the operational speed of the valvetrain can be severely limited, as can its lift and accelerations. It is only by careful design and production accuracy of the cam profile that a small-block Chevy valvetrain can be made as effective as current designs are proving to be.

In the pioneering days of engine design, and indeed, probably well into the inter-war years, because engine speeds were low most cam profiles were based on what was known as a three-arc design. This simple means of producing a cam profile design involved using an arc for each of the two flanks and a smaller arc for the nose. The dynamics of such a cam were

mediocre, but this was not a problem since engine speeds were low.

These days, small-block Chevys are turning up to and in excess of 10,000rpm, necessitating a valvetrain capable of opening and closing valves seventy-five times per second. This sounds amazing enough in itself; however, for more than half of that time period the valve needs to be parked on the seat during the compression and power strokes. The implication here is that the opening event takes place at a much greater rate than this. Considering the rate at which valves have to cycle in a high-performance engine

This device, known as an Optron, is often used to help analyze the various motions that take place in the valvetrain at high speed. This unit is the one used at Edelbrock to develop their offset trunion rocker. Similar systems are also used by several other cam companies.

gives some perspective to the problem of doing it in a controlled fashion.

The key to making a successful high-speed valvetrain work can be summed up with one word—smooth. To understand the techniques for generating smooth valvetrain operation, it's necessary to appreciate the major factors that must be dealt with to develop a cam profile for high output.

Horsepower Profile Requirements

To get good power output from an engine, certain valvetrain characteristics are paramount. The most notable of these is the area under the lift curve. The shaded area of figure 7-1 defines a lift curve, and it's often quoted in inches/degree of area. Calculating it with anything less than the required

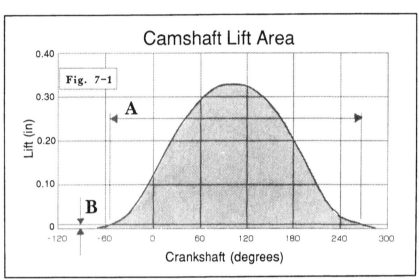

Figure 7-1: *The volumetric efficiency of a small-block Chevy engine is largely dictated by the lift/opening area. This becomes more critical as the displacement* of the engine increases simply because of a small-block's inadequate breathing capability.

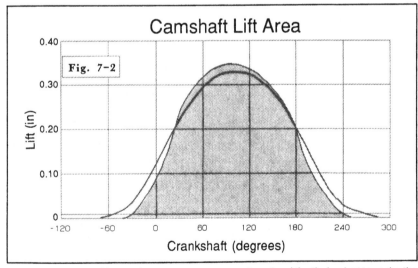

Figure 7-2: *Valve lift/opening area can be produced in two ways, either high lift over relatively short duration, or less lift with a longer duration. For a good power band width it is better to shoot for the high lift/short duration, but when this compromises valvetrain dynamics, it is neces-sary to extend the timing just to make the dynamics easier to deal with. When building a high-output street motor, it pays to think in terms of increasing the opening area by virtue of extra lift, rather than extra duration, as depicted by the shaded area in this graph.*

computer program is a pain in the neck, and it's not until recently that accurate assessments of a cam's lift area have been made to the public.

Essentially, the more area there is under the curve, the better the engine will breathe. Of course, the area can be developed in several ways. Either a lot of duration and moderate lift, or a moderate duration and a lot of lift can give the same results in terms of area available, but not necessarily power. Figure 7-2 shows how such curves differ.

In essence, it's necessary to compromise between lift and duration. Trying to put a lot of lift into a valve will impose excessive stress, especially when a shorter opening period is used. Under such circumstances the valve has less time to achieve the high lift and this leads to even more stresses. To reduce stress the valve can be opened slower, but for a longer period. Although this will cut stress on the valvetrain, the longer opening period will cause the engine to be more cammy and less responsive in the lower rpm range.

Although long-duration cams may be easy on the valvetrain, the price paid is reduced drivability and low-speed performance. As a result of these compromises a good cam designer's objective is to try and maximize the area under the curve, without necessarily overstressing the valvetrain, or producing a cam with too much duration. To achieve this goal it helps to understand why certain characteristics need to be built into the cam profile and first on the list is opening rates.

Fast opening of the intake valve is probably the most important factor facilitating good output. Lifting the valve off its seat up to about 50 thousandths (0.050in) can usually be achieved with greater accelerations than anywhere else in the lift curve. The principal reason is that acceleration up to about 1/3 lift is determined by the cam profile.

Achieving maximum valve velocity as soon as possible is important; however, the amount that can be put into the lifter to generate fast valve motion is not unlimited. The velocity that a flat lifter can reach is strictly determined by its diameter. Once the valve is up to its maximum velocity, the deceleration over approximately the top half of the cam is totally controlled by the spring. Velocity achieved on the closing side has to be bled off prior to the valve seating.

If the closing velocity of the valve toward the seat is too great, the valve can bounce off the seat. This will not only reduce performance, but also leads to rapid seat and guide wear, plus the possibility of broken valve springs, and damage to the rest of the valvetrain.

On the closing side of the cam profile, it's necessary to operate the valvetrain more gently. Setting the valve on its seat slowly preserves the valve seat, reduces valvetrain noise, and helps stop seat bounce. However, if closing is too slow it can cause reversion into the intake manifold, thus reducing torque throughout most of the rev range. The opening side of the cam has to fit different parameters to the closing side, which in itself has to be a compromise.

It shouldn't come as much of a surprise, then, that these requirements are best met by an asymmetrical cam profile. On a small-block Chevy, it's not uncommon for the closing side in the vicinity of the seat to be 20 percent less rapid than the opening side. Figure 7-3 shows, in an exaggerated form, what this means in the way of a lift curve.

Rate of Change

As I've already said, the key to making a valvetrain operate effectively at high rpm is smooth operation. To understand how a valvetrain operates smoothly, it's necessary to jump in with both feet, plough through the dynamics, and relate these to various points on a cam profile.

To start with, take a look at figure 7-4. If you've never been confronted with a cam lift curve and its first few derivatives, then this is going to look like a pretty complex graph. Fortunately, it's not as complex as it appears. As you can see, the profile is broken down into sections, and the dynamic characteristics of each section are then shown in graphic form.

The easiest curve to understand, of course, is the lift curve. This is simply the amount of lift that is generated at the follower in relation to the cam's rotation. But before going any further, we need to clarify an important aspect of the way cam lift data is generally viewed. Since an engine is a variable-speed device it is not convenient to quote valvetrain accelerations and velocities in terms of inch per second because they would continually change as rpm changes. However,

valvetrain motion can be directly related to the crankshaft rotation in degrees. In other words, the number of degrees turned will represent velocity

and irrespective of rpm, will produce a clear indication of how a valve is opening in relation to crankshaft rotation.

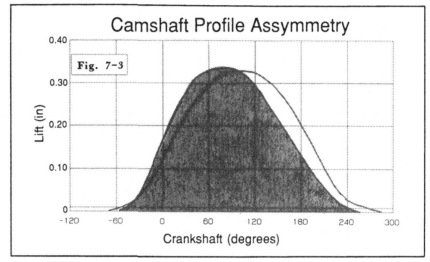

Figure 7-3: *The asymmetry in modern cam profiles is difficult to see in graphic form, and usually only studying the numbers produced from an accurate cam-measuring system will reveal any marked asymmetry to the profile. What we're showing here is the form in which the asymmetry takes on a typical cam profile. Basically the technique is to try and open the valve quicker on the opening side so as to satisfy the requirements at peak piston speed. On the closing side the valve needs to be set down slower as this reduces seat wear and valve bounce. From the performance aspect the area on the closing side is not as critical as it is on the opening side.*

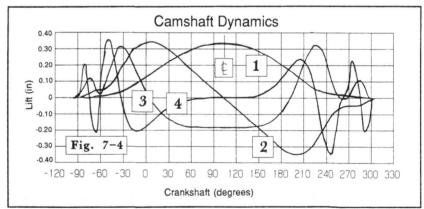

Figure 7-4: *Though you may not have any burning desire to design your own cams, it is a practicality without the need for a degree in mathematics and computer programming. The graph shown here is the output from Andrews Cam Profile Design program. This appears to be a versatile program, and allows the designing of both flat tappet and roller profiles. John Andrews, cam designer and author of this program, is considered an expert in the field of Harley-Davidson cams. His company produces a considerable number of these cams for suc-cessful racers and street bikes alike. At $2,500 (as of 1992) the program may sound expensive, but such an expenditure is little more than a drop in the ocean compared to the money that such companies as Crane, Competition Cams, and other major cam companies have spent developing their own computer programs. I have some limited experience using Andrews' program to design cam profiles. It's relatively easy to use and at this point in time I would categorize it as a useful tool for any budding cam designers.*

To see how this relates to the graph, consider curve 2. This represents lifter velocity, and is shown on the graph as inches per degree. A typical maximum velocity for a small-block Chevy, if it could utilize all of its follower diameter, would be 0.007356in per degree.

Just checking out the curve, you can see that the velocity continues to rise until the follower is almost halfway up the lift curve, and at that point the velocity begins to tail off. As it goes over the nose, the velocity reaches zero. From there on, the velocity of the follower is toward the cam as it drops to the base circle. Curve 3 represents lifter acceleration, and is measured in inches per degree per degree, sometimes written as inches per degree^2.

Looking at the lift curve, it isn't difficult to see that if there's a need for the valvetrain to run smoothly, the lift curve must have no abrupt changes in its form; in other words, the curve must be smooth and continually changing. In addition, the velocity curve must also be smooth and continually changing, that is, have no abrupt changes.

Careful inspection of the curves shows that the velocity curve is in fact a line representing the rate of change of lift in relation to crank angle; the steeper the lift curve is, the higher the velocity. Thus, the next step toward minimizing valvetrain vibration is to produce a smooth acceleration curve. This entails eliminating sudden changes of acceleration. If this isn't done it will lead directly to unwanted valvetrain vibration, which will ultimately limit the rpm possible on given springs.

A simple test to demonstrate what a sudden change of acceleration will do can be carried out in your car. The next time you're out driving, try this technique. Put your foot on the brake with a given pressure, whatever it takes to execute a normal, safe stop. Be sure not to move your foot or alter the pedal pressure until after the car has come to a stop. You will notice that this technique creates smooth retardation right up until the car actually comes to a stop. Then because the acceleration changes abruptly, since there's no more velocity to kill, it goes from a given acceleration, or in this case, deceleration, to zero in no time flat. This creates an infinitely fast rate of change of acceleration, and the passengers all jerk forward momentarily, and then back in their seats.

Whether or not you realize you're doing it, the normal technique for

stopping is to steadily increase the brake pressure until about ²/₃ of the way through the stop. Then during the end phase, brake pedal pressure is reduced so that the rate of deceleration eases up. As the vehicle comes to a stop, the brake pedal pressure is almost entirely released. The result is a smooth stop. Plotting out the change in acceleration from such a stop would show that it is a smooth curve.

It works the same way for a valvetrain. A sudden change of acceleration literally has the same effect as hitting the valvetrain with a sledge hammer. So, the buildup and decay of acceleration also needs to change smoothly and progressively.

One way to check that the acceleration curve is changing smoothly is to investigate what is known as "jerk," or the rate of change of acceleration. After that, we need to look at the rate of change of jerk, which is sometimes known as jerk 2 or quirk. Beyond this, however, the effect of smooth changes begins to have less and less impact on how smoothly the valvetrain runs. This is not to say these figures become meaningless. The more stages that are smoothed out, the more the accuracy of the cam becomes the overriding factor. Eventually, we end up with a formula that theoretically may be extremely smooth to run, but impractical to produce because the accuracy with which it would have to be ground would be beyond the scope of production machines, or even, in some cases, most prototype machines.

If you're being left with the impression that designing a cam profile means some heavy-duty mathematics, then you're right on target. In pre-computer days, even relatively basic cams would take about 100 hours of calculations. But calculators and computers have speeded up the process and a cam profile today can be done in a matter of seconds. The results of these curves can be analyzed by the computer, and the designer can make whatever changes are deemed necessary to the formula to generate the curve required.

In essence, the computer can be given any number of formulas that will generate smooth curves, up to a point. For instance, some relatively simple equations, based on sine waves, cycloids, and trapezoids, have been popular in the past. These days, however, most cams are based on what is known as a "polynomial equation." The beauty of this type of formula is that it allows

the cam designer a great deal of flexibility in the form of cam that is finally generated. Additionally, the polynomial equations are generally simple for computers to handle. However, there are certain things that do tend to complicate the issue.

Although it's relatively simple to figure out a computer program to design a cam on a polynomial equation, the cam does have to be split up into several sections to design it. The key to successful cam design is to match each section at the joining point, so that the transition from one computed profile to another is smooth, not only in terms of lift, velocity, acceleration, jerk, and quirk, but possibly for several other areas.

Dissecting the Profile: Base Circle

Now that we've got a fairly good idea of how the overall cam profile is generated, let's discuss each section in detail.

First, the base circle. This is the part of the cam profile where nothing is *supposed* to happen. Ideally, the base circle needs to be concentric; in other words, the base circle run-out should be zero. But grinding cams to a zero tolerance or a zero error is not practical, and for the most part, up to about 1 thousandth (0.001in) run-out on the base circle is acceptable. However, most competent cam grinders come in under this figure. Those utilizing the latest equipment can usually get down to within 0.0002 or 0.0003in on base circle run-out at the time they are ground. As stresses settle out, though, this figure may increase. Three months on the shelf may push it up to a thousandth (0.001in) or so.

Why aren't cams produced more accurately than this? Well, they can be, but will any further increase in accuracy be recognized by the valve? For instance, when cams are ground it is done between centers, but when the cam is running in the engine, it's running on the outside diameter (OD) of the bearing journals. A clearance exists between the bearing insert and the journal and varies with the load the particular bearing is carrying. As the cam goes through its cycle of events, loads are being applied and removed at various parts, causing the cam to bend and, as a result, the clearances to change.

This situation prevents the cam from rotating about its true center; instead, it orbits around the bearings. Therefore, even if the base circle was totally accurate, what the tappet would see is a base circle with a certain amount of error depending upon how much the cam flexes, and how much the bearing clearances are changing due to the loads exerted by each valve spring as it goes through its lift cycle.

The Ramp

The first part of the camshaft profile at which intentional tappet motion starts is the tappet or follower ramp. The ramp is a very important aspect of cam design and owes its existence to the need for a certain amount of valvetrain clearance to avoid holding the valve off its seat by virtue of combined cam errors and thermal expansion. Absorbing the tappet ramp clearance in a manner that's likely to generate smooth motion is extremely difficult, if not impossible.

If tappet clearance, or valve lash as it is often called, could be fixed accurately the problem would be minimized, if not potentially eradicated. However, because this clearance can vary, the point at which the cam follower picks up the rest of the valvetrain is going to vary. This means accepting some predetermined minimum shock as the valvetrain clearances are taken up.

The most common type of tappet ramp is called a constant-velocity ramp. With this type of ramp, the speed of the lifter is built up early on the lifter ramp and then held at a steady speed. Usually tappet ramps are 25–40 crank degrees long. Having reached onto the constant-velocity part of the ramp, the lifter will usually be moving between 3 and 6 ten thousandths (0.0003 and 0.0006in) per crank degree. In other words, the clearance is going to be taken up at this rate so that the follower will contact the rest of the valvetrain at a relatively low speed.

Where performance is the sole criterion, some cam grinders may use ramp speeds as high as 1 thousandth (0.001in) per degree on the opening side ramp. For the most part, lash clearances are best taken up just at the end of the ramp. Although you'd think that the valvetrain would run quieter by tightening up the valve lash, this is usually not the case because the tappet still runs into the rest of the valvetrain at whatever the tappet ramp speed is, if it's a constant-velocity ramp.

For flat-tappet Chevy cams this is the most common type in use, but some cam grinders are producing cams with constant-acceleration ramps. Although a constant-acceleration ramp may give marginally more area under the curve, it is more sensitive to precise valve lash, or parts breakages are likely to increase. Making the lash too wide means that the tappet or follower velocity as it takes up the clearance will be much higher, therefore the valvetrain will be noisier. Tightening the valve lash too much may reduce valvetrain noise, but the latitude for the expansion of various parts will be absorbed, and a valve could be left hanging open.

Another type of tappet ramp, probably the most complex of all, is the polynomial tappet ramp. This type of ramp seeks to bring the motion of the cam follower down to a very low level between certain limits of lash, say between 16–20 thousandths (0.016–0.020in). During this 4 thousandths (0.004in), which represents the operating window, the ramp velocity is slow so as to take up the clearance as quietly and as shock free as possible.

Hydraulic Ramps

With hydraulic cams the situation concerning the tappet ramp is a little different. The fact that the hydraulic lifter automatically takes up clearance means, on the opening side at least, a tappet ramp in the normal sense of the word is not needed.

If we accept that the lifter is compressible, which it will be because oil leakage is bound to occur, then it is more difficult but certainly not impossible to shock the lifter unless a substantial rate of change of acceleration is delivered to it. With a hydraulic cam, the gentle opening action is only needed for the first 3–6 thousandths (0.003–0.006in). From there on, the serious business of opening the valve as fast as possible can take place.

On the closing side, the tappet or clearance ramp needs to be rethought. The way the flank profile joins the tappet ramp on the closing side is important. With normal valve spring forces, if the valve approaches the seat at typically much more than 7–8fps (feet per second). That's about 2½ thousandths (0.0025in) per degree at 6000rpm, then we find that it is possible for the valve to bounce off the seat, and in some cases, break valves. This is the most common type of valve bounce, and leads to rapid deterioration of the valve seat.

Irrespective of the type of follower, a gentle approach to the closing ramp is

It's no problem checking out the lift profile of a cam. First, disassemble two hydraulic lifters, clean them up, and reassemble the units as shown here using Loctite to hold them in place.

very important. This applies to a hydraulic cam as well as a solid. During the lift process the hydraulic follower will have collapsed a certain amount. Even though the load is coming off it as the follower progresses on the downside of the cam, the valvetrain itself is likely to be too short to be totally without clearance as it approaches the base circle. For this reason the closing side tappet ramp on a hydraulic cam intended for quiet operation needs to be longer and higher than the opening side.

Flanks

Once the clearance ramp has been taken up, the follower moves on to the flank of the cam profile. This is where the opening action really starts. Here, acceleration is smoothly built up to a maximum so as to achieve maximum lifter velocity as quickly as possible, consistent with avoiding excessive valvetrain flexure.

Typically, the acceleration rate of the follower will build up to a maximum about 15 percent of the way into the opening side of the cam profile. From this point on, the acceleration will die off and reach zero at the point where maximum velocity occurs, which is approximately 40 percent of the way up the flank.

Until now, the way the valve has been opened, assuming an infinitely stiff valvetrain, has been totally controlled by the cam profile. The lifter has reached its maximum velocity and must be slowed by the spring. From here on, over the nose to about the same point down the flank side, the cam profile must be designed to be compatible with the spring. In other words, the motion of the valvetrain will ultimately be controlled by the spring. As soon as the spring has insufficient force to control the valvetrain at high speed the follower will launch off the end of the nose of the cam.

Cam profiles generally are designed using one type of mathematical equation, but the controlling numbers will be changed to generate forms to suit different sections of the overall profile. At the point where the valve spring takes control a different set of numbers, or sometimes even a different type of equation, may be used until the cam profile again takes control of motion on the closing side. The trick to making an effective cam is to ensure that each equation generates a shock-free blend with the sections before and after it.

Nose

To appreciate the next few points it helps to realize that the lift profile the

cam delivers is not due solely to the cam profile, but to the cam and lifter combination. For instance, changing the size of the base circle does not significantly change the lifter motion produced.

A camshaft having a larger base circle will also have a larger nose radius than a cam with a small base circle. Although the materials from which cams and lifters are made are hard, they are far from infinitely hard. Therefore as the lifter and cam surfaces touch, they deform to produce a contact patch of small, but nonetheless measurable area, rather than a theoretical line contact. The larger the radius of the cam lobe and the flatter the follower, the less surface deformation there will be to produce the required supporting area, and the lower the surface stress will be.

With typical cam materials there is a definite upper limit as to how much stress the surface can tolerate before fatigue and cracking occurs. As soon as the surface becomes overstressed, the profile literally wipes itself out. The key to getting a profile to live is to have a sufficiently large overall radius that stays within boundaries imposed by the material surface stress limitations. The worst surface stresses typically are produced at the tightest radii of the cam profile, usually over the nose of the profile.

Another factor to consider is that the stresses on the nose of the cam

normally are not maximized at high rpm, but do in fact reach their highest values at low rpm. This is one of the reasons why, until it's properly bedded in, a new cam shouldn't be idled at normal idle speed. Most cam manufacturers recommend breaking in a cam at about 2000rpm for twenty minutes or so. At this speed the nose stresses are significantly less than at 1000rpm, and the tendency for the lifter to rotate is increased.

At high speed, the highest loads in the valvetrain are seen on the profile flanks, where the accelerations are highest. Over the nose, the valvetrain unloads the profile because of its momentum away from the cam. Because the nose radius becomes smaller when the base circle is reduced, we find it is more likely to wipe out the nose.

It is common practice to grind cams with a 50 thousandths (0.050in) smaller base circle to clear the bolts on long-rodded 383s and 400s. This may be a much more temporary solution to the problem than grinding the rod bolts, and having them clear a stock base circle diameter cam because the bigger base circle will mean that the nose of the cam is more likely to live.

On some very long stroke engines the available rod-to-cam clearance cuts options somewhat. As a result, a 4.00in stroker may need the base circle of the cam reduced from 1.040in to as little as 0.825in. Only a roller will survive this.

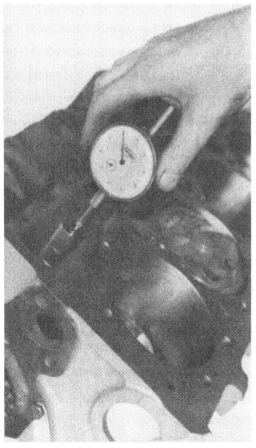

Then install the lifter and mount a dial indicator as shown here. All you need now is a large protractor wheel and you're in business.

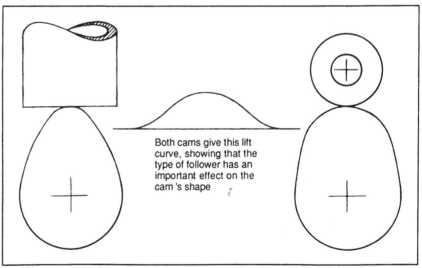

Figure 7-5: *Whenever a cam design is contemplated, it is important to remember that you are not designing a cam profile, so much as a curve of lifter motion. The shape of the lifter dictates* *what shape the cam profile will be. As can be seen from these two drawings, changing from a flat face lifter to a roller lifter affects the cam form substantially for a lift curve common to both.*

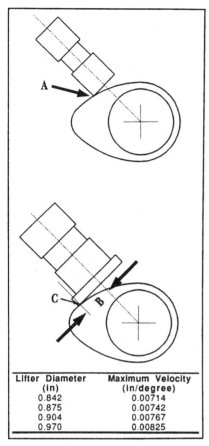

Lifter Diameter (in)	Maximum Velocity (in/degree)
0.842	0.00714
0.875	0.00742
0.904	0.00767
0.970	0.00825

Figure 7-6: *Here's why lifter diameter is so important. In the upper drawing you see the small-diameter lifter digs into the edge of the cam profile, and for that particular profile to work will require a lifter of far greater diameter. The lower drawing shows a mushroom lifter which provides the required diameter. Essentially, we see from the figures quoted here, that increasing the lifter diameter from the stock 842 thousandths (0.842in) to approximately 970 thousandths (0.970in) of a mushroom lifter, will allow over 10 percent higher velocities to be achieved. In terms of opening, this means that after about 20 degrees of the valve event has passed, the extra velocity capability of the larger lifter in conjunction with an appropriately designed profile, will allow the valve to be opened further. So, the critical phase of valve opening throughout the downward motion of the piston will present the cylinder with more valve opening area for better breathing.*

Followers

It's already been said that the lift curve generated by a given cam profile is dependent on the profile-follower combination. Making a comparison between flat and roller follower cams demonstrates this point.

These days, flat follower cams have reached a high level of development, but flat follower cams still have to contend with more friction than is often desirable. In addition, flat follower cams have velocity limitations imposed by the lifter diameter.

By substituting the flat follower with a roller design, two areas of potential improvement are made possible. First, valve opening velocities can be increased, and second, the amount of friction at the cam and follower interface can be cut, thereby reducing the potential of wiping out a cam profile.

Figure 7-5 shows the typical makeup of a flat-tappet follower, and some of the details that make it work, along with a simple roller follower. In both instances, the profiles generate the same follower lift curve. From the difference in the shape of the cam profiles, it's easy to see that the cam and follower combination produces a given lift curve.

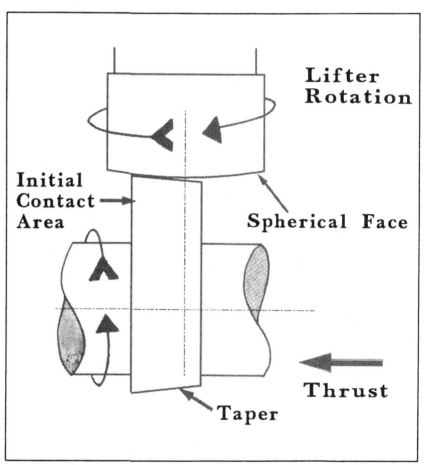

Figure 7-7: *There's more to a flat tappet lifter and cam design than you may think. Subtle changes in form make the difference between a flat tappet cam living for 100,000 miles or dying in 1,000 miles.*

Camshaft Mechanics

8

Part of an expert engine builder's education must include identifying, analyzing, and deducing prospective solutions for high-performance engine problems. Unfortunately, even a proficient enthusiast engine builder may not build enough engines to experience and solve certain problems. Some of the most difficult problems to find a cure for can occur in the valvetrain. To identify potential problem areas it's helpful to understand the basic mechanics and subtleties that contribute to extended camshaft life.

Camshaft Inspection

The first priority before installing a new camshaft is to carefully inspect the finish on the lobes. It's worth stressing here that basically, you get what you pay for. Many of the leading cam companies spend a fortune on their own research. If you insist on buying inexpensive camshafts, you will find that in one way or another, their quality or their performance has been compromised.

For instance, a number of big discount warehouses sell cams priced significantly under $50 and make a working profit on them. Retailing at such a cost, it's reasonable to assume they are produced for probably a third of that amount. Although it would be wrong to tar everyone with the same brush, I know for a fact that many of these cams have been ground on substandard castings. Their material specification is barely adequate for a stock Chevrolet cam profile.

To offset this, and to cut the chances of excessive returns, the profiles on these so called high-performance cams are "soft"; in other words, the acceleration rates and velocities used are conservative. Not only that, these cams are often produced in mass quantity, usually by people who work on "piece rate"—the more they produce, the more money they earn.

Producing an accurate cam is not something that can be rushed. Although the problem we are about to discuss is not found only on cheap cams, it is more prevalent among the lesser quality products. If the worker grinding the cam is in too much of an all-fired rush, they are not likely to let the cam grinding wheel spark out. Consequently, the profile produced will not accurately represent the master cam.

When grinding a cam profile it is necessary to feed the wheel in gently, rotate the cam slowly, and then, as it approaches finish size the infeed must be stopped and the grinding wheel allowed to finish cutting completely. If cuts are made too fast, or if the machine used is not up to scratch, or the grinding wheel out of balance, then a cam profile with chatter marks on it can result. If it hasn't sparked out properly the finish, although it may not have chatter marks on it, may look like a miniature ploughed field. Neither of these conditions are acceptable.

With many cams the Parkerising (the black finish put on it) tends to cover a multitude of grinding sins. To more easily reveal grinding problems use an oily rag and polish the cam profiles, then lightly oil them to produce a shine. Then, when the light falls on the cam just right, any chatter marks tend to be much more apparent. You should consider replacing any cam that has visible chatter marks on its profile.

Likewise, if the finish appears rough, it's probably because the cam profile has not been sparked out properly. If you end up with a cam like this, don't bother to try and refinish it yourself with emery or another similar product. Send it back with a note of complaint asking for a replacement cam that has been inspected by quality control, and a written inspection certificate to prove it.

If you cannot get a quality cam from the company you are dealing with, then you need to consider changing your supplier. Many of the large cam companies that have a fast-selling range of cams are finding it cost effective to produce large batches on fully automatic machines. This removes a lot of the operator-induced grinding errors, and consequently, the quality of such cams is far more consistent.

Dimensional Checks

Doing a visional check requires no other equipment than a pair of eyes, and maybe a magnifying glass, but if you're going to build engines seriously you need to go a little further before installing a cam.

Let's assume that what you are installing is a flat-tappet cam as these probably account for 95 percent of those used. To make a flat-tappet cam live, certain attributes have to be applied to the profile. Some of these attributes can be measured with a micrometer. One of the most important characteristics of a flat tappet cam is that it has a taper on the profile (see figure 7-7).

On a typical Chevrolet cam, there should be about 1 thousandth (0.001in) of taper across the width of the profile. This can be measured with a suitable 1–2in micrometer. You need to check that this taper exists, for without it, the profile will wipe out fairly quickly, especially if the setup employs strong valve springs.

Tapering the cam lobe looks like a sure-fire way of putting all the applied load on the cam profile edge in point contact rather than line contact. This would be true, except for the fact that a flat cam follower does not actually have a flat face.

Most cam followers have a spherical face which is between 30 and 100in radius. For a small-block Chevy a 45in radius is relatively common. Since that is a pretty big radius on a small-diameter lifter, it's not really noticeable; however, the fact that it exists proves to be the saving grace of a flat-tappet lifter setup.

If blocks, cams, and lifters could be produced accurately, the crowning of the lifter and the taper on the follower would not be a prime requirement. If all the parts were precision and infinitely hard, there would be theoretical line contact between the lifter face and the cam profile.

In practice, the degree of pressure applied dictates just how much the theoretical line contact flattens into a working area due to the surface flexure of the two components. If the middle of the cam operated directly in line with the center of a follower profile, the wiped area would be over the same part of the follower each time. This would mean that the amount of friction at the interface and the fact that it was always in the same place, would wear a groove across the face of the follower.

In the real world, cam followers are rarely square to the cam, and even if the profile of the cam was meant to be ground parallel, it's sure to be tapered one way or the other. Without a deliberate taper, just which way the cam profile would be tapered would be left largely to chance. As a result, the cam profile would have theoretical point contact on the follower, and thus would be likely to wear out quickly.

By having a deliberate taper, and crowning the follower, the contact patch on the follower can be offset from the center of the follower. What this means is that some degree of control as to where the follower contacts the cam profile is now achieved, irrespective of whether the follower bore is square to the cam or not. Also, having the contact patch offset from the center of the follower means that the follower will rotate, so to a degree, there is some rolling motion as well as sliding motion at the interface between the cam and lifter.

In other words, it's not a pure rubbing motion, and the fact that the follower rotates means that the lifter to cam follower interface does not see such high rubbing speeds. This of course extends the wear life considerably.

If you were to watch a typical stock cam operating a stock lifter, you would see that while the cam profile goes through the lift phase on the follower, the follower actually rotates about $\frac{1}{3}$ of a turn. Not only does this cut friction at the interface and extend the cam profile's wear life, but it also means that the wear pattern on the lifter is spread out, and therefore the lifter does not wear just in one spot, so its life is also improved.

The taper also helps keep a flat-tappet cam pushed up against the cam thrust face on the block. That's why a flat-tappet cam doesn't need a thrust button like a roller cam does. After a period of time, the two components will bed into each other, and, so long as excessive rpm or spring pressures haven't been used, a hard working skin can develop on both components, thus extending their potential life even fur-

ther. Without tapering on a camshaft, the cam is unlikely to go more than 1,000–2,000 miles unless spring forces are extremely low.

It is unlikely that your camshaft will have less than the required minimum of taper; however, this does not mean that it need go unchecked. On more than one occasion I have heard of cam companies grinding a popular range of cams in large quantities and shipping them out with no taper on, only to get numerous comebacks. For your own peace of mind, since it's such a simple check to do, put a micrometer on the cam, and check that it's tapered. Between $\frac{1}{2}$ and 1 thousandth (0.0005 and 0.001in) is common.

If you've reached the point of checking cam taper with a micrometer, you may be tempted to use it to check the consistency of the lift between lobes. This is definitely not the way to do it. Although practical to measure across the nose and base circle of profiles to find out how uniform they may be, it is not telling you what you want to know; this dimension does not necessarily have much to do with the amount of lift that exists. Having all base circles exactly the same diameter is not critical. If they vary by the odd thousandth of an inch will not detract from the cam's capability to put out horsepower.

The best way to check for uniform lift is to mount the cam between centers, or better yet, in V-blocks, and

check the lift of each lobe with a dial indicator. This will measure the difference in height between the base circle and the nose of the cam, a dimension referred to as the gross follower lift. It is entirely possible to see 2–3 thousandths (0.002–0.003in) difference in overall cam height using the micrometer technique.

Alternatively, the correct checking method with a dial gauge will reveal the true lift differential between one lobe and another, and may be down to less than a thousandth (0.001in). Certainly, if lift varies by more than 0.002in you need to consider that the cam manufacturer is not grinding the cams in as precise a fashion as it could be. On top of any profile errors, you will also have to consider the effect of base circle run-out (BCR). It is relatively common to see 0.001in BCR on a cam, so the effect should be allowed for when assessing the true lift.

Most enthusiast engine builders are not going to have a set of V-blocks

A magnetic dial indicator and a degree wheel are all you need to get a good working idea of your cam's timing and lift figures.

Checking base circle run-out is a relatively quick job with the cam installed. With a tall lifter and a dial gauge set up like this, you can run down both banks in a matter of minutes.

73

around or even centers in which to check their cams. The other alternative is to physically check the cam in the block. For this you will need a magnetic dial gauge base and a 1in travel dial gauge. A tall lifter, one that comes up pretty close to the deck of the block, will also be required.

The easiest way to acquire one tall lifter is to find two hydraulic lifters that are barely worn, disassemble them, and then use the core of one to join the two outer sections. If all the parts are degreased, Loctite them together permanently. This produces a lifter long enough to do the job of checking with a regular magnetic base and a 1in travel gauge.

Checking in the block, however, is not as accurate as checking with V-blocks or between centers. Various errors can creep in and affect the amount of lift measured. Such errors usually involve the cam bearings, however, and can be minimized by ensuring that the bearings are lubricated with a thicker type oil. So long as the bearings are in line, and not worn, the measurements achieved will be reasonably accurate.

While checking lift, another important parameter can be checked out, namely BCR. As mentioned, most cam manufacturers keep BCR to within a thousandth (0.001in) or less. Much more than this on a brand new cam should be viewed as less than precision cam grinding.

One aspect can blur the situation, however. If a cam is stored on the shelf for an extended period, some of the casting stresses can settle out and cause a slight distortion of the cam. This can show up as increased BCR. Such stresses can account for as much as 0.001in distortion.

Just how critical BCR is depends to a large extent on the cam itself. On occasion, I've seen cams that have been run in motors with as much as 5 thousandths (0.005in) of BCR. This distortion was not due to bad grinding, but rather was the result of an engine explosion which physically bent the camshaft. Although not all the lobes were out, many of them had a significant error. Upon replacing the bent camshaft with a straight one, only a marginal power increase was found rather than the substantial amount expected.

Such an outcome leads me to believe that when a bent cam is used to model BCR, the severity of the power reduction depends on which direction the cam is bent in. If the bend was such that it displaced all of the error on the closing side of the ramp, then power loss could be quite severe, as it could be if it was all on the other side. But, if the cam lobe is simply bent toward or away from the nose of the cam, then to a large extent, the effect of the base circle error can be offset by widening the clearance a little.

In general, we could say that with a solid lifter cam that is employing larger clearances—say 0.020–0.030in—the effect of base circle run-out on power can be minimal, and any loss in power would be on the order of 5–10hp on a 500hp motor. On the other hand, my limited experience with base circle run-out in a hydraulic cam reveals that the effect can be much more severe. Because a hydraulic cam doesn't have clearance ramps, the opening and closing points of the valve can be affected much more dramatically.

The effect of replacing a badly copied stock Chevrolet cam profile with a Crane blueprinted profile on a relatively stock motor was quite dramatic.

Although there were other errors, the main problem with the cheap copied cam was that it was not held between centers properly, and that there was a considerable amount of BCR on many of the lobes. The BCR quickly amounted to 3–5 thousandths (0.003–0.005in); replacing this cam brought the power of the motor up almost 30hp.

Since controlling the BCR is really a question of quality control, you can see that it pays to buy from a company that cares about quality. This may often mean paying a little more money, but what's the point of buying speed equipment that is below par? You may spend money for little or no power gain, in which case the whole exercise is pointless.

Computer Cam Checks

If you are a professional engine builder, you may want to get a far better idea of a cam's characteristics before putting it into a motor. Analyzing dynamometer and track results can be beneficial, but it's necessary to get even more sophisticated as far as equipment is concerned. I use a Cam Doctor to analyze cam profiles being dyno tested. This not only measures linear and angular dimensions of the cam to extremely close tolerances—40 millionths (0.000040in) and five seconds of arc being typical—but it also allows such things as the area under the curve to be measured, plus gives a comprehensive breakdown of the dynamics involved. Buying equipment like this, though, is a bit beyond the realm of most enthusiast engine builders.

This moderately hot 350 was run on my Superflow dyno over a period of time, testing various aspects of cams. During this session I got the opportunity to see the negative effect of a base circle run-out on an engine nominally making about 375hp.

I have checked cams for numerous people, both to determine where a problem lies or to relate the cam characteristics to the engine output seen on the dyno. So many different figures are used these days—especially with flat-tappet cams—to quote seat duration that it becomes difficult to compare one cam to another to determine which would work best on that particular engine. Taking measurements from the Cam Doctor, the engine builder is able to make direct comparisons by utilizing the same data points for all the cams tested.

Similarly, the Cam Doctor can be used to investigate problems. The type of problems that it can show usually relate to the dynamics of the cam.

For instance, one engine builder of some considerable experience came in with a camshaft that was breaking valve springs and followers. The cam profile itself was not a terribly aggressive one, as it was used for bracket racing, and it was only a question of getting enough power from the engine to do the job. The Cam Doctor analysis showed that the surface of the cam had a minute waviness in it. I suspected that this cam was ground with an out-of-balance wheel, as all the lobes exhibited a similar appearance when the acceleration, jerk, and quirk curves were inspected. The cam was returned to the manufacturer of origin, where it

To have a more precise idea of what's going into the engine by way of the cam profile, all cams prior to testing are checked out on the Cam Doctor. This measures the cam's profile to within 40 millionths and 5sec of arc. Not only do I get a printout of all the prevailing timing figures, but the computer also analyzes the lift curve in terms of velocity, acceleration, jerk, and quirk. As you can see, some of this information is displayed on the video screen shown inset.

was refinished, this time with great care to ensure complete accuracy.

The cam was installed back into the motor, and the lifter and valve spring problems were virtually eliminated. This proved to be a classic case where a lot of money could have been spent trying to discover the problem. But sophisticated equipment like the Cam Doctor led to a quick and inexpensive solution.

Reduced Base Circle Cams

If you are building a big-inch motor, that is, a motor with more than about 3.625in stroke, you will find that there is a potential problem of the connecting rod striking the cam lobes. The contact point usually occurs between the shoulder or the bolthead of the connecting rod and the flank of lobes on cylinders 2 and 7.

There are two ways to get around this problem: grind the cam profile smaller or widen the rod clearance.

When grinding the cam profiles smaller, the base circle will be reduced and so will the nose radii. If the cam uses an aggressive profile, this is certainly not the best way to go for a number of reasons. First, the surface stresses will be higher, and second, the grinding of the cam will cut further through the cam's surface hardening. Most cam manufacturers will supply a cam with the base circle reduced by 0.050in, but some are reluctant to do this and prefer any clearancing to be done by grinding the shoulder of the rod.

There may come a time, though, when it is necessary to grab all the clearance possible, especially in very big inch motors. If you elect to go with a reduced base circle on the cam, ask the manufacturer how their particular cam reacts to the reduced base circle; with some profiles, the cam life will be shortened. If you are using stock rods, you need to be aware that the 400 rod has the bolts set lower to clear the cam. However, a short center-to-center length makes it a bad choice.

End Float

The way a small-block Chevy cam is designed tends to eliminate end float in the stock setup. This is because the cam also drives the oil pump, and since the oil pump is driven by a skew gear the drag exerted by the oil pump tends to drag the gear in a screwlike fashion toward the rear end of the block. This movement, plus the taper on the cam, pulls the cam into the block, seating

the cam sprocket firmly on the face of the block at the front.

We don't need to consider any modifications concerning end float. However, any movement that does occur can be transmitted directly to the distributor. Therefore it's important to make sure that end float on the cam doesn't occur, so that ignition timing stays more consistent.

The easiest way to ensure this is by using a cam button in the end of the camshaft. The button simply bears on the case of the cam sprocket cover, and prevents movement fore and aft. Some water pumps have a cam bumper adjustment screw that allows the engine builder to adjust the screw until the clearance is taken up between the cam button and the cover. If you elect to use an aluminum cover it may provide for a cam bumper stop on the back face.

Although it's of some benefit to reduce the end float to a minimum in *any* engine, it becomes more important on engines that are dry-sumped. Such engines will have the oil pump driven from a point other than the camshaft, which means the natural tendency of

If you want a 5.70 rod to clear the base circle of the cam when the rod is installed with a 400 stroke crank, then it's necessary to grind the rod by chamfering the edge of the bolt down to ⁵⁄₈in at the point shown above. Although it's quite permissible to do it on all the rods to maintain balance, only two rods actually hit the camshaft.

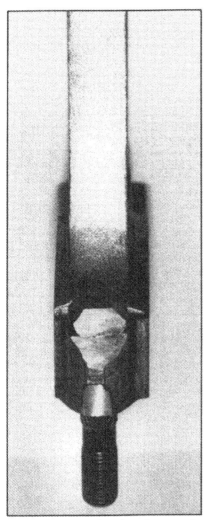

After being ground to clear the cam, the rod will look like this, and in case you're wondering, yes it is safe to use.

With a roller cam it is important to keep end float under control. A simple aluminum cam button will do the job, but if you're paranoid about cutting friction, bump stops built around needle roller thrust bearings, such as the one shown here, are available.

the cam to thrust into the cam face will be largely lost, and the tendency for the cam to use up the end float will need controlling. In this situation, a cam button is essential.

If roller cams are being used, and the cam bores are out of alignment, the cam can suffer what is known as "cam walk." It can either have a tendency to be pressed toward the back of the block—in which case it will run up against the cam thrust face—and not provide a problem, or it will tend to walk toward the front of the block. This situation occurs when the lifter bores are not perpendicular to the cam lobe surfaces.

To prevent cam walk, it's necessary to put in a bumper stop. Of course, if the cam walk is too evident, then the block needs to be machined to put the lifter bores square to the cam followers.

If a wet-sump is retained and a heavy-duty pump is used, the end thrust on the cam can be even greater than stock. If rpm is high, then it may be necessary to improve the lubrication or the bearing quality on the thrust face of the block to sprocket. Probably the simplest way of doing this is to drill a small hole in the face of the block, so that it connects with the oil gallery, and feeds pressurized oil to the thrust face. Also, a circular groove machined into the back of the sprocket that coincides with the oil hole will help distribute the oil over the entire face of the sprocket.

If this method of lubrication still proves insufficient, then a bronze shim can be installed between the two surfaces. Here, the thickness of the shim will have to be machined off the back of the sprocket. If you want to go whole hog toward achieving an adequate thrust bearing, the sprocket can be machined to accommodate a Torrington needle roller thrust race positioned between the thrust surface on the block and the sprocket. Going this route should end all problems associated with overloading the thrust surface.

Flat Tappet versus Roller Reliability

One of the most critical lubrication areas in a modern pushrod engine is the cam and follower interface. This applies not only to the small-block Chevy, but also to many other mass-production pushrod engines. Many of the oils blended these days have to be brought up to a specification capable of adequately lubricating the cam profile-lifter interface. If this requirement did not have to be met the oils would be more than good enough for the rest of the engine, bores, and bearings included.

On a small-block Chevy, the camshaft and lifter are probably the most unreliable parts of the engine in terms of wear. For this reason, it's a good idea to always change the oil and filter regularly. Doing so will extend the cam and lifter life. When a roller cam is installed, this critical lubrication point is removed, and the engine's demand for quality oil is likewise reduced.

So long as cam profiles and follower design are suitably done, a roller follower represents a big increase in valvetrain reliability. Roller lifters often like to be run at higher rpm to lube the roller bearing. Some companies have special street, marine, or continuous usage roller lifters, so if this fits your needs, then this is what you should use. Not only can the roller follower be more reliable, but also it can cut engine friction.

Just how much this improves power is debatable. Claims as high as 11hp have been made for General Motors' hydraulic roller follower setup, whereas some measurements in the aftermarket cam industry indicate a roller follower may only release 4 or 5 more horsepower at most. This assumes, of course, that the cams' lift profiles are identical.

When an engine utilizes a roller follower, it almost always needs a cam

Drilling a hole as indicated here, so that a pressure oil supply is fed to the cam sprocket thrust face, can cut wear at this point.

To control end float on production roller cams, a cam design change is made. See how the end of the roller cam (left) is different from that of the regular cam on the right. The roller cam requires a special thrust plate which is secured by screws to the block. The cam also takes a different style of drive gear. But, before you think you'll just interchange a factory roller into an older block, remember the blocks are different as well. It's possible to convert a newer block to a flat-tappet cam, but much harder to do it the other way around.

based on the steel billet. If a cam is ground on a regular cast-iron blank, the hardness and small diameter of roller can fatigue and crack the surface of the cast iron. When the factory changed to roller cams in 1986, it also changed the alloy the cam blank was cast from. This, together with a milder profile than most aftermarket cams, ensured that it would stand up to the action of the roller on the face. However, castable iron-based alloys for reliable operation with an aggressive roller cam profile are now becoming available.

For very high output cams, the aftermarket industry uses steel blanks as a starting point. Some of the high-performance street roller cams from companies such as Competition Cams and Sealed Power are based on upgraded alloy castings. Though not as good as steel, the profile design used makes the necessary allowances. Anytime a cast-iron blank is used, the price of the cam and roller kit drops dramatically. Another advantage is that these cams are compatible with a stock-type steel distributor gear.

However, if you intend using a roller profile based on a steel blank, it's necessary to change the distributor drive gear. The material used for the stock Chevrolet distributor drive gear is not compatible with steel. If a steel cam is used on the steel gear of the stock distributor, both cam gear and distributor gear will wear very rapidly.

To avoid this, it's necessary to use a bronze gear on the distributor driveshaft to retain material compatibility between the distributor drive and steel cam. With the bronze gear, most wear occurs on the gear rather than the cam. The bronze gear-steel cam combination does not have the wear life of the cast cam-steel gear combination, which is a good argument for using the high grade cast roller cams even if they are milder in action.

Apart from friction levels, why would you want to go to a roller cam? Well, if it's horsepower you're after, the greater lifter velocities at peak piston demand and higher lift values attainable with the roller cam can mean much better breathing.

You can elect to go in one of two directions here. You can retain the same opening period, and use a cam profile lifting faster and farther, or you can go to a slightly shorter cam so that the valve overlap triangle at TDC remains unchanged, or even becomes less. Either route will given more area under the curve to get better breathing and power, though the first option will give the greater top-end power.

However because the initial acceleration is slower on a roller setup it takes about 20 degrees for a roller to catch a flat tappet profile. As a result bigger overlap triangles are not seen with roller cams until duration exceeds some 290-300 degrees. For street cams up to 280-290 degrees a street roller almost always produces a better idle quality than its flat tappet counterpart.

In terms of additional power output, changing from a flat-tappet street cam of around 280 degrees to a street roller profile setup can be worth as much as 20hp. For an all-out race engine such a change can be worth as much as 50hp along with added reliability in all areas, except maybe the valve springs. Even this ultimately depends on the aggressiveness of the profile used.

Camshaft Types

9

You could install one of four distinctly different types of cam and cam follower assemblies into your small-block Chevy: a flat-tappet cam with either hydraulic or solid lifters, or a roller cam design for either hydraulic or solid lifters. Assuming for the moment that budget is not an operative factor here, which cam is going to work best? If, from experience, you found that a 280 degree flat-tappet hydraulic cam provided the sort of power curve you wanted, what could you do to get more from the engine? I'm also assuming the 280 degree cam gave the bottom-end power required, but like most hot rodders, you want more mid- and top-end power if it's possible.

Fortunately more power is possible, but it means replacing the hydraulic flat-tappet cam with one of the other three alternatives. Now, most hot rodders are going to assume that they can select a 280 degree cam of one of the other designs and still look for the same low-end power, but also expect a gain in whatever areas the other designs seem to show advantages, such as in faster opening rates and higher lift. However, selecting a cam on this basis may backfire since each cam's characteristics could vary substantially and, as I'll show, a direct comparison based solely on catalog figures is at best no more than a rough estimate.

Simple Camshaft Comparison

Before comparing cam types, let's contrast hydraulic cams to see which is likely to give the best performance. First, we've already established that opening the valve as fast as possible is a required characteristic of any cam. Of course that has to be tempered by mechanical limitations, and obviously trying to put too much acceleration into a valvetrain is going to cause undue stress and wear, usually at the cam and lifter interface. However, in today's marketplace there are a wide range of cams available which, at one end of the scale, have very slow acceleration rates compared with those at the other end of the scale.

The easiest way to compare hydraulic cams is to look at the hydraulic intensity. To do this you need to check the seat duration figures which are normally quoted at 4 thousandths (0.004in) tappet rise. These figures are sometimes called the advertised duration. From this subtract the duration at 50 thousandths (0.050in) tappet rise. The number you arrive at is the hydraulic intensity.

Many of the older profile designs have as much as 75 degrees difference between these two numbers, indicating that they have relatively lazy opening and closing rates. On the other hand, the more modern designs can have hydraulic intensities around 50 to 60 degrees. The slower lifting cams tend to be more trouble free, as demands on the valvetrain and lifter performance are less.

However, the faster opening cams can be made to live; it's a question of following installation requirements to the letter. This means making sure the cam is lubed properly, that excessive spring pressure is not used, and that the break-in procedure is strictly observed.

Hydraulic versus Solid

If the typically lower noise level delivered by a hydraulic cam is not an issue, then you may decide that a solid flat-tappet cam looks like a better bet in terms of performance. The cam specifications indicate that for about the same seat duration the 0.050in figure of a solid or mechanical flat-tappet cam is greater. This cam promises to retain much of the low-end power but with a bigger 0.050in timing

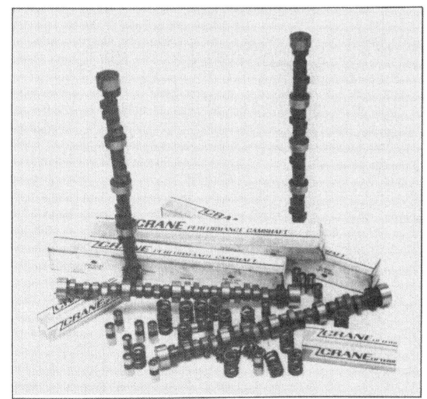

With all the literature printed by the cam manufacturers you'd think it was easy to make comparisons between various types and brands. In practice this proves to be far from the truth.

and more lift, it looks like it'll make more top-end power. None of this sounds like an unreasonable assumption, but unfortunately, due to the nature of solid and hydraulic cams and the way their duration figures are measured, a direct comparison just does not give a true idea of the valve events that will take place in the engine.

Take, for instance, a 280 degree hydraulic cam, say the Competition Cams 280 Magnum. The specs for this cam are given at 6 thousandths (0.006in) lift and 50 thousandths (0.050in) tappet lift. For a 280 degree mechanical cam, the figures are given at 15 thousandths (0.015in) lift for the advertised duration, and 50 thousandths (0.050in) tappet lift.

The starting figure for each has been chosen because in the first instance, it is reckoned that the hydraulic cam will have a follower that collapses a maximum of about 6 thousandths (0.006in) as it puts pressure on the valvetrain to open the valve. With a solid cam, the 15 thousandths (0.015in) tappet rise represents the motion on the tappet clearance ramp. Remember that lash is set at the valve, and since a 1.5 rocker ratio is operative, a 0.015in tappet rise at the cam is equivalent to 0.0225in lash between the tip of the rocker and the valve stem.

A 280 degree cam in either hydraulic or solid could have virtually the same seat timing, but the next point of measurement reveals some big differences. For a hydraulic cam the 0.050in tappet rise point is 44 thousandths (0.044in) farther on than the advertised duration. With the solid lifter cam, if the advertised duration was at 15 thousandths (0.015in) tappet rise, then the 50 thousandths (0.050in) duration is only 35 thousandths (0.035in) on from that point.

In other words, we're looking at the advertised duration when the cam has only raised the lifter a further 35 thousandths (0.035in). Because it has not had to move the lifter as far, the 0.050in lift duration figure for a solid lifter cam will appear greater. The only real comparison that can be made here is to see what duration a solid lifter cam has when it has moved the valve 44 thousandths (0.044in) on from the lash point.

Checking Some Examples

When measured on the Cam Doctor in figure 9-1, the Competition Cams 280 H delivered 283.4 degrees of timing at 6 thousandths (0.006in) lift. At 50 thou-

sandths (0.050in) tappet rise—that's 44 thousandths (0.044in) farther on—it delivered 231.4 degrees of duration. Maximum lift was 0.471in.

Now let's see how the Competition Cams 282 S stacks up against this. Seat timing proved almost the same; it was measured with 15 thousandths (0.015in) clearance at the tappet because of the 1.5 ratio that represented 0.0225in at the valve. The delivered seat timing was 283.3 degrees—44 thousandths (0.044in) farther on from that—and the cam delivered 229.6 degrees of timing. We're now making a back-to-back comparison between the 280 H and the 282 S.

On the other hand, Competition Cams' catalog quotes the 0.050in tappet rise figure as 236 degrees. Based on the catalog figures, you could easily be led to believe that the solid lifter cam was opening the valve faster and farther because the gross lift quoted is also higher. But from the gross lift we have to subtract the tappet clearance, so immediately 0.022in comes off the top.

Assuming that a hydraulic lifter collapses no more than 0.006in, the comparison between the 280 H and the 282 S reveals that they are very similar in terms of lift area and duration. Initially, the 282 S is a little slower at opening and closing, but right at the end it succeeds in lifting the valve marginally more, thus giving both cams virtually the same opening area.

Okay, let's throw the 280 R into the equation. Here we have a roller cam, and the justification for rollers is that they allow higher velocities to be achieved because they are not limited by the tappet diameter. Ultimately the only limitation that a roller follower has is the amount of side thrust that it

can absorb. The true seat timing of the 280 R, as measured on the Cam Doctor, proved to be 280.5 degrees; 0.044in farther on from that, it delivered 230 degrees, so as yet it's still slightly shorter than the hydraulic.

Competition Cams' spec quotes the 0.050in tappet lift at 236 degrees, but bear in mind that's the lift from the base circle, the valve itself doesn't start to move until the lifter has traveled 15 thousandths (0.015in) up the clearance ramp.

So, comparing all the cams at the point at which they have lifted the follower 44 thousandths (0.044in) higher than where they started reveals that they are all pretty close to 230 degrees.

Moving on to the next step at 94 thousandths (0.094in) we see that still most of the cams are showing just a tad shy of 200 degrees period. It is not until the next step, when the tappet has risen 144 thousandths (0.144in) from the point at which it first started to open the valve, that any significant divergence appears. The roller cam is now starting to show its form. At 194 thousandths (0.194in) above the point at which the valve started to open, the roller cam is definitely on the winning side, with 148.4 degrees duration compared with 141 for the hydraulic and surprisingly, only 138.1 for the flat-tappet cam.

At the next two lift stations, the flat-tappet solid and hydraulic cams both show comparable figures. On the other hand, the roller cam proves to have considerably more duration at these lift figures. As far as peak lifts are concerned, the two flat-tappet cams lift about the same, assuming the hydraulic lifter does not collapse any more than 6 thousandths (0.006in). The

Figure 9-1: Comparison of Valve Event Duration Figures

	Lift	280H	282S	280R
	0	283.4	283.	280.5
	44	231.4	229.6	230.0
(+50)	94	199.8	196.5	198.5
(+100)	144	171.0	167.5	173.3
(+150)	194	141.0	138.1	148.4
(+200)	244	106.5	105.1	121.7
(+250)	294	58.4	58.4	89.3
Max. lift		471.0	472.5	530.45
Area		24.65	24.65	27.24

Figure 9-1: *Study the figures in this chart and you'll appreciate there's much more to making a cam comparison than simply looking at catalog figures. Although a catalog may give you a guide as to what you're buying, mental adjustments have to be made based on the fact that standards for measuring duration vary from cam to cam and manufacturer to manufacturer.*

roller 280 R, however, has pushed the valve to 0.530in lift.

Dropping down to the next line on the chart in figure 9-1, you can see that the area under the lift curve is much greater at 27.24 rather than at 24.65 for the other two cams. This represents a 10.5 percent increase in flow area during the lift cycle. The cylinder is receiving much of the additional valve lift when it most needs it, that is, when piston speed down the bore is around its maximum.

So much for my tests on these cams. Though I feel they were reasonably accurate, the one problem I had was setting the tappet clearances precisely. The Cam Doctor program does not (as of 1992) allow the mathematical subtraction of a specified lash at the lifter, so I had to physically introduce it. To get around this problem I asked Competition Cams to run a similar test on their profile computer. Figure 9-2 shows the results.

You can see, then, that the mechanical attributes of a camshaft as derived from a manufacturer's catalog cannot be used without making some allowances. Comparing the lift-duration figures of the hydraulic and the solid flat-tappet cam, there is little justification for using a solid lifter cam since the hydraulic one will produce the same kind of valve opening area for the same duration. In addition, it's necessary to make an allowance for hydraulic follower collapse. Just how much it collapses depends on its leakdown rate. Most lifters collapse somewhere between 0.002 and 0.005in. Dyno tests between these two 280 degree camshafts, one solid and one hydraulic, produced similar power figures.

What has been said so far may make the solid flat-tappet cam design look redundant. Not so. For a race situation a flat-tappet cam with maximized accelerations and velocities will make more power, but it may not have sufficient life for a street motor. As of about 1988, a new breed of tight-lash solid lifter cams has been introduced. These can be hard on valvetrains, but they live long enough to win races.

Figure 9-2: Comparison of Competition Cams 280 Profiles

Part #	Appl.	Type	1	2	3	4	5
12-212-2	Magnum	Hyd.	—	280	0.006	290	0.006
12-223-4	Magnum	Solid	0.022	282	0.028	272	0.015
12-221-5	Race	Solid	0.026	280	0.032	276	0.020
12-702-8	Street	Roller	0.020	280	0.026	276	0.015
12-430-8	Street	Hyd. rol.	—	280	0.006	289	0.006

Part #	Appl.	Type	6	7	8	9	10
12-212-2	Magnum	Hyd.	280	230	0.050	235	0.118
12-223-4	Magnum	Solid	282	236	0.061	230	0.101
12-221-5	Race	Solid	280	242	0.636	225.6	0.115
12-702-8	Street	Roller	280	236	0.0593	234.8	0.107
12-430-8	Street	Hyd. rol.	280	224	0.050	225.2	0.100

1. Lash
2. Advertized duration
3. SAE specified lash for quoting SAE duration (lash + 0.006in valve lift)
4. SAE duration at valve
5. Lobe lift used for Competition Cams seat (advertised) duration
6. Advertised duration
7. Duration at 0.050in tappet rise
8. Total tappet rise after specified lash has been taken up, plus 50 thousandths. With a 1.5 rocker this means that valves in all cases will be 75 thousandths (0.075in) open, assuming a totally rigid valve train.
9. Duration at 50 thousandths tappet rise after specified runnng lash has been taken up. This is a true comparative figure, as all equate to 75 thousandths valve lift.
10. Lift at TDC at valve on intake with all cams set to 106 degrees to full lift.

Figure 9-2: *Cam testing is one thing, but knowing exactly what you're testing is another story altogether. Looking at the specs of a cam will not reveal much about the important characteristics of the profile. Listed here are five cam profiles all from the same manufacturer, Competition Cams. This company lists more information than most manufacturers on their cam profiles, yet even that falls short of conveying to the engine builder exactly what it is they're using. If you're a serious engine builder, you need to precisely determine the cam characteristics your engine favors, then you will need to accurately determine the profile lift, velocity and acceleration curves. The only affordable equipment I know, as of 1992, that will do this is the Cam Doctor.*

Lifters

10

Hydraulic Lifters

Hydraulic lifters seem such a good idea that you're almost bound to ask, Where's the catch? The fact that a hydraulic lifter pumps up to absorb the clearance in the valvetrain means it can also leak down during the lift phase. This factor prevents the full-opening envelope of the cam to be realized at the valve. The question is, How fast do they leak down and is this amount significant?

At first this characteristic would appear to be a strike against the hydraulic lifter as a performance item. Seemingly another problem that hydraulic lifters have, and we've probably all heard of it, is lifter pump-up. Pump-up is assumed to happen when rpm gets high enough that the lifter physically pumps up faster than it leaks down, and holds the valve off its seat. In truth, it is not the hydraulic lifter that produces lifter pump-up.

What happens is that when the valvetrain is on the verge of valve float either from the valve bouncing off the seat or the follower leaving the profile nose, the lifter expands to take up the excess clearance. Because lifters are valved to take up clearance faster than they bleed down, they end up holding the valve off its seat. The principal cure for this is to install slightly stronger springs or damp spring surge.

This doesn't mean to say that there is no difference between anti-pump-up lifters and regular lifters; for the most part, anti-pump-ups have a slightly quicker leakdown, and a slightly slower pump-up rate. This tends to slow down the rate at which they take up the extra clearance when valve float is encountered.

Although I've never tested it, some cam industry claims indicate that the stock GM lifter is good for about 200rpm more before it pumps up than some aftermarket lifters. However, usually hydraulic lifters that run to higher rpm often do so because they bleed down quicker. This may help low end, but rarely top-end power. Some cam companies such as Competition Cams and Crane have gone to great lengths to make sure that as far as possible, lifter-to-profile combinations are matched. Avoid the temptation of buying cheap lifters of unknown quality

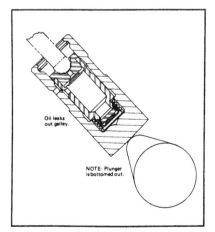

Operation of a hydraulic lifter. Stanadyne, Inc.

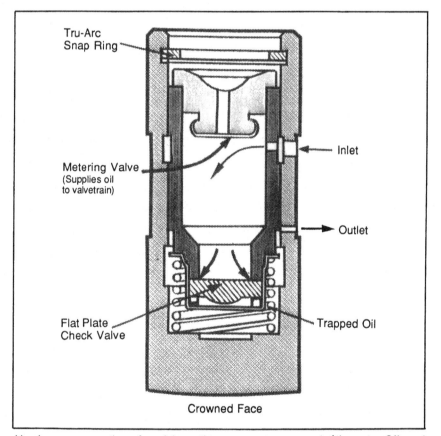

Tru-Arc Snap Ring

Metering Valve (Supplies oil to valvetrain)

Inlet

Outlet

Flat Plate Check Valve

Trapped Oil

Crowned Face

Here's a cross section of an Isky anti-pump-up lifter. It's a good safety valve to have on your engine, but remember that if you're a competent driver and don't over-rev your engine there is no need for an anti-pump-up lifter. Of course there may be circumstances where the driver has substantially less control over whether or not the engine's over-revved. A good instance here is marine use, where the prop may come out of the water. Off-road racing is another example as wheels are often way off the ground and the engine will run into an over-rev situation. Then, an anti-pump-up lifter can be justified. But, when there's time to watch a tach and shift at the appropriate rpm, there is little excuse for over-revving the engine —other than driver incompetence.

High-Performance Hydraulic Lifters

The number of regular lifters sold under the guise of anti-pump ones may represent the biggest scam of the high-performance industry. Though you may find it hard to believe, many lifters sold as anti-pump up are nothing more than stock off-the-shelf lifters. Because some unscrupulous retailers know that the typical hot rodder cannot tell one set from the other, they get away with it. If you don't want to be caught out then you should know what an anti-pump lifter is supposed to do and how to identify it.

Shown here is a cross section of an Isky anti-pump lifter. Though there are other ways to do the job, this is typical of the method of function. With a normal lifter, oil is pumped into the inlet port from the oil galley that passes through each of the lifter bores. This oil goes into the central body and pushes the flat plate check valve at the bottom of the inner cylinder off its seat. Although a check plate is often used in the design shown here, on some lifters a ball check valve is used. When this valve opens, oil passes into the lower chamber.

Unlike the anti-pump lifter shown here, most lifters have no outlet port. This means that the lower chamber fills up until the pressure in it equals the pressure fed from the inlet port. At this point the spring pressure just seats the check valve. There is now no lash existing in the valvetrain. It will have been taken up by the oil pressure in the lower chamber moving the central piston up.

Additionally, the fact that there is oil pressure in the lifter's lower chamber means that a small force of 2-3lb is applied, which is attempting to open the valves. This in effect backs off the valve seating force exerted by the valve spring. However, since it is way short of the delivered spring seat force, it has minimal effect on the valvetrain other than to reduce the noise level.

As the cam rotates and pushes the lifter upwards, so the trapped oil in the lower chamber makes the unit act, in effect, as a solid lifter, transmitting the entire cam motion as dictated by the profile. The only factor acting against the hydraulic lifter is leakage, other than this, it reacts just as a solid lifter until rising rpm causes separation to take place somewhere in the valvetrain. When such separation occurs, because the load on the bottom of the follower is relieved, the pressure of the trapped oil drops to that of the chamber above it or less.

If it drops below, which will be the case when approaching valve float, then oil will flow into the lower chamber and try to take up the rpm induced lash of the valvetrain separation. In other words, the lifter sees valve float as an increase in system lash, and adjusts accordingly in an effort to compensate. Doing so now prevents the intake or exhaust valve from seating properly because the valvetrain is now "too long," and the valve no longer seats. This results in a loss of compression either on the compression or firing stroke, and the engine runs rough, misfires, and does things that it shouldn't.

With an anti-pump-up lifter, if the inner piston goes too far up it releases oil pressure out through this small outlet port. However, such a lifter does require more precise initial adjustment.

This shot clearly shows the difference between the wire retaining ring and the True Arc snap ring. The True Arcs are the way to go if you anticipate the engine running into valve float for whatever reason. If not, the True Arc is of no real advantage.

be made, in effect, an anti-pump-up lifter.

By adjusting the valve lash so that it's only say, 0.005in into the hydraulic adjustment, the lifter is restricted from expanding (pumping up) by more than a like amount.

Some form of compensation is needed to counteract this effect. The chart in figure 10-1, gives an idea of the situation pertaining to a typical street cam. Most small-block Chevy street cams are ground on 110–112 lobe centerline angles because this produces good idle and cruise vacuum. Let's take 110 then as our base requirement. For regular lifters such a case would run best when set at 4 degrees advance. However this timing would not pertain until the rpm had reached a high enough value for the leakdown to cause an insignificant loss of duration. If the cam is timed in conventionally, then at low rpm it will change due to leakdown.

In the first column we have the cam timing at 2000rpm, assuming a 10 degree bleedoff on the exhaust. We'll use cam timing figures known to be optimum for a 110 degree lobe centerline cam, that is, with 4 degrees of advance. So, the timing figures we need to shoot for are as shown in the first column. At high rpm the cam needs valve events to take place at slightly different points.

To see what happens to the timing figures, check out column 1. When engine rpm drops to 2000, the lifter bleeds down and delivers only 270 degrees of exhaust timing. All the re-

and leakdown rate. They may cost power and the cam warranty!

So to avoid lifters pumping up, the moral is to make sure the right springs are used in the valvetrain. If lifter pump-up is still encountered, it is a fair bet you are turning the engine at too many rpm. A properly set up hydraulic system, even with a fairly big cam, is capable of running to over 7000rpm.

I estimate that probably better than 50 percent of lifters sold at a premium price as anti-pump-up are, in fact, the regular type. So what constitutes an anti-pump-up lifter? Talk to various supply sources, and you'll get a lot of questionable answers. Why? Probably so that the general public will go on buying regular lifters re-priced and re-labeled as anti-pump-up.

One of the first types of genuine anti-pump-up lifters featured a groove ground into the inner body to bleed off pressure once the lifter had expanded a certain amount. To make this work it was necessary to adjust the valve lash with the engine running. The lash would be taken down until valve noise just stopped, indicating that the lash was only marginally less than zero. However, a stock off-the-shelf lifter can

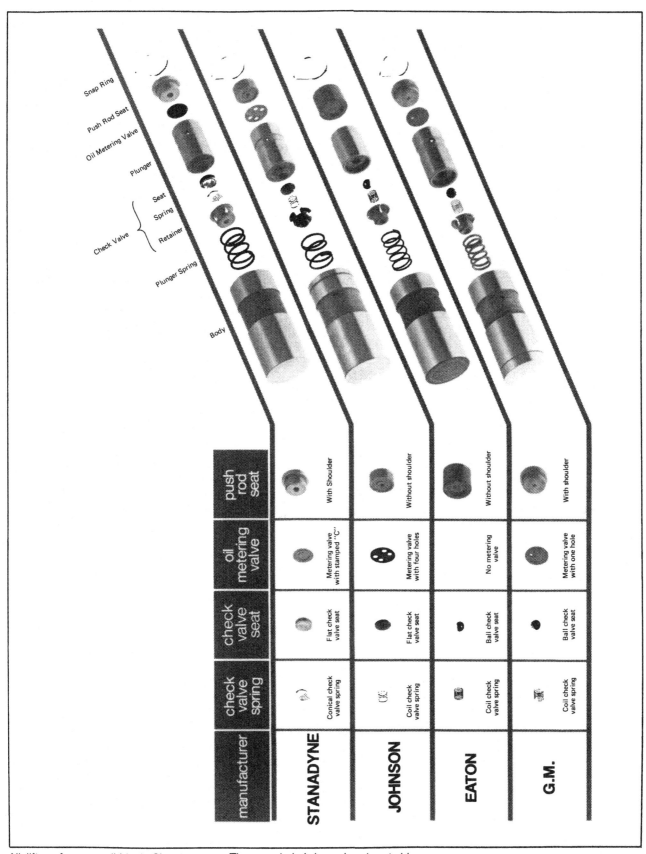

All lifters for a small-block Chevy are manufactured by one of four companies.

These exploded views show how to identify the different brands. Stanadyne, Inc.

duced exhaust timing is taken from the closing side of the exhaust event, thus reducing the overlap period. In other words, nothing is changed except the exhaust valve now closes 10 degrees sooner. This has the effect of spreading the LCA to 115 degrees, and putting the advance from 4 degrees to 9. From what we know about cam timing in a small-block Chevy, we can say that an LCA of 115 degrees is farther than 110

from the optimum of 106–108 for the 350 small-block requires. So from that point the engine now has less-favorable cam timing. Fortunately, the cam has now advanced, and has less overlap. Both factors usually help low end.

A small-block Chevy typically favors about 4 degrees of advance, and usually, setting the cam at that produces the best spread of power. However, there is a tendency to favor top-end

power if the cam is retarded slightly, and to favor low-end torque if the cam is advanced slightly.

The potential exists to change the cam timing to even more favorable values at the top end. In our first example if the cam timing was right at 6000rpm, it's going to be a little too advanced at 2000rpm. For that reason, if lifters are installed on the exhaust only, the cam usually needs to be retarded the odd 2-4 degrees. As changing the advance from 4 degrees to 1-2 degrees at high rpm can often help high rpm output, changing the cam advance from 9 to 5-6 degrees *can* make a measurable difference in low-end power in most instances.

If the lifters are used on both the intake and the exhaust, a whole different pattern emerges as the rpm climbs. Assuming that lifters are used on a 280/280 cam, but deliver 270/270 degrees at 2000rpm, then timed in with 4 degrees of advance when zero collapse is assumed the cam will exhibit the figures in column 4.

As rpm drops to 2000, so we see the picture change. First, the timing delivered advances by a whole 5 degrees. Second, the intake centerline moves from 106 degrees to 101, but the LCA stays the same. We now have a situation whereby the cam is looking smaller at 2000rpm, but the cam timing it's producing is also not what the engine ideally needs at this rpm.

Here a compromise needs to be struck to make the most of the top- and bottom-end capability. Retarding the cam 2 or 3 degrees may not subtract from the top-end power significantly, but when a cam is 9 degrees advanced at the low end, retarding it can make a big difference in low-end power. So, the golden rule here is that if you're installing lifters that bleed down rapidly on the exhaust only, you need to look at 1–2 degrees less cam advance. If you're putting them on the intake and the exhaust, then you need to look at 2, maybe as much as 4, degrees less advance than normal.

Of course, you do have another alternative. Instead of catering to the bottom end you can time the cam to produce maximum top-end power. Let's take a look at the resulting timing figures on a 108 LCA cam and see how they pertain to situations as we described in figure 10-1.

In the first instance the 108 LCA 270/280 degree cam is timed in to produce optimal events at 6000rpm— pretty much as in column 2 of the chart

Figure 10-1

| | Ex | | In/Ex | |
	1	2	3	4
RPM	2000	6000	2000	6000
Period In/Ex	270/270	270/280	270/270	280/280
In Open	29	29	34	34
In Close	61	61	56	64
Ex Open	74	74	74	74
Ex Close	16	26	16	26
Intake Cert.	106	106	101	106
LCA	115	110	110	110
Advance	9	4	9	4
Overlap	50	60	50	60

Figure 10-1: *Assuming a 10 degree loss of duration at 2000rpm, and a zero loss of duration at 6000rpm, the figures for the cam timing change as shown here. However, when cam timing figures change, it changes many other factors, the most important of which are the cam advance, LCA, and overlap.*

Figure 10-2

	1	2	3	4
RPM	2000	6000	2000	6000
Period In/Ex	270/270	270/280	270/270	280/280
In Open	31	31	36	36
In Close	59	59	54	64
Ex Open	72	72	72	72
Ex Close	18	28	18	28
Intake CL	104	104	99	104
LCA	110$\frac{1}{2}$	108	108	108
Advance	5$\frac{1}{2}$	4	9	4
Overlap	50	60	54	64

Figure 10-2: *Most people assume that the only advantage of a rapid leakdown lifter is that it will allow the use of a bigger cam. In essence this is only part of the story. If good cruise and idle are priorities, then these can be achieved together with better top end power that a tighter lobe centerline angle cam will deliver. So, not only do the rapid leakdown lifters allow the selection of a bigger cam, but can also be used on slightly tighter lobe centerlines. As you can see, to get the optimum from rapid leakdown lifters is not just a question of installing them on a big cam.*

shown in figure 10-2. This would tend to produce the best top-end output. At the low end the cam timing would change to that in column 1; that is, exhaust valve closure would change from 18 to 28 degrees. The change reduces the overlap from 60 to 50 degrees.

Thus, there is a trade-off here. The overlap situation is far better for 2000rpm, however; the lobe centerline angle is a little bit on the wide side, though this is not necessarily a disadvantage at such low rpm. In column 4 the timing figures are at 6000rpm where the 280/280 degree cam is timed to produce optimal power at that rpm. When the engine is slowed down to 2000rpm, such a cam would produce the figures shown in column 3. Here, the lobe centerline angle stays fairly optimal, but the cam is advanced by 9 degrees, which is a little too much.

The overlap is more favorable, though, at only 54 degrees instead of 64. Nine degrees is too much advance, though, and if the cam is retarded

slightly, it won't significantly affect the top end but it can make a bit of difference in the bottom end.

Consequently, if you're going to use rapid leakdown lifters, you need to consider retarding the initial cam setting slightly. If they're used just on the exhaust, time the cam in more or less as if they were solid lifters, or at most, up to 2 degrees less advance. If rapid leakdown lifters are used on both the intake and the exhaust, then figure that you'll need 2, possibly as much as 3 degrees of retard compared to conventional lifters. This means that for the most part, cams will go in timed at 1–2 degrees of advance instead of 4.

Our discussion thus far is based on the assumption that you're using rapid leakdown lifters sold by Crower, Rhoads, or Competition Cams. If you're using the Crane or Competition Cams lifters, which leak down far slower, any adjustments you make on the cam timing have to be moderated with that in mind. These two lifters leak down slowly enough that you can afford to put the cam in about where it's meant to be with regular lifters, or maybe with a degree of retard at most.

Lifter Leakdown Rate and Engine Output

Lifter leakdown rate and engine output are closely related. Before deciding on a cam and lifter combination involv-

ing rapid leakdown lifters, you need to be aware of the effects and their proportions that various rates of lifters are likely to produce.

Slow and rapid leakdown rates have been discussed at length, but as yet, all references to the rate of leakdown have been in general terms. Now is the time to look at numbers and apply them to test cases.

Undoubtedly, there are existing industry standards for methods of measuring hydraulic lifter leakdown. However, I have a Jennings precision valve spring tester that produces accurate comparisons. The comparisons were done by first priming the lifter and then applying a precise load to collapse the lifter. The load of 200lb was applied for 30sec. The amount of collapse was noted, from which the collapse rate in inches per hour was calculated.

My tests confirmed the inconsistency I suspected occurred in any one batch of lifters.

I also found I could measure low rates of leakdown with extreme accuracy, but the rapid leakdown rates proved more difficult to measure. When the 200lb load was applied, the lifter collapsed so quickly that timing it was difficult.

For these tests, all the lifters had been used in engines for a period of not less than one hour and rarely more than six hours. The lifters tested can be

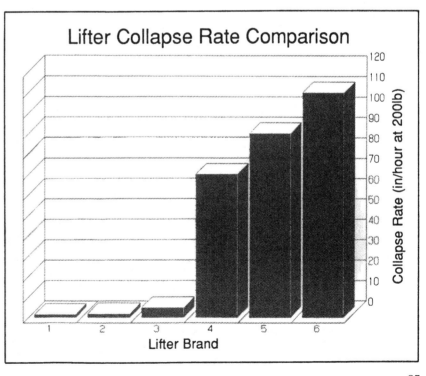

Using this precision Jennings Equipment valve spring tester in conjunction with a stopwatch, I found I could produce accurate measurements of the leakdown rates of the slower or stiffer lifters. Less accuracy was achieved on the rapid leakdown lifters because of the short time period involved.

considered broken in. The lifters tested for column 1 had a stiffness rate between 1in and 2in per hour, but several of them had leakdown rates approaching 3in per hour. The variation amounted to almost 300 percent, but the average for the entire test batch was 1.44in per hour.

The next group of lifters tested were the type sold by both Competition Cams and Crane. Here something of a minor mystery developed. The Crane high-intensity lifter, which supposedly has a faster leakdown than a regular lifter but slower than a Rhodes, had the same manufacturer's part number as Competition Cams' regular lifter.

Of the lifters tested there was little difference other than the normal spread expected among the regular Crane lifter, Crane's high-intensity lifter, and Competition Cams' regular lifter. Based on what could be learned from Crane, the desired leakdown rate for their high-intensity lifter is achieved by selective assembly to a set of tolerances a little different from regular lifters.

The leakdown rates I measured for the Competition Cams' Magnum and Crane high-intensity lifters versus the Competition Cams' regular lifters did not average out significantly different, although the average leakdown rate of the Magnum and high-intensity lifters did prove marginally faster. Since the dyno produced different test results with only a marginal change in lifter bleeddown rate, the lifter leakdown rate is apparently far more important than assumed.

The lifters tested for column 3 were those marketed by Iskenderian. Among this batch of lifters, leakdown rate was considerably faster than either the Crane, Competition Cams, or GM lifters. Additionally, leakdown spread between the slowest and fastest was only about 20 percent, as opposed to variations up to 300 percent for brands tested in column 1 & 2. Before putting too much emphasis on this low spread, it's worth mentioning that we had only about half the number of lifters to test with here, and they were about the lowest time for use of any lifters tested. These factors may have skewed our statistics, so obviously we will need to do some more tests for forthcoming reprints.

Column 4 shows the results of a true fast leakdown lifter. The graph shows, in no uncertain terms, just how much faster these lifters collapsed than the regular type. On average, the rates are typically fourteen times greater. However, remember these rapid leakdown lifters collapsed so quickly that it compromised the accuracy of the timing of the collapse. As a result the accuracy of our measurements may be no closer than 10-15 percent. Again, because of the limits of accuracy, we could not get a true idea of the spread of the leakdown rates.

Column 5 shows the leakdown rates of the regular Rhodes lifter, which proved comparable to the rapid leakdown lifter sold by Crower and the ultra rapid leakdown lifter sold by Competition Cams.

Column 6 shows an extremely rapid leakdown lifter that was marketed for a while out of California, but it is no longer available. These figures cover what we perceive as the market extremes as of 1992. Now using a simple comparative A versus B test, let us examine the effect of lifter leakdown on power output.

The above graph depicts the potential gains possible on a short-period cam. The cam used was a Competition Cams 268 HE. Shown here is the power output of a set of lifters with an average leakdown rate of approximately 2.5in per hour compared to a set of lifters with a leakdown rate of about 100in per hour. Several other rates of leakdown were tested, and all the figures fell between the two extremes shown.

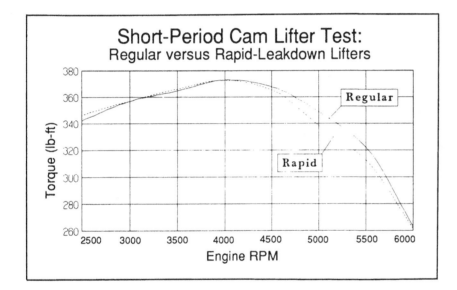

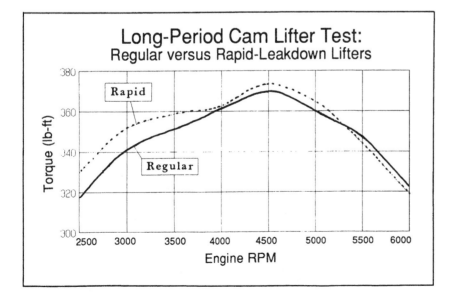

This graph shows the limits between a relatively stiff hydraulic lifter and a lifter with a high degree of collapse. With a short-period cam, simply replacing the lifters with faster leakdown lifters made only marginal improvements in the bottom-end power yet reduced output quite noticeably in the mid top-end rpm range.

The moral here is that using rapid leakdown lifters on a short-period cam is not going to achieve very much. If you want the extra vacuum and low-end performance of a rapid leakdown lifter, then you should have chosen a slightly shorter cam with selected stiff lifter to get all the top end possible!

In using a longer cam, such as the Competition Cams 292 HE shown here, quite a span in the torque output produced by regular lifters compared to that of the rapid leakdown lifters. On a cam of this duration, it is not until 5,200rpm that the regular lifters outpace the output of the rapid leakdown lifters.

It's important not to overlook cam optimization. This is a simple A-B test where no retiming was done. Bear in mind that the tests with regular lifters would have near optimum cam timing, whereas the rapid leakdown lifters would have less than optimum cam timing as demonstrated in figure 10-2. Because of this you can reasonably expect them to deliver slightly better results if the cam were suitably retimed.

However, there's another point to consider. Where would the torque output lie if a slightly shorter cam with stiff lifters had been selected? The power curve implies that a slightly shorter cam has the potential on a larger cam to give the same bottom end and top end as rapid leakdown lifters. If this is the case, it will make the rapid leakdown lifters redundant.

Unfortunately this question has not been adequately answered by any tests conducted in the industry so far. Such tests will need to be exhaustive and probably costly. They will inevitably involve many different tests to establish trends more precisely. At this time, no one in the performance industry seems in any great hurry to conduct such tests, and therefore we may have to conduct our own tests.

One of the points emphasized so far is the variation in lifter performance, which means that if lifters are not tested in comparison to other lifters, we can only look at the results in terms of trends. In other words, you can only

measure whether you'll get gains or not. For this we need to look at some further test results, again using a 268 HE Competition Cam and a 292 HE Competition Cam.

This test makes a comparison between a fast leakdown lifter and an infinitely stiff lifter, as represented by a solid lifter. For these tests, a solid lifter

with 6 thousandths (0.006in.) lash was used to generate the baseline figures. This lash was used because it closely simulates the 4 thousandths (0.004in) lifter collapse typically seen in a hydraulic unit.

The curves in this graph show the gain or loss in pound-feet of torque using a set of lifters with an average

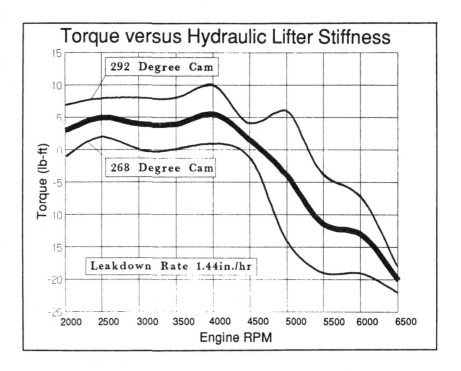

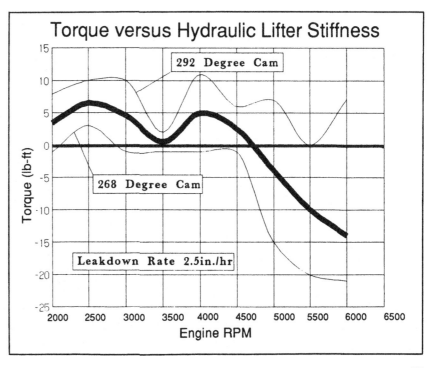

leakdown rate of 1.44in per hour. The zero line represents the baseline output given by the solid lifters. For both the 268 and 292 degree cams, the low-end torque output was better with the hydraulic lifters than the solids were. This can be accredited to the intake valve closing earlier, which increases low rpm charge, trapping and reducing

exhaust intrusion into the intake phase during the overlap event.

As rpm increases, the situation changes. At 4500rpm, the hydraulic lifters delivered less power on the 268 degree cam, while the hydraulic lifters on the 292 degree cam proved superior until 5300rpm, at which point they delivered less than the solid lifters. The

heavy line is the average gain/loss and should be used as a trend guide for this rate of leakdown lifters compared to infinitely stiff ones.

With a 70 percent increase in lifter leakdown rate, the results shown below were produced. The average leakdown for this test was approximately 2.5in per hour. Again, notice the trend line. The faster leakdown produced better low end but less top end than the solid lifters.

The leakdown rate of the lifters for the first test of the ultra rapid leakdown lifters averaged out at about 70in per hour. The use of these lifters resulted in a fairly good gain in low-end torque, but once again, as the rpm increased, the situation reversed.

For the large cam, the breakeven point was between 5500 and 6000rpm, whereas on the small cam it was a little less definable. But anything over about 3500rpm showed that the rapid leakdown lifter did not produce any positive results. The solid black line is representative of typical cases so over 5000rpm the engine's output is reduced when rapid leakdown rates are employed.

The last two graphs show the results for lifters of approximately 90in and 100in per hour leakdown. The solid black line shows that as the leakdown rate becomes greater, the rpm at which the advantage ceases is reduced.

Let's consider the data presented up to this point. Proponents of the rapid leakdown lifters claim an increase bottom-end torque. Based on these tests, such a claim is well substantiated. However, these tests do not show the full potential of rapid leakdown lifters. To do so, the cam timing would need to be optimized as described in the main text. In essence we are looking at the minimum gains possible.

In addition to low-end increases, the industry claims that the bottom-end torque is increased without a loss of top-end horsepower. As of 1992, my own limited test plus industry tests have failed to substantiate this claim. Theoretically, this can only happen if the lifters rectify less than optimal timing figures and truly do react as near solid lifters at high rpm. Currently, neither I nor the industry have tested cams suitably retimed to make the best of rapid leakdown lifters.

Vacuum and Valvetrain Dynamics

By now you should have in perspective the power gains achievable with

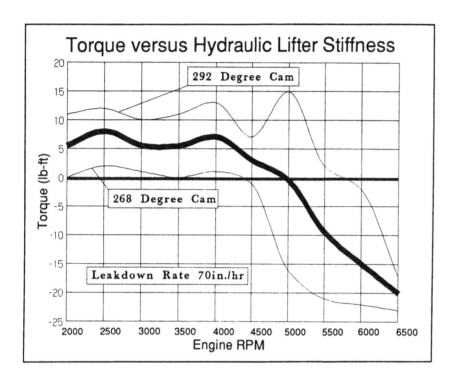

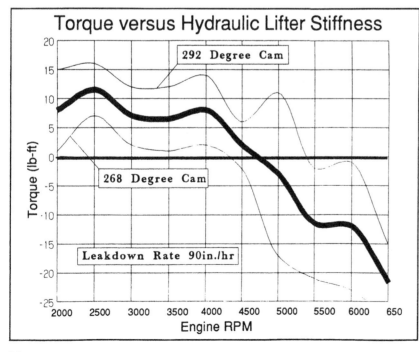

rapid leakdown lifters. Yet other aspects need to be considered. Not unreasonably, we can assume that if a lifter collapses, then, as the cam/lifter interface comes around to the base circle, a certain amount of lash will be left in the system. This cannot be taken up until the lifter has refilled.

This unwanted lash generates noise from several sources. First, and probably the most prominent, the valve is set down on the seat while the lifter is still on the deceleration flank of the cam rather than on the actual closing ramp. This plus the extra lash existing in the system means that rapid leakdown lifters can produce a considerable amount of additional valve train noise until higher rpm is reached.

The bar graph shown here will give you an idea as to the noise levels you can expect. These noise levels were not measured with a sound meter but judged by a number of people—experienced at listening to dyno engines—who averaged out the perceived noise. This chart should be used only as a guide.

Column 1 shows the noise level of a typical solid lifter. Remember, this is not a solid lifter on a cam designed for such, but a solid lifter set to 6 thousandths (0.006in) lash at the valve on a hydraulic cam. Column 2 shows how the 1.44in per hour leakdown rate lifter faired in these tests. Column 3 shows the 2.5in per hour results, and so on.

Notice the subjective noise at 1000 and 2000rpm. From these tests the rapid leakdown lifters prove noisiest at idle, but as the rpm increases, the noise drops. Again, these are average figures. The noise generated on your cam may vary from these tests because the type of closing ramp on the cam can have a significant effect. As mentioned, Rhoads 1992 designs have taller and longer closing ramps, specifically designed to complement a more rapid leakdown lifter. Such a ramp design reduces the noise from a rapid leakdown lifter considerably. None of the cams for the tests shown here had the luxury of a special closing ramp other than that normally used for a regular hydraulic lifter.

Dynamics

Obviously, noise in a valvetrain means the dynamics of the valvetrain have considerably altered. Most cam designs do not make a significant allowance for considerable lifter collapse during operation. As a result, a rapid leakdown lifter can display con-

siderably different valve float rpm, as compared to a regular lifter. Depending upon the characteristics of the cam profile and the leakdown rate involved, valve float rpm compared to regular hydraulic lifters can either increase or decrease.

Typically solid lifters on a hydraulic cam will run 600 to 1000rpm higher before valve float occurs. On the other hand, rapid leakdown lifters usually, but not always, run a slightly higher rpm than a regular hydraulic lifter before valve float occurs. This is usually due to lower valve lift because less total velocity and accelerations are put into the valvetrain.

On occasion, valve float may occur at a lower rpm, because the valve spring is not exerting enough seat load

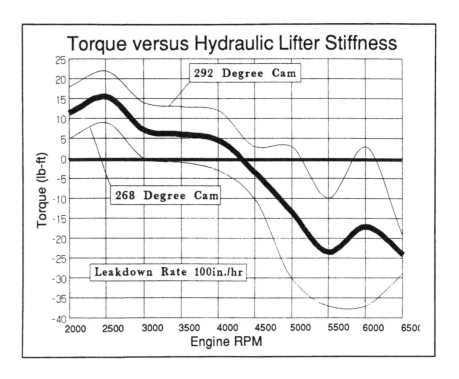

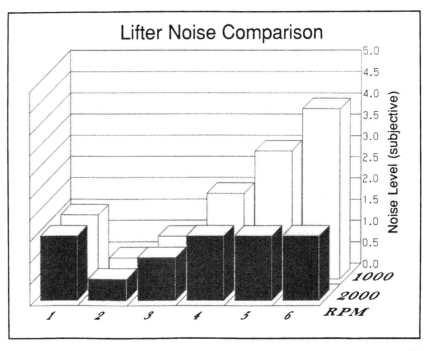

on the valve. Under these circumstances, the closing velocity of the valve onto the seat is high enough to cause it to bounce from the seat rather than the valvetrain separate elsewhere.

Vacuum

Because a rapid leakdown lifter shortens the cam timing, it also affects the vacuum at idle and cruise speeds. The bar chart shown below represents typical results of a 280 degree by 110 degree LCA cam in a 350 small-block. A number of variables affect the amount of vacuum seen at idle, including compression ratio, carburetion, and exhaust back pressure. This chart shows trends rather than hard and fast data. However, it is representative and so can be used to good effect. As for previous charts, the numbers refer to the rate of leakdown of lifter involved in the test. The importance of the vacuum depends on the car accessories that rely on it for operating. To an extent, a vacuum reservoir, such as that marketed by Cam Dynamics, can compensate for a low vacuum.

New Developments

Although I've not tested them, even in prototype form, there are some new developments as of 1992 in the pipeline concerning rapid leakdown lifters. Rhoads has taken out a patent on a system that seeks to achieve greater cam profile compatibility to the rapid leakdown lifter.

What Rhoads is doing is adjusting into the lifter so that there is at most 23 thousandths (0.023in) of hydraulic action left. This works in conjunction with a camshaft that has a much higher tappet ramp than normal, its height being about 27 thousandths (0.027in). Once on the constant-velocity part of this ramp, it moves the lifter at approximately 0.00075in per degree, which is relatively rapid as ramps go, but still slow enough to ensure quiet operation of the valvetrain. By making the ramp taller than the amount of bleeddown available, they're able to keep the valvetrain quiet under normal operation and actually able to introduce more rapid bleeddown rates into the bargain.

Rhoads' new experimental lifters bleed down at about twice the rate of their regular lifters. By being able to bleed off say, 0.020in from a typical hydraulic cam, they are shortening up the opening period, depending upon the profile used, typically 8 to as much as 15 degrees. This system looks like it will allow slightly bigger cams yet to be used successfully in street vehicles, and it also holds promise for better mileage and vacuum on emission control cars as well as adding more horsepower to the engine's output.

Solid Lifters

If hydraulic lifters are so good, why is there any need for a solid lifter? Essentially a solid lifter offers advantages in as much as it is slightly lighter, and less problematical for high-rpm applications. At high rpm it is difficult for a hydraulic lifter to deliver the exact dictates of the cam due to whatever collapse it may have. A solid lifter, in this instance, represents an infinitely stiff hydraulic lifter.

The down side of mechanical lifters is the noise they produce. This of course is due to the built-in valve lash typically designed into a valvetrain using solid lifters. However, since the late 1980s there has been a new trend

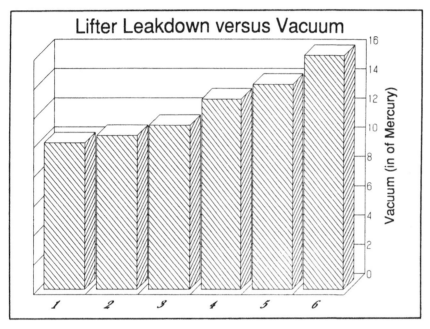

Here are the three types of flat-faced lifters. Far left is a regular hydraulic lifter; center is a regular solid lifter; and right is a mushroom solid lifter.

toward designing cams with what are becoming known as tight lash profiles.

Traditionally, small-block Chevy profiles were designed to run with lash figures of typically some 20-25 thousandths (0.020–0.025in) with some requiring as much as 28 thousandths (0.028in). In contrast, tight lash profiles may require as little as 9 thousandths (0.009in) lash. Such tight clearances will not necessarily make these valvetrains quieter.

It is often believed that if the valvetrain lash is closed up the valves will make less noise. However, this is to a large extent not true. If a cam profile has a constant velocity ramp, then over a major proportion of the tappet ramp, the tappet will take up the valve train clearance at a given velocity irrespective of the clearance involved. So we can say that whether the clearance is 30 thousandths (0.030in) or 15 thousandths (0.015in), if it's still on the constant velocity part of the ramp it will generate the same amount of noise, because contact velocity remains unchanged.

In simple terms, all the parts hit each other just as hard whether the lash is wide or tight. It is only when lash figures reach impractically tight values that valvetrain noise starts to significantly diminish. At such clearances, problems will occur in terms of power development, and reliability due, most likely, to burnt exhaust valves.

For a race engine or an engine intended for serious high-performance, the fact that a solid lifter makes more noise may not be a significant factor. If this is so, then the advantage of a solid lifter installation producing the same intended valve opening characteristics is that it often produces more top end power than its hydraulic counterpart. This power advantage is due to the elimination of pump up, and/or of lost motion due to lifter collapse.

As was explained earlier, some lifter collapse can help the low end power, and if cam and lifters are optimally matched, a hydraulic lifter-cam combination does have the potential to produce better results. However let's not delude ourselves into thinking that perfecting such a combination is as easy as a snap of the fingers. It isn't. At least with a solid lifter/cam combination you have a better idea of what is going on and when.

It is quite normal to find that for the same intended lift profile at the valve, the solid tappet cam will tend to make less low end power than the hydraulic

one. Again, this is not a problem where competition and outright performance are the main criteria.

Lifter Diameter

At this point, it's probably a good idea if we take another look at the lifter diameter in relation to the valve velocity that can be generated.

One theme has been prevalent throughout our investigation of the small-block Chevy valvetrain so far. On numerous occasions we've discussed the need to open valves as high and as fast as possible because of the typically inadequate breathing characteristics of the cylinder head, especially for the larger-displacement engines. At this point let's reconsider the effect of lifter diameter on the opening area of the valve train.

To refresh your memory, take a look at the sidebar relating to lifter diameter in chapter 7. This shows how the lifter diameter affects the maximum velocity that can be attained. The way we can look at the dynamics of the valvetrain here is that the faster the contact patch moves from the middle to the outside of the lifter, the faster the acceleration. The further it moves from the center of the lifter to the

outside, the greater the velocity available. As you can see, it does, in essence, crudely simulate a crank arm. The maximum velocity possible can be calculated quite simply from the formula given in the diagram.

A stock Chevrolet lifter is 842 thousandths (0.842in) in diameter. If the block of the engine you're using is a serious effort, it's almost certain to need the lifter bores accurising. If the race rules do not specifically prohibit such a move, then there are several other sizes of lifters larger than this that can easily be adapted.

For instance, the next common size up is 875 thousandths (0.875in), as used in the small-block Ford engine. The next common diameter above that is used in American Motors' engines and has a tappet diameter of 904 thousandths (0.904in).

However, with any of these diameters you could of course go for a hydraulic or a solid lifter, but probably the easiest way to get an effective large lifter diameter is to use a mushroom lifter, where the head of the lifter is much bigger—about 970 thousandths (0.970in). If you decide to go this route there can be a problem with interference of one lobe to an adjacent lifter.

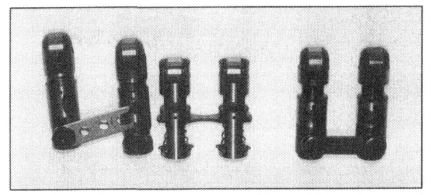

The type of roller lifters on the far left are permanently paired together. Problems with just one of the roller lifters means scrapping the pair. In the center is a pair of Crane roller lifters. Failure with any one of these, and they can be separated since they are not fixed to the link bar. Another technique is to use the forked-end link bar, as shown in the set on the right.

A roller cam needs to be ground on a steel blank rather than on a cast-iron one. Until about 1990 all roller cams, regardless of who ground them, were produced from billets made by a subsidiary of Crane Cams. Around 1990, Competition Cams began applications for changing over to their own cast-steel blank.

To avoid problems it's necessary to install the cam and lifters and check a suitable clearance of about 15 thousandths (0.015in) exists. To hold this constant, make sure that the end float of the cam is tightly controlled. If a mushroom lifter is used, the velocity can be increased proportionally, and this gives the engine the potential to produce that much more horsepower.

Roller Lifters

It doesn't take much inspection to reveal the fact that a roller lifter is a far

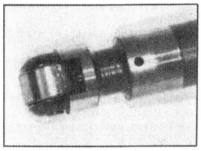

Look at this roller and you'll see it's been severely damaged. This can happen for a number of reasons. The most common is running the engine into valve float and brinelling the roller on the cam. Another possibility is that some debris may have gone around the engine and become trapped between the roller and the cam lobe. Lastly, it could just simply be a bad roller.

more complex piece than a flat-faced lifter. If we're to use the roller lifter then, this complexity must, in one way or another, be justified. So, what are the advantages of a roller lifter over a flat-face lifter?

Probably the number one reason for using a roller lifter is that the profile can be made to live significantly longer when the stresses and loads developed from the heavy valve springs that are needed for high rpm are used. In practice we find that a flat tappet cam is really on the ragged edge in a small-block Chevy when over the nose spring loads approach about 350lb. On the other hand, a roller-cammed valvetrain can cope with valve springs in excess of double this figure.

Additionally we find a roller cam is also able to develop greater valvetrain velocities, and do so with lower friction levels. All this adds up to the fact that with a roller it's possible to generate higher lifts, more rpm, and still have the valvetrain survive.

Of course the most obvious disadvantage is cost. It is necessary not only to make a far more precision, and therefore more costly, follower, but also it's necessary to grind the cam on a steel blank rather than the normally used cast iron for flat-tappet applications.

At first sight, apart from the cost aspect, there would seem to be little disadvantage to roller followers. In

terms of performance, though, there is one notable disadvantage—the acceleration rates that can be delivered to the valvetrain with a roller follower are ultimately limited by the developed side load that can be tolerated.

It is important to realize the fact that the acceleration rate of a flat-tappet cam can, though hardly good design practice, be made infinite. All that is necessary is to design the profile so that the contact line on the follower moves from the center to the edge instantly. To visualize how this can take place, watch a cam rotate and check out the motion of the contact point. The flatter the cam flank is, the faster the contact point moves from the center of the lifter to the edge.

On the other hand, to do this with a roller would take a lobe that contacted the roller at 90 degrees to the lift motion. This represents a pressure angle of 90 degrees and instead of lifting the follower it would simply snap it off. In practice, pressure angles of about 30 degrees are considered about maximum.

For a simple comparison between roller followers and flat followers, we could say that a roller type is acceleration limited, whereas a flat follower is velocity limited. Initially if we're talking about short-period cams, the advantage in terms of performance can go to the flat follower. But, when longer periods and high lift are considered, then the advantage goes to the roller follower.

Another aspect of roller followers that you have to consider is that the profile is less tolerant of grinding and dynamic errors than a flat-faced follower. Fortunately these days the quality of grinding from reputable cam manufacturers has reached the point where profile errors are rarely a problem. Rarely though, is not the same as never.

For instance, I had one racer come into my shop with a problem of a cam which repeatedly destroyed all sixteen lifters. It had done this three or four times even with a change of brand of roller lifters. Eventually it was traced to the fact that the grinding wheel used to grind the cam was out of balance. This produced minute surface errors which set up a vibration in the valvetrain. This I felt to be at a frequency that the rollers could not contend with. Consequently they lived for only about a dozen passes down the dragstrip.

If you've taken time to look through a number of cam manufacturers cata-

If you intend doing a lot of cam changes in your roller-cammed small-block Chevy, then the Crane followers are useful inasmuch as they lift the rollers up past the base circle due to the spring loading on the link bar.

logs, you may have noticed that roller profiles are typically required to run with much higher spring loads than their flat-tappet equivalent. Apart from some dictates due to profile dynamics, part of this is due to the fact that roller followers will not tolerate valve float. If valvetrain separation occurs, the closing velocities can be so high that the rollers brinell the surface of the cam. Over a period this can lead to vibrations very similar to those generated by the out-of-balance grinding wheel just mentioned. To avoid such problems, some of the extra seat load is there to make sure that valve float does not become a factor to contend with.

Another point you need to consider is that with a roller cam the profile surface must be parallel to the cam's centerline, as opposed to the slight taper that is used on a flat-tappet cam. This means that if the lifter bores are square to the cam centerline, there is no natural tendency of the cam to walk towards the thrust face between the block and cam sprocket. Therefore, it is necessary to control the end float of the cam. This means that a cam button is virtually essential.

Hydraulic Rollers
During the mid-1980s Ford introduced a hydraulic roller cam for their 5.0 liter HO Mustang engine. It wasn't too long before GM followed suit, and during 1986 a roller-cam version of the small-block Chevy became available.

Unlike aftermarket designs, the factory roller cams used a substantially different method of pairing the followers to constrain the rollers so they always ran on the profile at a true 90 degrees to the cam's centerline. This necessitated a change in block design, making it impractical to adapt the factory setup onto earlier blocks. Not only is the roller mechanism itself different, but also the cam differs in as much as the drive-sprocket-mounting diameter and the sprocket itself is different for the hydraulic roller cam.

About the same time that the original equipment manufacturers were working on hydraulic roller cams, the aftermarket industry was gearing up to introduce a hydraulic roller cam for pre-1986-style blocks. Sealed Power probably instigated much of the work in this area and their hydraulic roller lifter followed the normal pattern of using a link bar to maintain alignment of the lifters with respect to the cam.

Initially there were a few false starts on hydraulic roller cams for the small-block Chevy. I experienced, in the early days, one or two problems with hydraulic-lifter failures. To be fair though, this was mostly with pre-production items made for us to test before general release to the public. The hydraulic roller lifter as it now stands is a reliable piece.

Although costing more money to equip out a valvetrain with an aftermarket hydraulic roller, one asset you can virtually count on is that cam lobe problems will be a thing of the past. For anything over about 265-270 degrees, the hydraulic roller offers a definite performance advantage over its conventional counterpart. By the time we're looking at cams of some 280-290 degrees, then performance dif-

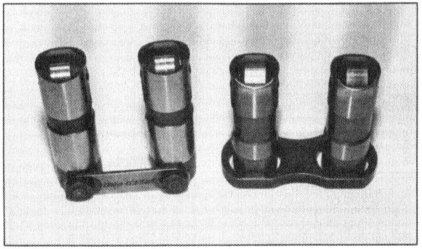

Pictured here is the basic difference between an aftermarket hydraulic roller follower (left) and a factory one (right). The factory one is prevented from turning by the special slotted plate, and its shorter length permits the use of a stock-length pushrod, whereas the Sealed Power design, as with many others, requires a shorter pushrod.

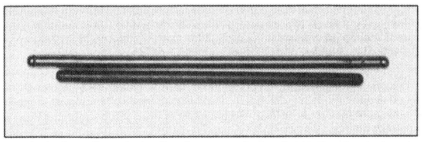

This photo, shot from underneath the cam valley, shows how the rollers have moved up into the block to clear the cam, thus allowing the cam to be withdrawn without any interference.

If you're buying a Crane hydraulic roller cam and kit, this is how much shorter the required pushrod is than the stock pushrod.

ference can be, depending on the size of the engine, 15-25hp, with the advantage going to the roller.

Sounds too good to be true? Well, you could run into a problem with the center body forcing the normally used wire retention clip right out of the body the first time the engine is run into valve float. To avoid this, replace or only use those lifters having a regular-type heavy-duty snap ring retaining the center body.

Only a close inspection here will reveal any functional difference between these lifters. The center lifter has a small flat ground on the lower section of it so that oil can pass down here to help lubricate the cam lobe. I have no idea how effective this can be, but I believe there is enough oil flying around inside the engine to lubricate the cam lobes under most circumstances anyway.

Lift Loss

Many engine builders contend that because hydraulic lifters bleed down, they reduce the area under the lift curve, and therefore present a potential source of power loss. Well, this may be true, but the leakdown on a hydraulic lifter can be very slow. The question is, How much can this affect the power?

Just to find out, I ran an experiment whereby *selected stiff* hydraulic lifters were substituted for solid lifters. These would represent a hydraulic lifter of infinite stiffness. The clearance with the solid lifters was carefully set to between 0.005 and 0.006in hot, and the subsequent power runs showed that the solid lifters may have given a little more top-end power, and a little less low down. The emphasis here is on "a little" because the differences that were recorded were of the same order as the engine's capability for producing consistent power figures. If pressed to put a number to it, I'd have to say that there was probably less than 5hp in over 400.

It's important that you take stock of this experiment because it will bear on an issue we'll discuss later. We compared a very stiff hydraulic lifter to an infinitely stiff one. The bottom line is that there is little justification for running a solid tappet-type cam in a street application. It's only where the absolute power of the engine is at a premium, such as in race conditions, that a solid lifter can be justified.

Aeration

If you are to get the best from hydraulic lifters, you must check the condition of the oil. Referring to the charts showing gains and losses over a solid lifter, you may wonder why there are substantial peaks and troughs in the curves. Probably, these extremes are due to the use of a stock oil pan on the test engine.

A rapid leakdown lifter has a far greater through flow of oil than a regular one. If the pan design allows the crank to beat the oil and aerate it, compressible oil will be fed to the lifters. This results in lifter collapse not only from leakage but, also, compressibility. If straight oil is fed to the lifters, then compressibility is held to low levels.

Generally, the 4 thousandths (0.004in) tappet motion used to determine a hydraulic cam's duration represents a good estimate of lifter col-lapse due to oil compression taking up the valve spring seat load. However, if the oil contains air, it now becomes a spring and can have a dramatic effect on valvetrain dynamics. It is possible, with aerated oil, for the lifters to run the valve train into a surge condition long before normally acceptable valve float.

In other words, to use rapid leakdown lifters successfully, you must pay attention to the bottom end of your motor. The use of an effective pan and an oil scraper system will limit power loss both from the valvetrain dynamics as well as reduced windage losses.

An equally important factor is the type of oil used in the engine. Some oils have a greater tendency than others to aerate. Best results will obviously be achieved with oils with anti-aeration additives. Most racing oils are blended with this factor in mind.

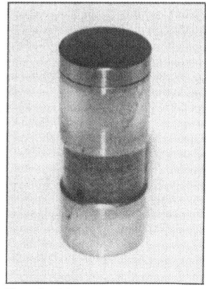

These hard-faced lifters are almost bulletproof. GM knows it and prices them accordingly. Your Chevy dealer is the source.

Certainly for the street, the fact that a hydraulic cam is maintenance-free and much quieter seems to make up for the fact that, under certain circumstances, it *may* give up a small amount of power. But before deciding what type of cam you should equip your engine with, be sure to read about the various types of lifters available, later in this chapter.

Wear

One of the prime concerns of building a valvetrain for a hot small-block Chevy is that you'll need to consider the wear that could occur at the cam and follower interface. This subject has been touched on before, but the first rule of thumb is to make sure that new

followers are used on a new camshaft, and that the break-in lube and procedure is followed to the letter. Remember, the modern faster lifting cams are more prone to wearing if proper assembly and break-in procedures aren't followed. The key to their success is to make sure they are used correctly.

If you want to reduce the likelihood of cam and valvetrain wear to a minimum, then it's not a bad idea to use a heat-treated cam. Companies such as Iskenderian offer, at an additional price, heat-treated cams having a harder lobe surface. If the service is available in your area, a Tuftrided cam works very well.

Usually the problem with the lifter-cam combination is not so much the lifter wearing initially, but the cam profile itself, and once the profile starts to go it simply chews up the lifter. If you can cut down the likelihood of the cam scuffing in the first place, then the possibility of reducing lifter wear is considerably increased. If you want to ensure that lifter wear isn't going to be a problem, it's practical in most situations to use the hard-faced lifter offered by GM, part number 5232720. But be warned—they are up to three times the cost of the more common iron faced lifters.

Rebuilds

If you have to buy sixteen lifters, although they may not be expensive per unit, sixteen of them can run the cost up quite a bit. To save money you

may be tempted to buy so-called rebuilt lifters. For the most part, rebuilt lifters are not. The typical process of producing a rebuilt lifter is to reface the front of the lifter, and then flush it with a solvent to clean out the deposits. If the lifter then works on a test rig, it's considered rebuilt. If it doesn't, it's trashed.

Simple economics dictates the use of this procedure. To actually disassemble a lifter by hand and rebuild it is a more costly process than supplying a brand-new lifter, and most lifters fail not because they wear out, but because they get too dirty inside.

If an automatic cleaning process does not restore the action of the lifter, it is not cost effective to do anything about it. So your rebuilt lifter is no more than a refaced and cleaned part —which does not necessarily make it a bad part. However, you need to consider that though rebuilds may be cheaper, they may not be up to snuff for a really hot cam. But for moderate street applications, say up to 270 degrees, my limited experience indicates that they are adequate so long as the rebuilder is reputable. Although I suspect the majority are, I've been burned a couple times. One firm I recommend is Motor Machine & Supply in Tucson, Arizona, but ask yourself if it's worth taking the chance on your cam warranty just to save a few bucks.

Rapid Leakdown Lifters

If there's any point that could cause controversy in this book, this is going

---

New Lifters—Always

With any flat-tappet cam design, you should, if you make a change in cam, use new lifters on that cam. Failing to do so can cause a rapid rate of wear of both cam and lifters.

The only exception to this is if you remove a low-mileage cam and you make sure that the lifters go back on the same lobes. However, this rule does not apply if the cam changes from one block to another. Because of errors in the machining of the lifter bores, the lifters may sit on the cam lobe in a slightly different position, and therefore will not resume their original, bedded-in attitude to each other.

What you see in the photo here are some lifters which were run about 1,000 miles on a new camshaft. The lifters previously had only about 2,000 miles on them and had shown no unusual wear, but here they were used instead of new lifters on a new camshaft. You can see what happened in as little as 1,000 miles. Now this may be a rather more extreme case than usual, but it does emphasize the point.

When installing a new cam lubing the profile is important. Cam companies may use a variety of lube mixes for their particular cam, it's not necessary to use only one brand of lube mix for that particular cam, most of these lube mixes work across the board.

I tend to use Moly grease on the cam lobes if we're making a lot of cam changes on the dyno. However, if I'm building the engines from scratch then during the engine build we will use Crane Cam Lube in most instances.

Rhoads Lifters did much of the pioneering of rapid leakdown lifters.

to be it. The subject of rapid leakdown lifters and their pros and cons has been bandied about for many years.

One of the principal protagonists for the fast leakdown lifter is Jack Rhoads of Rhoads lifter fame. For many years Rhoads lifters, pioneered by James Rhoads, Jack's father, were the only type of fast leakdown lifters on the market. In the late 1980s, it seemed almost everybody in the cam business saw the potential and decided to get on the bandwagon. For years, though, there had been a great deal of skepticism in the industry as to whether this type of lifter actually did improve engine output. Can a fast leakdown lifter be made to work? What, if any, are the advantages of a rapid leakdown lifter?

A fast leakdown lifter *looks* like a good way to reduce power output from an engine because it is simply cutting the valve lift envelope area, but as we know, this is not necessarily good for power since it will increasingly restrict the breathing as rpm increases. If this is the case, then how can they be justified?

We've already considered a test whereby a solid lifter was substituted for a hydraulic, and a little more top-end power was gained. But there is much more to this than meets the eye, and under the right circumstances, a fast leakdown lifter can be advantageous for an engine. It's basically a

question of knowing how to use fast leakdown lifters.

Let's look at the concept behind it. If the lifter leaks down rapidly, then we find at low rpm when it has more time to leak down, it will effectively shorten the cam timing. As engine rpm climbs, less time exists for the lifter to leak down. As a result, the delivered cam duration more closely approaches the camshaft profile. Let's face it, at low rpm the engine doesn't need long-period cams—long-period cams are for high rpm.

So, does the rapid leakdown lifter promise us the same performance low down as a short cam while retaining the attributes of a long cam at high rpm? The answer is yes, it does have the potential to do that, but it's the combination that counts if the rapid leakdown lifter is to be made successful.

There are a number of factors to consider here, the two most important being the duration of the cam and the rate of leakdown of the lifter. Obviously a short cam is going to promote good bottom-end power anyway, so putting a rapid leakdown lifter on such a cam is unlikely to do anything other than reduce the top-end horsepower unless it fixes less than appropriate valve timing. There are cases of this happening, especially with late-model emission engines which usually have

the cam retarded from optimum. As we shall see later, rapid leakdown lifters tend to advance the effective intake centerline and this can result in more power on smog engines with retarded cam timing. However, let's get back on track.

Next, we have to consider which of all the valve events is most counterproductive toward producing low-end horsepower. The answer to that question is that the most counterproductive part of any valve event at low rpm is intrusion of the exhaust valve opening into the intake stroke as this can push burnt gases back into the intake manifold.

We also need to consider at what point the intake valve closes at the end of the induction cycle, and equally important, at what point the exhaust valve opens.

Of all these factors, which would a rapid leakdown lifter affect most? It's easy to assume that a rapid leakdown lifter simply shortens the duration of the cam, as shown by curve 1 in figure 10-3. But this is not the case. The lifters pump up far faster than they bleed down, so at the start of the valve opening period the lifter has taken up all the clearance. The lifter starts to bleed down again after the lift cycle has begun and it tends to alter the cycle, as shown by curve 2 in figure 10-1.

The point to notice when comparing curves is that a fast leakdown lifter at low rpm cuts the duration and moves the center of lift toward the opening point. In other words, the timing experienced at the valve is shorter and more advanced than the specification ground on the camshaft. Not only that, but because the intake and exhaust valves are closing earlier, but the opening events take place more or less as they would have with a regular lifter, the timing becomes shorter as well as more advanced as rpm drops. The advance comes about due to the fact that a cam's position in the engine is referenced from the lobe centerline angle.

Let's take stock of the situation. Basically, what we see is that at low rpm the cam timing is shortened and advanced. At high rpm the duration of the cam and its timing tend to return to whatever figures were ground on the cam. A look at low-rpm valve events reveals that the overlap period is shortened by the early-closing exhaust valve. This cuts the amount of exhaust dilution that the intake charge experiences at low rpm, which has a dramatic

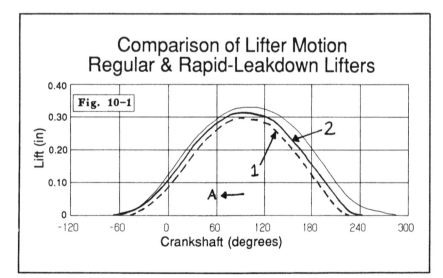

Figure 10-3: *Most people are under the impression that rapid leakdown lifters shorten the cam timing in the manner shown by curve 1. That is it simply reduces the entire lift envelope as seen by the valve. In reality this is not so. The lifter produces the initial opening points that a regular stiff lifter would, and then bleeds down throughout the lift cycle. This means that the amount of duration and lift that it subtracts gets greater as the event goes on, so all the additional timing comes off the closing side of the profile.*

effect on low-end power if a big cam is used. This aspect is probably the number one asset of the fast leakdown lifter.

The opening of the exhaust is barely affected; however, looking at the intake side we find that the opening of the intake is relatively unaffected but at low rpm the intake valve closes sooner. At low rpm there is more time to fill the cylinder; the intake valve does need to close sooner, otherwise it will start pumping some of the indrawn charge back out through the intake valve. That's point number two in favor of a fast leakdown lifter.

In practice, it seems that it is the change of overlap that usually has the biggest effect on output. Installing fast leakdown lifters only on the exhaust normally produces the biggest gains in terms of low-end power, vacuum, and idle quality. However, this does not mean that putting fast leakdown lifters on the intake is a worthless exercise. On the contrary, but there are more critical factors to be taken into account if all the possible benefits are to be accrued.

A rapid leakdown lifter alters the dynamic cam timing, and the installed cam timing will almost certainly need to be different than that used for stiff lifters to get optimum results. Also, the type of rapid leakdown lifter used can have an effect on the optimum cam timing used. Advancing cam timing tends to favor the bottom-end power, simply because the intake valve closes sooner. Retarding the cam seems to favor the top-end horsepower because the intake valve closes later, allowing more time to fill the cylinder. Also, at high rpm more overlap promotes better exhaust scavenging. A rapid leakdown lifter can supply these requirements, but it most likely won't need the same timing figures as a cam utilizing regular lifters to get the best power curve.

Though it may vary from engine to engine depending upon the specification, it would appear that for the most part (but certainly not always) using and optimizing a rapid leakdown lifter requires the cam to be set in a degree or two different. The basic reason for this is that it is only above about 3500–4000rpm that a high-rate rapid leakdown lifter (of the type sold by Competition Cams, Crower, and Rhoads) returns the valve timing to anything like the same as a stiff hydraulic lifter would. Because of the lifter's natural tendency to advance the low-speed

timing at the valve, the static cam timing may need to be set to compensate. We'll deal with this in detail later in this chapter.

Another aspect of rapid leakdown lifters that makes them good for street work is that since they cut overlap, they tend to improve economy. Assuming optimized cam timing in each case, a rapid leakdown lifter will not give your engine any more power than a stiff hydraulic lifter, but they will bump low speed torque. What it will do is allow you to choose a bigger cam than you would have normally run, and it allows that bigger cam to run as if it were a much smaller cam at low rpm. Yet the engine will enjoy most (but rarely all) of the benefits of the longer timing at high rpm. In essence, the rapid leakdown lifter allows a broadening of the power curve, and therefore you need to choose an engine specification that complements this capability.

If your engine needs a certain amount of low-end power to pull a stock torque converter, you may have to limit cam duration to say, 270 degrees. Because of the low-end requirement, you're now stuck with whatever top-end power a 270 degree cam and regular off-the-shelf lifters will give. On the other hand, a 280 degree cam with

rapid leakdown lifters can produce the benefits of a 270 degree cam at low rpm, with almost all of the additional power a 280 degree cam can deliver at the top end.

However, there's more to making the most of rapid leakdown lifters than just simply using them on a cam that is basically too big. The point is that the engine may only be able to utilize a cam a little too big for the bottom end and still satisfy top-end requirement because of a compression ratio limitation. Remember that if insufficient compression is used the engine won't benefit from a long cam, irrespective of the type of lifter used.

If only a slightly longer cam than required to develop the low-rpm power is installed, you may need a rapid leakdown lifter that has a slower leakdown rate. On the other hand, if your engine is tuned so that the compression ratio is compatible with a bigger cam that is too long for low-speed requirements, then the more rapid leakdown lifter would, in most cases, be better.

Before going the rapid leakdown route, you need to remember there is always more than one technique for skinning a cat. The other side of the coin is that if a rapid leakdown reduces top end, a stiffer lifter will increase it. It

Comparison of 280 Hydraulic Flat Tappet and 280 Hydraulic Roller Cam

	Flat Tappet	Roller	% Difference*
Lift in.	0.474	0.528	+ 11.4
Duration seat @ 0.006in	280	280	0.0
Duration @ 0.050in	230	224	− 2.6
Opening area	7879	8030	+ 1.9
Overlap area	310.4	232.7	− 25.0
After BDC area	856.4	774.0	− 9.6
Lift in. @ peak piston velocity	0.415	0.462	+ 10.2
Lift in. @ TDC	0.121	0.109	− 9.9

Refers to gains of roller over flat tappet.

Looking at these figures comparing roller and flat tappet, the change in engine characteristics becomes obvious. First a 280 roller cam tends to make more mid-range torque together with a little more horsepower. This is because the mid-range volumetric efficiency is increased due to more than 10 percent greater valve lift at peak piston velocity. This is where the most demand is put upon the breathing capability of the head. The reduced overlap area can be a mixed blessing. For a street machine, it will produce a better idle quality, but it will

also reduce any scavenging that would occur if the exhaust system were tuned to extract the combustion chamber residuals. However, most street machines are equipped with mufflers, which, in one form or another, usualy produce some back pressure. If this is the case, the reduced overlap area can reduce the amount of intake pollution from backflowing exhaust. Therefore the advantage now goes to the roller. As the duration considered becomes longer, so the advantage goes more and more to the roller.

is practical to go for a shorter cam to get the bottom end required, and use it with a stiff follower to make the most of the top end. That's a good argument for lifters being solid in calibrated sets just so you know what you are getting.

What's Available

As of 1992, cam manufacturers marketing rapid leakdown lifters include Crane, Competition Cams, Crower, and Rhoads. To lump all these companies under one heading would oversimplify the situation, however, as each firm's products differ slightly. Crane and Competition supply the slowest leakdowns, the Hi-intensity and Magnum, respectively. They can be used effectively on almost any cam over about 265–270 degrees. You can expect some increase in idle vacuum and low-end power.

Moving up the scale to the next level, the Rhoads and the Crower lifters, we find there's a considerable difference between them and the first two lifters. These moderate leakdown lifters collapse considerably faster, will provide a larger increase in idle vacuum, and on a big cam make a significant difference in low-end power. I estimate that at 2000rpm they will, from a typical 280 degree cam, bleed off 10 degrees.

Next on the list is the Hi-Tech lifter sold by Competition Cams. With three different lifter leakdown rates—that is, a regular lifter and a moderate plus rapid leakdown lifter—Competition Cams are well able to supply the needs of the performance enthusiast. Its tech line will give you solid advice based on many hours of dyno testing. Heed their advice; I have found it to be first class. The high-tech unit is Competition Cams' ultra rapid leak down lifter, intended for use on relatively large cams.

A negative side effect of lifters bleeding down very rapidly, that is in the range of 40-100in per hour, is the fact that it will leave the valvetrain too short on the closing side. As a result, the valve strikes the seat at a much higher velocity than it would with a regular tappet. This, plus the additional clearance, can cause the whole valvetrain to generate a click at each valve closure.

Though they have shortened up, the slower leakdown lifters, which with 200lb load, typically leak at a rate of about 2.5in per hour, are still on the taller closing side ramp of the cam profile and thus do not exhibit a ticking noise at idle. However, the fact that the rapid leakdown lifters can tick on a cam intended for regular lifters can be circumvented.

For instance, Rhoads offers their own cams that have a special taller closing ramp to accommodate the characteristics of their lifter. This profile design technique reduces the ticking noise because the lifter and the valve are set down more gently.

Gain Sources

The fact that rapid leakdown lifters can be made to work is not in question here, but it's still worthwhile to look into *why* they work. Where do the gains come from? Probably the most beneficial aspect of using a rapid bleeddown lifter is that it reduces valve overlap, and this in turn reduces the exhaust intrusion into the intake cycle. This probably constitutes the biggest single advantage of a rapid leakdown lifter.

About 75 percent of the advantage is gained due to the earlier closure of the exhaust valve at low rpm. Therefore, it's possible to achieve about 75 percent of the benefit of a rapid leakdown lifter by installing them on the exhaust side only. By doing so, a change is made in both the effective lobe centerline angle and the advance timing position at the valve. By using them on just the exhaust, the cam timing from low rpm will change as rpm increases.

Rocker Arms

11

Rockers and Pushrods

The stock rocker setup on a small-block Chevy is both simple and reliable—at least on a stock motor. If a change to a more radical cam is made, some details will need to be taken care of if a stock-type rocker is expected to survive. Assuming a low-budget engine rebuild and the need to use only partly worn existing rockers, you'll need to do whatever it takes to make those rockers work.

First it's necessary to establish whether or not the slot in the rocker is long enough to accommodate any additional lift the cam may have. If it isn't, the slot will have to be extended to avoid butting up against the stud. (See figure 11-1.)

Next, inspect the pad that bears on the end of the valve. Unless the rockers have seen very little use, there will be a step formed at the end of the worn section of the pad. Depending on how the rocker met the valve, this step could be on both ends of the wear section. If they exist, these steps must be removed. If they are left on and the new cam delivers a higher lift, a problem can arise. As the rocker moves through its arc on the tip of the valve, as it contacts the end of the valve tip the step section will put a side load on the valve. Not only will this cause a noisy valve action, but it also will cause the valve guides to wear much quicker.

So long as the wear step is no more than 5 thousandths (0.005in) or so it is possible to dress the step off with a stone. In the process, try not to remove any metal from the existing worn section, as the case hardening on a stock-style rocker is minimal. It varies from brand to brand, but figure about 0.020in.

Once the step has been stoned off, the rockers are ready for further use, but check to see what type of ball pivot the rocker used. On some stock motors the ball is plain. To survive use at higher rpm, and with stronger springs, a grooved ball is necessary. The grooves allow oil to lubricate the interface between the ball and the rocker much more effectively.

Without these grooves the rocker can, with stronger springs and higher lift, burn and partially seize. When this happens, it dumps fine metal into the oil, which eventually spreads to the rest of the engine. Whether grooved balls are essential or not depends on the cam and valve spring combination. A long-period cam doesn't change what's needed for the ball, but cams with high lift and strong spring loads do.

Grooved balls should be used anytime more than 0.450in valve lift is envisaged, and/or springs of more than 250–270lb over the nose are used. If you have a set of rockers that need modifying for high performance and are equipped with the plain pivot balls, you should seriously consider buying a new set of rockers since the grooved balls are not sold separately. Both Sealed Power and TRW as well as most of the cam companies market a quality grooved ball rocker having a longer slot to accommodate higher lift.

If broken in with plenty of molybdenum grease in the pivots, this style of rocker can tolerate about 350lb of over-the-nose spring loads with valvetrains with up to about 0.500in lift.

Rocker Ratios

The stock Chevy rocker is quoted as having a nominal 1.5:1 ratio. This means it should deliver a peak valve lift 1.5 times higher than the lift on the cam. What is not commonly realized by inexperienced engine builders is that the rocker ratio changes as the valve goes through its motion because the valve-to-rocker geometry changes as lift progresses. This geometric change is a variable we can do little about short of designing our own rockers, but there are important facets of valve lift that we do have control over. Let's first establish the importance of valve lift.

The flow curves of typical modified small-block Chevy cylinder heads show that almost irrespective of the type of cylinder head, flow increases up to about 600 thousandths (0.600in) lift. If it's an all-out race head, the flow increases up to 700 thousandths (0.700in), and maybe a little more on really effective heads.

Since the valves in small-blocks are too small to start with, limiting the lift will serve only to further restrict the breathing. Almost any small-block Chevy needs generous valve lift to make horsepower because of cylinder head limitations. Not only is it necessary to lift the valve as far as possible, but also to move the valve off its seat as quickly as possible, the most important valve being the intake.

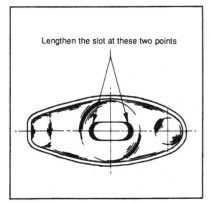

Figure 11-1: *If a cam change is made to one having a higher lift and the stock rockers are retained, be aware that the pivot slot may not be long enough, and will need to be ground as indicated here.*

Lengthen the slot at these two points

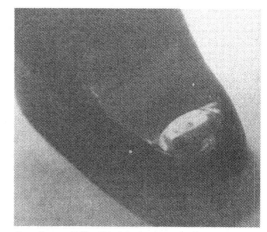

A rocker pad like this has been worn too much for further service. Once it's gone through the case hardening, it will not last long.

Valvetrain Stiffness

Many engine builders often suppose the pushrod is the weak link in a pushrod overhead-valve engine, such as the small-block Chevy. The pushrod, due to its length, looks like it should be the most flexible item in the valvetrain. Fortunately, it takes loads in a manner that minimizes the effect of bending, until, that is, buckling occurs.

Indeed, if straight, the pushrod is a relatively stiff part of the valvetrain. The weak link in any pushrod valvetrain is, in fact, the rocker, and rocker stiffness is an important factor toward developing horsepower.

I did some tests on a number of rockers to ascertain their stiffness; the nearby chart shows the results. You'll notice there is not a great deal of difference from one type of rocker to another. Secondly, many of the more expensive rockers have no more stiffness than inexpensive rockers, such as the Competition Cams' Magnum rocker.

This particular rocker proved to be an exceptionally good value for as much as it delivered. Over the stock rocker, the Magnum rocker had 20 percent increase in stiffness, an 80 percent increase in overall strength, and, at a 1.6 ratio instead of 1.5, a 9 percent increase in opening area. All of this isn't bad considering this is a budget piece, and if used within the recommended spring poundage, it is about as near to a bullet-proof speed equipment part as you can get.

Another aspect of rockers and their flexibility is that when they bend they act as a spring. This energy is stored during the opening phase and released as soon as accelerations go from positive to negative. This can cause the valvetrain to run into a vibration problem if the cam profile doesn't make an allowance for it, and many cam profiles don't.

Instead the rocker is assumed to be virtually infinitely stiff. This means you need a rocker that has some inherent

So, you want to check out rocker ratios and stiffness? First, check how much cam lift exists.

Next, install the cylinder head with the rocker you intend to test, and using a light valve spring, set the appropriate lash; then check to see how much valve lift occurs. To get the full lift rocker ratio, divide the amount designating cam lift into the amount for the rocker lift.

To test rocker stiffness, it's necessary to do a test like this using both a heavy and a light spring, and compare how much less valve lift there is with the heavy spring. A 10 thousandths (0.010in) loss of valve lift is not uncommon.

damping capabilities. Consequently rocker assembly stiffness is not the only factor. If you want a high-performance rocker, you need to know that both stainless steel and aluminum have better internal damping properties than the steel stock rockers. In other words, neither stainless nor aluminum make good springs.

So, if you're building an all-out motor, you should look for the stiffest rocker available, in either aluminum or stainless steel. For what it's worth, titanium, although it has the properties of lightness and strength, would probably not make a good rocker unless it could somehow be heat-treated to be less springy. On the other hand, a carbon fiber rocker, although expensive to make, would probably be the ultimate way to go.

Here's a fixture I made up to test rocker stiffness. This fixture was put under a press, and the load to deflection of the rocker was measured.

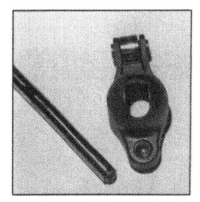

Competition Cams advises the use of a new pushrod when you install their Magnum rockers. Previously worn pushrods may cause a failure as seen in the pushrod cup of this rocker and on the end of the pushrod.

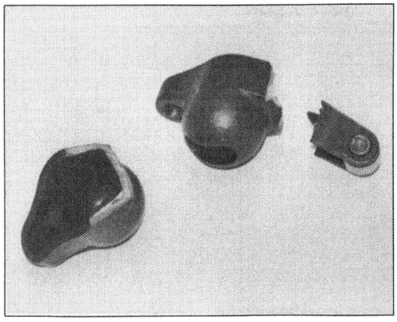

The Competition Cams' Magnum rockers proved to be stout pieces. They took almost twice the load the stock ones took before breakage. This strength equaled and even surpassed several of the more expensive aluminum rockers.

My press-deflection tests have also indicated that the Crane/Cam Dynamics Strongarm rocker is well named.

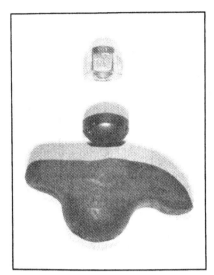

Here is the stock rocker setup for the small-block Chevy. It's changed little from day one. It's simple, reliable, and fits Detroit's main criteria in that it's cheap to manufacture.

If valve lifts over 500 thousandths (0.500in) are envisaged, a roller rocker of some sort is the way to go. Without it, the heavier side loads produced by a non-rollerized tip will cause guides to wear out abnormally quickly. Used within their specifications, these Competition Cam roller rockers are as near bulletproof as you could expect.

Rocker Ratios

What you think you are buying is often not what you get! I have had the opportunity to measure numerous brands and types of rockers. All are certainly not born equal—as the accompanying chart shows a substantial deviation from the quoted ratio can exist.

If you are looking for maximum output then, regardless of whether you are working within the confines of a budget, you should check the ratio your rockers are delivering.

Before starting this you need to set the pushrod length to some standard consistent with delivering maximum lift. My best recommendation here is to use the Manley pushrod length checking tool.

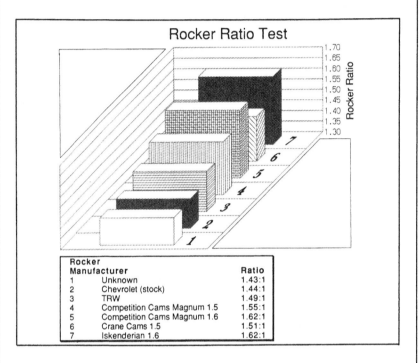

Rocker Manufacturer		Ratio
1	Unknown	1.43:1
2	Chevrolet (stock)	1.44:1
3	TRW	1.49:1
4	Competition Cams Magnum 1.5	1.55:1
5	Competition Cams Magnum 1.6	1.62:1
6	Crane Cams 1.5	1.51:1
7	Iskenderian 1.6	1.62:1

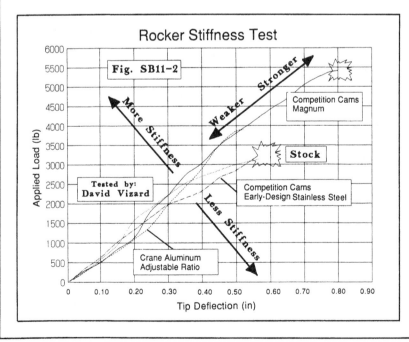

On a typical 350ci 275–300hp small-block, which is probably short on lift, losing 0.020in of lift on an already low lift cam may subtract as much as 10hp from the engine's output. Armed with the right information, that 10hp need not be lost.

Although rated at a 1.5:1 ratio stock, many of the aftermarket or OEM replacement rockers do not measure up to this. Test results have revealed ratios as low as 1.40 on a stock cam. Using a rocker with a 1.40 ratio as opposed to a full 1.5 will easily account for a 10hp loss. With an engine having a relatively big cam, there is a real possibility of losing as much as 15hp.

What we're talking about here is potential losses on a typical application. Just how much power is lost or gained by attention to the rocker ratio does depend on engine displacement, the camshaft used, and the flow characteristics of the heads, but we'll deal more with that later.

At this point it's worthwhile to make sure the rockers you buy have as near the designed ratio as possible. You'll find that most rockers when checked at full lift fall below the 1.47 mark, and actually getting a true 1.5 ratio stock-pattern rocker is difficult. Part of the reason is that they only deliver their true design ratio about halfway through the lift.

Proven rocker designs of 1985 may not be up to scratch in 1995. In the past I have had good results with TRW and Sealed Power rockers, and as of 1992 at least, strongly suggest these companies or, better yet, some of the leading cam companies as a possible source.

If you are buying a reputable brand from a local parts store, I suggest initially buying just one rocker while making sure a full set of sixteen can be obtained from what can reasonably be presumed to be the same batch. If the first rocker checks out okay, you are reasonably assured of getting a set of identical rockers. If the sample rocker delivers an acceptable ratio, figure that anything above about 1.47 is hard to get, then go ahead and buy the additional fifteen. If the sample measures out low, take it back to the store and explain that it doesn't deliver the right ratio for your needs and find another source.

If you are in the market for a new set of rockers and can stretch the budget a little, Crane has a stamped steel rocker with a quoted 1.6:1 ratio. You can figure that 1.6:1 rockers will give you the best horsepower per dollar return when used on the intake only.

If you want to step up a rung, the Competition Cams Magnum rockers do a fine job and are very reliable if the spring poundage limitations are observed. Crane also has a stamped-steel roller-tip rocker that is inexpensive. As it happens, most flat-tappet cam and spring combinations are compatible.

Most of the horsepower increase from increased rocker ratios comes from opening the intake valve faster and farther.

If you have a dual-pattern cam that is ground on a fairly wide lobe centerline angle, putting a 1.6 rocker on the intake and staying with the 1.5 rocker on the exhaust works very well, especially if the heads have been ported to some extent.

Knowing when and where high-lift rockers will work might just look like a little black magic, but the reasons why rockers react in certain ways is next on the agenda.

Ratios and Cam Timing

So that you can make an informed choice among the many styles of high-lift rockers on the market, let's talk in detail about their effects on performance engines. Incorrectly used, high-lift rockers will lighten your wallet without necessarily producing any additional output.

The easiest way to deal with this subject is to set some ground rules. They will pertain to not only enthusiast engine builders, building an engine or two a year, but also to professionals who have a dynamometer at their disposal.

Over the years I have seen many professional engine builders test high-

During my cam tests, a lot of use was made of these Crane adjustable 1.5-1.6 rockers. One set was used for over four years in over 7,000 dyno pulls with rpms up to 8,000. Not one failure was experienced. I finally retired them when they started looking scrappy from repeated removal and replacement from the engines. Scratches through the gold anodizing did not make them the most photogenic pieces in the shop!

Here's the Crane/Cam Dynamics strong-arm rocker. This is a relatively inexpensive cast-aluminum rocker for street applications. It has its limitations, as outlined in its instructions, but used within those limitations, it appears to be a cost-effective, reliable piece.

lift rockers and come to erroneous conclusions concerning the rockers' capability to produce extra power. Often such conclusions are based on tests using an engine having optimized cam timing with 1.5 rockers. In such a situation installing 1.6 rockers can cause, as I've seen on more occasions than I care to mention, a decrease in power. This looks like fairly convincing evidence that high-lift rockers *don't work*.

In reality, the test procedure was at fault. To understand why, consider first what effect high-lift rockers have on cam timing engine requirements, and second, whether or not the high lift is justified.

For smaller cubic inch engines, high valve lift is not as important as it is for larger cubic inch engines. Consider this: If a camshaft delivers enough lift for a 300ci engine, and then displacement is increased to 400ci, it's fairly reasonable to assume that another 25 percent air demand will be required at

any given moment in the lift cycle to retain the status quo. Unfortunately, this air demand cannot be easily met because the lift is now insufficient. So anytime displacement increases, valve lift needs to increase by a proportional amount.

I must emphasize that though not practical to increase lift in proportion to displacement by changing rockers, a big cubic inch engine is, nonetheless, much more sensitive to having adequate lift than a small one. With a 300ci race engine having say, 0.600in lift with 1.5 rockers, changing to high-lift rockers and gaining some 0.050in lift is only likely to deliver a fraction of the horsepower increase it would on a 400 incher. In fact, on a 300ci engine, there may be no gain in power until 6000rpm or more is achieved. So displacement is a prime ingredient to take into account when considering high-lift rockers.

But, there are many other equally important interrelated factors. For instance, as the rocker ratio is increased

there is a need to spread the cam lobe centerline angle. If the lobe centerline angle was optimum with 1.5 rockers, then basically changing to 1.6 rockers requires 1 to 2 degrees at the most spread in the lobe centerline angle, and if the same low-end characteristics are required the cam timing should also be shortened by about 4 degrees, especially on the intake.

How about high-lift rockers with a stock cam? Because of the relatively slow opening rates on stock cams, the valves do not lift as much as they do with an aftermarket cam. This means that the response produced by the engine to high-lift rockers can be a greater percentage increase in power. So if you don't want to make a cam change, a set of high-lift rockers will still produce good results.

Sticking with the intake for a moment, let's discuss where high-lift rockers work best. For a typical street 350 with a moderate off-the-shelf street cam, I find that with the normally wider than optimum lobe centerline angles used, high-lift rockers deliver good results.

Making the move to high-lift intake rockers serves two useful purposes. It has an effect similar to closing up the lobe centerline angle slightly, bringing it nearer to optimum. And it brings about the much needed added lift required of most street cams, a limitation brought about by restraints imposed by the lifter diameter. As a result, using high-lift rockers with a relatively short, wide lobe centerline street cam is usually a very effective way to grab more horsepower without necessarily causing a significant loss in low end.

What do I mean by short? Typically, cams around 260–280 degrees on 110–114 degree LCAs will respond well, especially if in a 350. Such timing and LCAs cover most of the range of off-the-shelf cams. Under these circumstances you can expect a power increase typical of that shown in figure 11-2.

If the cam is a short single-pattern cam then there is a little, but not much, extra power to be had by putting the high-lift rockers on the exhaust. With short cams a high-lift rocker extends the effective timing, and also cuts the amount of power taken to expel the gases out of the cylinder on the exhaust stroke. You can figure that with cams up to about 270 degrees, there is possibly two to three additional horsepower in high-lift rockers.

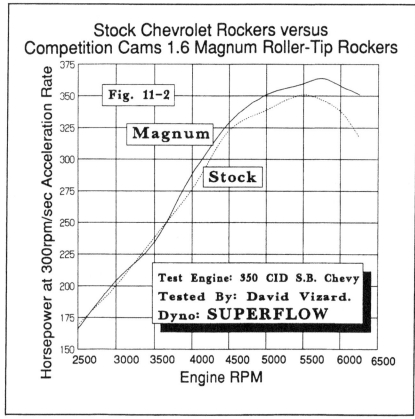

Figure 11-2: *On an air-starved small-block Chevy with a relatively short cam, high-lift rockers can represent an easy way to substantially increase top-end horsepower. The test shown here indicated that a direct change to Magnum* rockers was worth some 16hp on the top end. On bigger engines we've seen gains of as much as 22hp by making the change from a stock 1.5 GM rocker to a 1.6 Competition Cams Magnum rocker.

A better way to go rather than use high-lift rockers on the exhaust is to use cams with a longer exhaust than intake period and stay with the 1.5 rockers. If a longer opening exhaust period is better, why don't all cam grinders employ such strategy? Well, nothing comes for free. Single-pattern cams generally deliver slightly better fuel economy and some additional low-end torque over their dual-pattern counterpart. Dual-pattern street cams usually pay off from about 4000rpm upward.

For the most part, exhaust profiles have a greater effect on power when their opening area is extended by increased duration rather than increased valve acceleration and lift. When using a cam with 280 degrees on the intake and about 285–290 degree exhaust timing, you will often produce better results when high-lift rockers are installed on the intake only. Using them on the exhaust often cuts the power throughout most of the rpm range (see figure 11-3).

On cams sporting 290/300 degrees, a 1.6 on the shorter intake and a 1.5 on

the exhaust usually adds up to about a 7–10hp increase on an average high-compression 350 small-block Chevy. These kinds of test results indicate that most cams have adequate exhaust valve accelerations.

Many cam companies market dual-pattern cams. In some cases (Crane, for example), the longer period exhaust valve opening used is an intake profile. As such they not only lift longer, but also higher. As a consequence, the exhaust valve is in less need of a high-lift rocker, as the longer period allows more time to reach a higher lift.

On occasion, I've had the opportunity to test camshafts such as those from Competition Cams that have dual-pattern timing, but the cam lift is very similar intake to exhaust. Even under these circumstances it is hard to see much, if any, advantage of a 1.6 rocker as opposed to a 1.5. Ultimately, it's a question of economics.

Unless you want to spend money on numerous sets of rockers and dyno time, take my recommendations. This means high-ratio rockers all around if a short single-pattern cam is used. If a long single-pattern cam—280 degrees or more—is used, then depending upon the degree of modification of the head, the 1.6 should work on the intake. The same cannot always be said for the exhaust. You have about a 50:50 chance that they may do the reverse. With a dual-pattern cam, the situation becomes clearer. Thus, it appears the best technique to use is 1.6 or more on the intake and 1.5 on the exhaust for optimal results.

If you're a regular visitor to the drag strip, then an opportunity exists to test the effect of high-lift rockers on both intake and exhaust without buying more than sixteen rockers. Crane produces an adjustable rocker that can be set to 1.5 or a 1.6 ratio.

The easiest way to determine and dial in to your engine's needs is to start with all rockers set at the 1.5 ratio. Adjust mixture, timing, and so on, until you've achieved the best from the car. Once some consistent baseline figures have been established, set the intake to 1.6. After optimal results have been achieved with a 1.6 ratio intake, and comparisons made, continue with the exhaust set to 1.6. This should give you a good idea which combination gives the best results within the limitations of fixed cam timing.

Ideally, at each rocker ratio change the cam advance and retard should be

reevaluated. With a dual-pattern cam the timing *usually* needs to be retarded 1 or maybe 2 degrees when higher ratios are used on the intake only. However, this assumes the cam's LCA is optimal or at least nearly so for the engine in the first place.

To make testing in this area easier, read chapter 13 on cam drives. To do such testing the Crane rockers, be it strip or dyno, are a little more expensive than similar regular rockers. Refining the engine's cam and valvetrain in this way is well worth the effort, though. I have used the Crane adjustables on numerous occasions to simplify optimizing the rockers needed for any particular cam.

Optimizing Geometry

Until now we've talked about the effect that high-lift rockers have on horsepower, but what about its effect on valvetrain dynamics? What is an optimal ratio? It's difficult to answer those questions since so many factors affect it, and until the time when computers were used to model valvetrains accurately, it was difficult to say what was optimum.

Only trial and error methods pointed toward optimal ratios. Pushrod valve operation became widely used in the mid 1950s, and its rapidly increasing popularity meant a lot of research was done. By the end of the decade it was

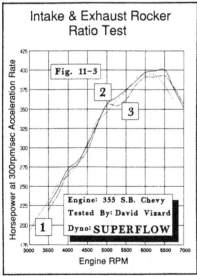

Figure 11-3: *If the cam you're using has extended exhaust timing, the use of a 1.6 ratio rocker on the exhaust may actually be detrimental to power. Study the figures in this graph for the typical result of such a move. Curve 1 is the output of the engine with 1.5 rockers on the intake and exhaust. Curve 2 is 1.6 on the intake, 1.5 on the exhaust. Curve 3 is 1.6s all around. Note that fitting the higher-ratio rockers to the exhaust negated all gains made on the intake. If in doubt, always use 1.5s on the exhaust.*

The graph in Figure 11-3 shows:

Intake & Exhaust Rocker Ratio Test

Y-axis: Horsepower at 300rpm/sec Acceleration Rate (175 to 425)
X-axis: Engine RPM (3000 to 7000)

Engine: 355 S.B. Chevy
Tested By: David Vizard
Dyno: SUPERFLOW

Some rocker designs require relieving here to clear 1.50-1.60in diameter springs. I've seen rockers machined like this fail at this point and do not particularly recommend it.

realized that a pushrod and rocker valvetrain actuation produced the best results when the rocker ratio was between 1.5 and about 1.75.

To see why having a mechanical advantage at the rocker pays off, let's consider a basic rocker system where it's a 1:1 ratio. Looking at the weight of the valvetrain components reveals that a major proportion of mass is in the lifter and pushrod. Only about 35–40 percent of the effectively moved mass resides in the valve retainer and spring. Essentially, the business of the valvetrain is to open and close the valve. An unwanted by-product is that it has to also move a lifter and pushrod.

The rationale here is to arrange things so that the valve motion is maximized, while minimizing the lifter and pushrod motion since it represents a major proportion of the reciprocating weight. If the valve is operated through a rocker arm ratio, there's less total back-and-forth motion of the mass involved.

Another point in favor of a high-ratio rocker is that it gives a mechanical or lever advantage over the pushrod and follower. Assuming a 1.5 rocker ratio for the moment, we see that at any point in the valve lift event the pushrod and follower experience a returning force holding it in contact with the cam 50 percent higher than that exerted by the spring.

If the seat load is say, 100lb at the moment that lash takes up, the spring force exerted on the pushrod and follower is 150lb. If the spring exerts 250lb at full lift, then the force returning the pushrod and follower back to the valve's closed position in its seat is 375lb. This leverage ratio from valve spring to follower allows control of the valvetrain mass much more effectively than if a 1:1 rocker ratio had been used.

Since a rocker change from 1.5 to 1.6 develops more lift, one would assume the engine rpm capability before valve float would decrease. However, using rockers with the same effective mass shows this not to be true.

Unless influenced by other factors, such as spring surge, changing from a 1.5 to a 1.6 ratio should marginally *increase* the rpm limit of the engine. But don't expect to find the rpm limit increasing when a change is made from a 1.5 stamped steel rocker to a heavy-duty aluminum 1.6 or 1.65. The greater mass of the aluminum rocker is not usually offset by this more favorable rocker ratio, and typically you'll find about a 200rpm drop in engine speed before valve float occurs.

Rocker Types

Because the stock rocker looks so simple and performs its job so effectively, it's easy to lose sight of just how much an appropriate rocker design can contribute to power development, especially very high outputs. There is more to selecting rockers than just looking for one that delivers a high ratio.

Irrespective of its construction, comparing a high-ratio rocker that incorporates other potential assets to a stock 1.5 ratio rocker, the difference could mean as much as 75hp. So, choosing an appropriate rocker can significantly affect the success of your engine.

Let's start with the simpler attributes needed for a high-performance

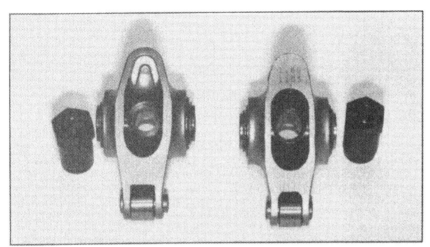

Here are two examples of stainless roller rockers from Competition Cams. The type shown on the left are slightly lighter and a later design.

Shown here is basically an evolution of rocker design. On the left is the original 1.5 rocker designed to clear the typical springs common some years ago. It still suits the majority of applications, but when modified to a 1.6 ratio, a spring-to-main-body clearance problem can arise. This has led to the development of the offset trunion rocker (right), where the entire body is moved in relation to the hole in the trunion, thereby moving the body further away from the spring. This allows more clearance on a larger spring. For high-rpm applications using a large spring, the offset trunion rocker seems to be the preference.

rocker. Aftermarket rockers are available to suit two common stud sizes, 3/8in which is usually the typical stock size for a small-block Chevy, and 7/16in. The 7/16 stud offers a potentially stiffer valvetrain. If the engine is only required to turn up to about 6500rpm, the 3/8in stud will do.

It's worth questioning, though, the cost effectiveness of roller rockers on what is probably a budget motor with only a 6500rpm capability. Sure, there is some justification for roller rockers, but if horsepower is the number one priority, a good set of reworked heads is almost mandatory. While the heads are stripped it makes sense to install 7/16 studs. But there are exceptions to this line of reasoning.

Viewed on a cost-effective basis, some of the less expensive high-performance rockers can justify their existence on 3/8in studs. Two that come to mind are the Competition Cams stainless-steel roller-tipped Magnum rocker, and the Crane/Cam Dynamics Strong Arm rocker.

Rockers and Big Ports

Even limited experience in porting small-block Chevrolet heads quickly reveals that a major obstacle in achieving a high-flowing port at high-valve lift is the port width constriction imposed by the pushrod location. Although this constriction isn't critical, even with highly reworked stock castings, I find a well-developed head based on a high-performance aftermarket casting can have an intake valve capable of flowing more air than the pushrod constricted area will allow. The result is that the pushrod aperture becomes a constriction.

Rockers with pushrod cups offset sideways up to about 1/4in are available from a number of manufacturers. Moving the pushrod sideways gives the head ports more scope for generating extra port width. On an all-out race engine turning a very high rpm this asset may be worth as much as 20hp. But for the most part, offsetting the rocker by a small amount does not cause any undue pushrod-rocker-valve alignment problems. However, large offsets will cause the rocker to want to skew slightly on the valve's end, but the pushrod location will restrain it.

With offset pushrods, though, there is more side load on the pushrod itself, so the fit in the guide plate becomes more critical. If large offsets are used on the rocker, at least a degree of offset should be used at the follower. Of course, this will have to be the roller type because offsetting a follower that rotates is a fruitless exercise.

Among others, Iskenderian produces a roller follower with an offset, which helps bring the pushrod back to the vertical position. If you're looking for rockers that have offsets and high ratios, a few companies to check with include Competition Cams, Crane, Crower, and Iskenderian. Over the years I've used all of these brands with varying degrees of success.

Aluminum versus Steel

By far, the most common high-performance roller rocker is the forged or extruded aluminum type. Though very bulky, aluminum is reasonably good in terms of its mass/stiffness ratio. The difference between a well-designed aluminum rocker and a steel one in terms of stiffness versus reciprocating

mass proves minimal, much less than is often supposed. Aluminum is popular because it is easy to machine, whereas the stainless-steel alloys normally used for rockers are extremely tough.

Often the question arises as to how long aluminum rockers will last in a street machine. Will fatigue kill them before achieving a reasonable mileage? The answer depends largely on the spring forces involved and the rpm the engine is taken to.

Contrary to what you may have read before, a properly designed aluminum rocker can be an extremely reliable street piece, so long as the spring stresses imposed by the valve don't go out of sight. Anytime spring forces start to escalate, the chances of rocker fatigue failure become more realistic.

The question is, which rockers are more prone to breakage than others? Unfortunately, I haven't been able to run through a comprehensive series of tests on the subject, but there are some things to watch for. Any rocker that has to be machined to clear a large-diameter valve spring is going to fail sooner than if it didn't have to be machined. Large valve springs require some rockers to be machined, and this leaves them thin at the junction between the arm on the rocker side and the main body. Rockers that have seen a lot of service are the ones I've seen break the most. However, I won't be too specific here because the number of breakages I have seen is too few to base any statistics on.

In an effort to allow for valve spring clearance without undercutting the body of the rocker, some manufacturers have located the hole in the trunion of the rocker farther forward, so that the pivot point is actually behind the stud centerline, on the pushrod side of the stud. This allows high-ratio rockers to be more easily accommodated in

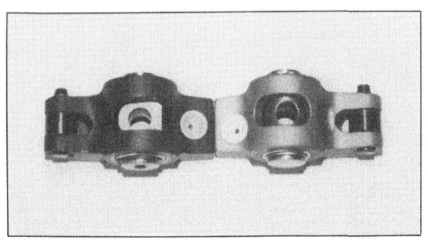

Here's the difference between a regular rocker with zero offset and a rocker designed with 1/8in offset. Both examples are from Isky.

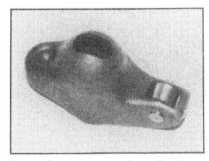

Here's Crane's inexpensive roller-tipped rocker. Basically it's a pressed-steel rocker suitably heat treated, with a roller added.

the space available on a typical small-block Chevy head. Edelbrock rockers have popularized the concept, and are available with ratios ranging from 1.5 through 1.7.

Though aluminum rockers can take a pounding, the fact that they ultimately fatigue can mean that a race, especially a long-distance race, could be lost by the breakage of a rocker. For this reason, many engine builders prefer to use a stainless-steel investment cast rocker. Although they don't necessarily offer increased stiffness, they do have a definite edge in terms of fatigue life. For engines expected to run in 500 mile races, stainless-steel rockers would be my choice.

Shaft-Mounted Rockers

The pivoted stud-mounted rocker is certainly a stroke of genius as far as a production line engine is concerned. However, when we get to really exotic valvetrains requiring offset pushrods, high ratios, and so forth, certain shortcomings begin to arise.

Probably the most important drawback of a high-tech stud-mounted rocker is that without adequate support, an offset rocker tends to load up the valve and the stud at an angle. Also, the roller does not have a true rolling motion over the end of the valve, but there is a certain sideways component as well.

Though this deficiency need not necessarily be a major drawback, a shaft-mounted rocker is generally a better bet. It can be made stiffer, and the fact that the shaft can control any off-center or side loads ensures straight-line motion at the end of the valve.

There are two types of rockers in this category, the pseudo shaft-mounted rocker, and the authentic article. That comment is not meant to put down the first category because some pseudo shaft-mounted rockers have proved very successful.

In this type of setup the rockers are paired off, with each pair mounted on a short shaft. The assembly then mounts on the studs. There are various designs available, with some being more true shaft-mounted than others. True shaft-type rocker assemblies are not legal for Winston Cup racing as of 1992, however.

Companies that carry these types include Erson, Crower, and Crane. The Crane pseudo shaft design was new as of 1990, and has some novel features. It

These Isky rockers don't look much different except in color. In actual fact, Isky uses color coding to differentiate the blue 1.5 from the black 1.6 rocker models.

Although stainless steel is significantly heavier than aluminum, it is also significantly stronger. Even though cast, stainless steel still retains most of the strength of forging, but the casting process allows the material to be put to best use, so less material is along for a free ride. The end result is a rocker which has good durability for the weight involved.

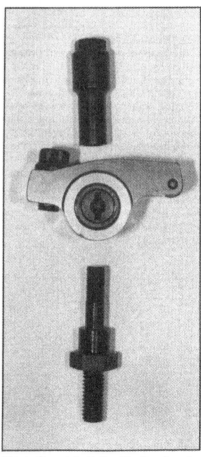

This is Crane's Imitation Shaft rockers for Winston Cup engines and any other class of racing where shaft rockers are banned. For all practical purposes it simulates the effect of a shaft, although no shaft is present.

This stainless-steel Crower rocker, in its earliest design form, was one of the first stainless-type rockers to be introduced to the performance industry.

seems to be proving itself worthy of inclusion in some of the top Grand National and Winston Cup engine builders' parts assembly lists. At the time of this writing no in-house tests have been done on the pseudo shaft rockers.

Suppliers of true shaft-mounted rockers include Jessel Engineering, T&D Machine, Crower, and Zorian. Again, I've not tested any of these rockers personally, but the first three companies have a reputation for producing high-quality products, and their equipment is used by some of the top engine builders in the nation.

Although I've had no dealings with Zorian, I've never heard any negative comments about their products either. In fact, it's been more the reverse.

Over the years, Jessel has established a good reputation with its shaft-mounted rockers. T&D is, in effect, the new guy on the block; however, Larry Torres, the boss at T&D, is well respected in the industry, having been a racer of high repute himself, and having set many track records. Crower's reputation is based on forty years experience in this field. Suffice it to say that you can get high-quality products from all of these companies, but it's worth noting the T&D rockers are the least expensive. All these companies will custom-build the rocker assemblies to fit your cylinder heads. For the most popular styles of cylinder heads, pushrod offsets, and so forth, they carry the required parts in stock.

Pushrods and Guide Plates

In the more mundane stock heads, the pushrod location and hence the rocker orientation over the valve is controlled by slots in the heads. Better location can be achieved by moving the pushrod location point nearer the rocker.

On factory high-performance Chevrolet heads, the slot-in-head technique is done away with in preference to a steel guide plate located directly under the studs. When steel pushrod guide plates are used, most stock pushrods will wear excessively at the point where they pass through the guide plate. To offset this you will need to use the pushrods with hardened ends. Most aftermarket pushrods are of this type. There is also a choice of guide plates available. Most are flat but some, as per Competition Cams items, are stepped to move the pushrod location

T&D Machine specializes in making rocker setups for various engines. They have a wide range available for almost all the different cylinder head configurations of the small-block Chevy. Pictured here is a shaft setup with 1/4in offset on the intake, so as to allow the port width to be widened. The Pontiac Chevy head is deliberately cast so the port can be made wide. Here the large offset on the T&D rocker allows that port width to be accommodated without problem. This T&D rocker setup is relatively typical of the principles used to convert from a stud rocker setup to a full shaft setup.

Although most rocker manufacturers use needle roller bearings on a shaft setup, they are in fact unnecessary. The rollers prove to be little more than icing on the cake. Their main advantage is that they need little oil, and therefore, the oil at the top end of the engine can be limited. However, valve spring cooling becomes the factor that dictates just how much oil must go to the top end. Spring cooling requirements dictate the lower limits of flow and not the lubrication needed by a roller bearing or guide. In many respects, a plain bronze bearing would be just as effective, and it won't shed rollers.

Here is an installed full shaft setup.

point to a position immediately below the ball end of the pushrod.

Pushrod stiffness is an important factor, especially with today's rapid acceleration cam profiles. For a good street machine you need to consider that the main requirement of any pushrod you may install is that it be straight—the slightest bend is exaggerated as the valve motion takes place, and one pushrod bent out a few thousandths inch can easily rob the engine of a measurable amount of power.

To put some figures to that, I've seen a bent pushrod with about a 0.030in bend in it take 8hp off a 300 degree hydraulic-cammed bracket motor. Increasing the stiffness of the pushrod makes little difference when talking about cams of the normal street variety; the biggest factor to concentrate on, as I've said, is the straightness of the pushrod. But when spring loads exceed about 400lb over the nose, then there is real justification for looking at pushrods with greater stiffness than a typical $^5/_{16}$in pushrod delivers. My recommendation here is, if there is room to accommodate a $^3/_8$in pushrod, then go that route.

Finding ways and means of reducing pushrod weight is important for any valvetrain. The pushrods used in small-block Chevys typically are made of tubular chromemoly and stainless steel. Although they don't weigh much in themselves, remember that in operation they are full of oil. Efforts to cut reciprocating weight have mostly been directed toward making satisfactory aluminum, titanium, or carbon fiber pushrods.

A few years ago Manley introduced carbon fiber pushrods, but they did not seem to achieve any great acceptance in the industry. Although I've not used carbon fiber pushrods in small-block Chevy engines, I have had experience with them in small European high-rpm four-cylinder engines.

A carbon fiber pushrod does have potential; however, you must buy from

The Crower shaft rocker assembly uses stainless-steel rockers.

Continuing to draw on their expertise in the cast versus aluminum rocker area, Crower used this technique to make a shaft-mounted rocker. In this shot of the Crower setup, you can see how $^1/_4$-in offset is accommodated on the intake rocker.

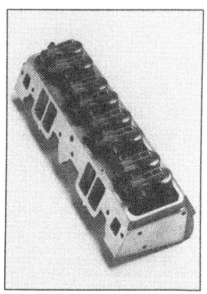

This Crower setup on a Brodix -11 head certainly looks the business. It's the sort of setup you would expect to see on a high-output alcohol motor. Although I've not done any tests, stiffness of a shaft rocker setup is said to be appreciably higher than that of a conventional stud-mounted installation.

a company that has the necessary technology to make a reliable piece because there's more to it than simply making a carbon fiber pushrod with a couple of steel inserts in the end.

Several companies currently manufacture these pushrods in small quantities for select race teams who are, at the time of writing, being relatively close-mouthed about the degree of success achieved. If you're interested in carbon fiber pushrods, I recommend contacting PRD.

If you take a look at the nearby test charts, you will see that carbon fiber

pushrods can dispose of something like 60 percent of the weight in the pushrod compared with a steel pushrod, and still be in the region of double the stiffness. In addition, because the wall thickness is greater on a carbon fiber pushrod, the amount of oil contained inside is less, so in operation the advantages of a carbon fiber pushrod are even greater.

The last point to concern yourself with is that carbon fiber does not support vibrations very well, and in effect, a well-designed carbon fiber pushrod can not only act as a very stiff

means of transmitting cam motion to the valve, but also as a reasonably effective noise and vibration damper.

Although titanium works effectively for a pushrod because of its relatively high stiffness-to-weight ratio, it does have one disadvantage: it makes a good spring material. The only titanium pushrod test I know of showed a *reduction* of power. This may have been due to the fact that the titanium supported or even aggravated valve-train vibrations.

If you are building a serious competition motor it's a good idea to consult a cam company that's in a position to manufacture custom pushrods. Obviously, if you're ordering a cam for an all-

One of the advantages to a shaft rocker setup is that high-ratio rockers can be made to clear more easily large-diameter valve springs. Rocker ratios up to 1.75 can be had in shaft installations.

If offset pushrods are used, the slots in the guide plate will no longer fit. It used to be common practice to saw guide plates in two, then re-weld them. Isky came up with this idea: no need to weld, just bolt them up, set them at the right pitch, and tighten.

If the pushrod is offset in the rocker, then obviously it will run at an angle from the pushrod button centrally located in the cam follower. If roller cam followers are used, I find that since they don't rotate, it is practical to offset the pushrod button in the roller follower, thus bringing the pushrod back in line for a more direct approach to the rocker. Pictured here is a centrally located and an offset pushrod button-type roller lifter from Isky.

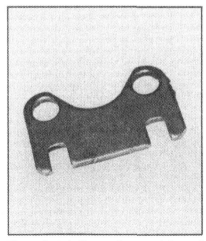

Shown here is the most common type of pushrod guide plate; it's also about the cheapest. If you need something special, then there are other options.

This Manley pushrod-length checker makes setting pushrod lengths a quick and easy task. No engine builder's toolbox should be without one.

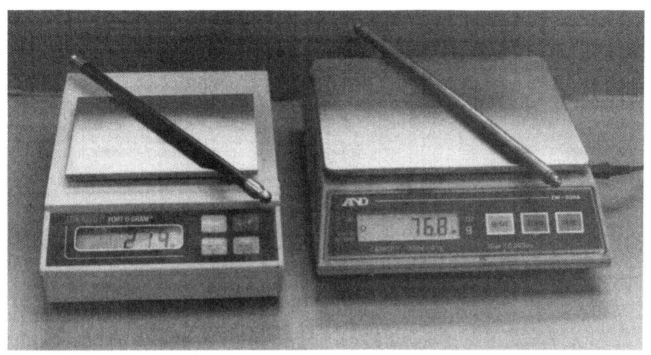

So how much can carbon fiber save? These scales only tell half the story. The carbon fiber pushrod on the left weighs in at 27.4 grams, while the steel one on the right is 76.8 grams. What the scales don't tell you is how stiff each item is. The carbon fiber, even though it has substantially less mass involved, is actually almost double the stiffness of the chrome-moly steel one.

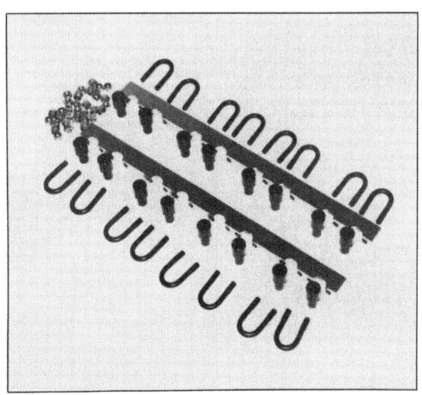

When I look through cam manufacturers' catalogs, there seem to be a hundred different designs of stud girdles. Though they may vary in price and appearance, they all seem to do the job to about the same degree. For my tests I've used this type.

out race engine you'll need to coordinate your valve gear, so it's a good idea to consult the cam manufacturer on whether or not to use an ultra-stiff pushrod. Many cam manufacturers can custom-build pushrods to various lengths and diameters.

Ordering pushrods should be one of the last jobs done on an engine build. Block decking and variations in cylinder head thicknesses due to milling for compression mean the stock pushrod will not be of the right length. If the length is incorrect, valve lift will be lost.

In addition, the geometry of the rocker over the end of the valve can mean a dangerously close approach to one of the edges. With the high-point loading typical of a roller-tipped rocker, this can cause failure of the valve end.

If you're building an all-out race engine, I recommend that you choose a spring retainer and lock that can accommodate a hardened lash cap, so that the rocker tip bears on to a larger area. If titanium valves are being used, then a lash cap is almost mandatory.

To get the correct pushrod length you will need to buy an adjustable pushrod, which is available from almost all of the big cam manufacturers.

Using this pushrod, adjust the length until the valvetrain delivers the maximum valve lift consistent with the tip of the rocker sweeping over the middle of the valve. Once you've set the length, measure the pushrod and order rods to suit. A great help in speeding up selection of the right pushrod length is the Manley setting gauge. This very inexpensive item could save you a lot of time.

Stud Girdles

One of the shortcomings of the stud-mounted rocker is flexure due to increased spring loads. To offset this, a stud girdle can be used to tie in all of the studs to one supporting member. Because loads are transferred and shared among studs, flexure is reduced. As to how much horsepower this may be worth it's difficult to say since I've done no back-to-back tests, but stud girdles typically are used on any engine expected to peak at 7000 or more rpm. If the engine is expected to peak at less than 6500, you need not be concerned with a stud girdle. Inevitably, engines that peak at the lower rpm are well-mannered road engines. Any money that may have been spent on a stud girdle could be more effectively used elsewhere.

As to whether stud girdles contribute to extra power or not is debatable, but they can definitely improve reliability and extend the life of the valvetrain. By stiffening it up, it seems that the incidence of valve spring breakage and keepers pulling through retainers is reduced. This could be because the aluminum of the stud girdle acts as a kind of valvetrain damper. If by damping out spurious vibrations the cam profile is more closely adhered to, the chances of spring or retainer failure should be reduced.

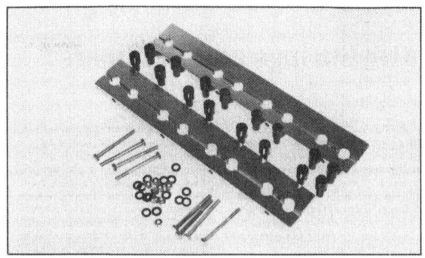

I have also used this type without any apparent advantage in going from one to the other.

Remember if you're going to use 1.6 rockers, they're best used on the intake. Save the 1.5s for the exhaust, which for most applications should have slightly longer timing.

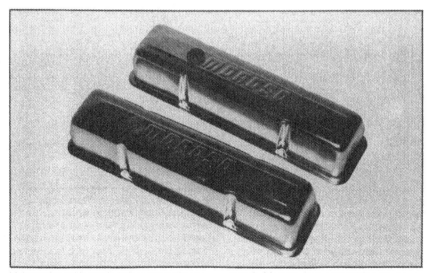

Valvetrains with stud girdles are going to require taller valve covers to clear. As usual, Moroso has something to cover the racer's need in this area.

Valve Springs and Retainers

12

The sole function of a valve spring is to store energy for the purpose of returning the valvetrain and valve to the seated position. It must perform this function to the dictates of the cam profile as closely as possible. At low rpm this presents a minimal challenge. Just a few pounds of spring force is all that is necessary to keep the elements of the valvetrain in contact.

Valve Float

When high engine rpm is required, a spring with insufficient force will lose control of the valvetrain. Just before any audible indication is apparent, engine power begins to drop rapidly. If the engine is allowed to rev further, this phenomenon, known as valve float or bounce, becomes audible.

On a muffled engine, valve float usually sounds like the clattering you would expect of a valvetrain out of control. If the engine is on open exhaust any mechanically audible signs are lost, but the exhaust note becomes very ragged because the intended valve events have now become artificially extended in more or less a random manner. It's obvious that the motion of the valve is no longer following that intended by the cam profile. Figure 12-1 depicts the typical deviation from intended valve motion.

Most people's first perception of valve float is that the follower is simply parting company from the nose of the cam lobe. If and when this happens it's because the combination of mass and imparted velocity is greater than the delivered spring force can control. This is not an unrealistic assumption, but usually initial loss of valve motion control is due to the valve bouncing off its seat at the end of the closing phase.

In figure 12-1, the valve motion has some bumps in it just after the point of closure prescribed by the lobe. What's happening is that the valvetrain's component separation may be imminent but the closing velocity of the valve toward the seat is too high, allowing the valve to actually bounce off the seat in the head. Normally, this is the most common type of valve bounce and its action eats into the compression cycle and extends exhaust opening farther into the intake cycle during the overlap period.

An obvious conclusion is that the delivered spring force is inadequate. Such inadequacies are not necessarily due to the spring's over-the-nose poundage, however. More often they result from the delivered seat load being too low.

Although the assumption of inadequate spring force may be correct, the effect of valve bounce may be postponed without necessarily adding extra delivered spring force. Some events occurring in the valvetrain tend to defy most conceptions of what is mechanically possible.

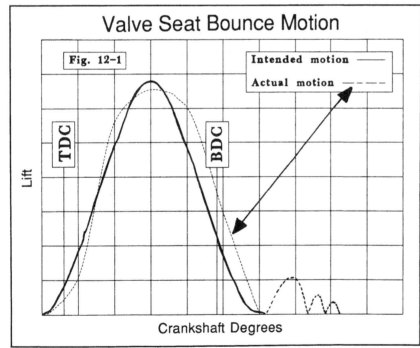

Figure 12-1: *This graph depicts a typical valve bounce situation. Note how flexure of the valvetrain prevents the valve from actually flowing its intended motion. Worse yet, valve bounce because of a too high seat closing velocity and possibly problems with the spring causes the valve to bounce from its seat well into the compression stroke, thus reducing power. Sometimes adding as little as 5lb of extra spring load on the seat can make a significant difference to seat bounce. An additional 5lb of seat load can cut bounce from four to five cycles down to one cycle.*

Here's a spring and retainer setup from a Corvette aluminum head. essentially the same springs have been used on all small-block Chevys since day one.

Some years ago, one of the major motor manufacturers was investigating a valvetrain problem with the aid of a camera capable of 8,000 frames per second. To put this into perspective, that meant that at 7500rpm the camera was able to take a photo every 5.6 degrees of crankshaft rotation. This method proved more than adequate to study the valvetrain motion at the cylinder head.

The engine, equipped with a pushrod valvetrain, utilized a double-valve spring that delivered some 280–300lb of full-open force. This was on a cam profile intended to produce 420 thousandths (0.420in) gross lift at the valve.

At low rpm the valve motion was as intended, but as rpm increased the situation changed dramatically. At 4000rpm, still well below the engine's intended maximum range, the spring went into a "surge" condition, a situation where the available spring force becomes incapable of controlling the mass of the spring itself, let alone any of the valvetrain components. At this rpm the camera showed that during the lift cycle, the base of the spring was bouncing off its seat and moving toward the retainer.

At the same time the top of the spring, still in contact with the retainer, was moving down on the opening sequence. In other words, the spring was dynamically collapsing in on itself in spite of the fact that there were some 80–90lb of static spring force available to keep each end of the spring firmly planted in position.

Though technically speaking the spring was out of control, for the most part the engine ran as if nothing unusual was happening and by 5000rpm the spring had more or less stabilized. At about 6000rpm it was evident that once again, spring surge was about to influence a control over the valve spring. And at 7500rpm, the spring totally lost control of the valvetrain and the valve motion caused the engine to spit back through the carburetor, misfire, and send large flames out of the exhaust. Since there was nothing unusual about this valvetrain, it's reasonable to assume that its action could well be typical.

This was a valvetrain that was supposedly functioning acceptably. Had the spring been a little more problematical, the precision of the valvetrain motion would have decayed to the point of an engine malfunction.

The obvious cure for the loss of valvetrain control is more delivered spring force. Unfortunately the indiscriminate use of added spring force brings a rash of attendant problems, especially for the small-block Chevy. Over-the-nose spring force much in excess of 330lb or so can dramatically accelerate flat-tappet cam wear. Even cams used in an accurately machined block may live only 2,000–3,000 miles with a 350lb spring force over the nose.

Added to this, there is the problem of increased valve guide wear. With a cast-iron guide and a stock-type rocker, stepping up spring force by 50 percent from 200 to 300lb can result in a 500–1,000 percent increase in guide wear. Installing heavier springs also causes the valvetrain to draw more power to drive it, so less is left at the flywheel.

Depending on oils, profile design, mass of parts, and so on, a 50 percent increase in spring force at the levels we're dealing with can sap between 2-4hp from the crank. The added friction shows up as increased oil temperature. These power-loss figures can be considerably greater under less than ideal conditions. Since added spring force can carry so many negatives along with it, there is an obvious need to make the most effective use of available spring force.

As it happens, arriving at a workable spring package for the rpm range concerned is not by any means totally force related. The strange antics of the spring described earlier proved to be a classic demonstration of spring surge, and this can be a significant factor in reducing a spring's capability of controlling the valvetrain. Surge occurs when an outside force excites the spring at its "natural resonant frequency."

If you've never taken any engineering classes you may feel that throwing in this term is a bit like rushing you into a dark, windowless room with a medi-

The most common problem with a dual-damped spring setup is the damper itself. Often these can wind their way out from between the coils. Rounding off all the edges, as seen here on the left-hand spring, and chamfering the sides of the coil tend to cut this problem.

The most common type of high-performance spring setup for a small-block Chevy is a dual-damped spring combination. On the left, the two springs and the flat-wound damper are displayed. On the right, these components are shown assembled.

cal insurance contract all in fine print. So let's break it down. The natural resonant frequency of an object or a system is its vibration frequency. A clock pendulum serves as a good example. The bigger the mass of the pendulum and the longer its suspension, the slower it oscillates from side to side. A pendulum is used in a timepiece because the frequency of its swing is fixed by virtue of its mass and the pendulum length.

The resonant frequency of a system, then, depends on its mass and stiffness. An example most can relate to is guitar strings. Plucking a string causes it to vibrate at its natural resonant frequency. Making a higher pitched note is achieved by shortening the string on the finger board. This slightly increases the stiffness of the part of the string allowed to vibrate and reduces the mass subject to vibration. The net result is a higher frequency vibration producing a higher pitched sound.

In the same way, a spring can vibrate. Beating the end of the spring causes a vibration wave to travel through it. Beating the end of the spring at the right frequency causes a wave to build up and ultimately the spring loses control of its own mass. The frequency at which a spring loses control should be one that is higher than any it's likely to be subjected to during use.

For instance, if the vibration can go from one end of the spring and back twice without dying out, hitting the spring every other time will still cause it to resonate. The frequency with which it resonates and the degree of severity or amplitude of the resonance depends on the spring's stiffness and mass. Increasing stiffness or reducing mass increases the natural resonant frequency of the spring.

A cure for the ill effects of too low a natural resonate frequency can be brought about by designing a spring with a natural frequency so high that it doesn't interfere with the valvetrain motion within the operating rpm range used. Cure number two is that the unwanted motion can be damped.

Spring Dampers

To achieve valve control at a given rpm there are obvious limitations as to how stiff or light we can make both the spring and valvetrain components. But by adding a spring damper into the equation and some thoughtful spring design, many potential spring problems can be overcome. This now raises the question as to how spring damping can be achieved.

The simplest way to damp a spring is by means of friction. The most common technique to damp valve spring vibration is to incorporate a flat-wound damper into the design. A flat-wound damper fits snugly inside the spring so that as the spring assembly compresses, the sides of the spring coils rub against the damper. Most stock Chevy valve springs use this technique, however, many other techniques exist.

For instance, a flat-wound damper doesn't actually contribute much to the spring force and its function can be carried out by an inner spring having an interference fit with the outer spring. By winding the coils in opposite directions, the action of compressing the spring causes relative motion and friction between the coils. This produces a damping effect similar to a flat-wound damper.

Using dual springs presents another advantage in that we're now dealing with two springs, each having a different vibration frequency. The smaller inner spring will usually have a higher resonant frequency than the outer one because of its reduced mass. Additionally, if we achieve a given spring force with two springs instead of one, the mass of *each* spring in the two-spring system will be significantly less than the one spring used in a single-spring system.

The first point in the rpm range at which a vibration frequency is likely to

From right to left, here's a range of springs from stock through high-performance street to endurance race, and finally to a high-rpm, pro stock-style setup. This shows just how much more spring a radical roller cam would take than a stock flat-tappet cam.

A triple spring provides the most optimal performance; to make this package function with a conventional spring, effectively is not easy and draws heavily on the skill of the spring designer.

compromise the valvetrain will be at a higher value with the dual-spring system. A thoughtfully selected split between the force delivered by the inner and outer spring can produce a spring package that allows significantly higher rpm to be obtained without necessarily delivering any more total spring force than that produced by a single-coil spring and damper.

Of course, we could take this one step further by adding a flat-wound damper between the inner and outer spring. However, at this stage the additional advantages of installing a flat-wound damper into a dual spring are far less than in a single. My contention is that an optimally designed dual-spring package is far less likely to need a flat-wound damper.

If two springs are better than one, what is the situation concerning three springs? A triple-valve spring can show an improved surge to delivered force performance over a dual spring. Unfortunately, a law of diminishing returns and escalating costs influence the situation because of the need to nest one spring inside the other. However, for a long-distance motor the wear and tear on the springs from an interference fit with a flat-wound damper is usually less than without.

What it boils down to is, duals with a damper are first choice, closely followed by duals without, so long as the "package" is well suited to the application. Yet for high-rpm applications typical of an all-out drag race engine, a correctly designed triple spring is probably the best way to go.

The importance of damping spring surge cannot be overemphasized and is probably worth illustrating here. Some years ago, I conducted some tests for Iskenderian on a cam that was one of a new range they were about to introduce. The cam intended for heavy-duty truck usage proved to be capable of producing up to 5500rpm, but a big dip in the power curve was noted at 4750rpm. On the shop dyno, figures are taken every 250rpm, yet at that time, Iskendarian was taking power figures at only 500rpm intervals. Thus, taking power figures at 4500 and 5000rpm missed recording the dip in the power curve.

Initially, I suspected the dip was the result of either a fueling or induction-related resonance. Inspection of the power curves run when the heads and cam were first installed showed no such dip, but as the figures were traced through repeated tests the dip became

more apparent. This pointed a finger at the valvetrain: the springs had experienced the almost inevitable initial relaxation.

As a temporary fix the springs were removed and the fitted heights were set a little tighter to increase the seat load. This increased the output at 4750rpm by no less than 11hp and in doing so, eliminated the dip.

Spring surge had proved to be the culprit and the added spring force was sufficient enough to change the vibration frequency to eliminate the loss of valvetrain control at 4750rpm. The outcome was that Isky changed both the specification of the spring used with the cam, and their procedure to test every 250rpm so that errors such as this wouldn't slip through the net. The situation demonstrates how important having the correct spring for the job can be, and how just a few pounds' difference in load can make a significant difference in the power curve, as can be seen in figure 12-2.

Apart from dampers and multiple springs, spring surge can be countered

by other means. For instance, barrel-wound springs, though designed for installational purposes, have a degree of surge resistance. Although they have never gained popular acceptance, they do have some specific advantages, at least for a warmed-up street motor. To understand the thinking behind a barrel-wound spring we must look at the necessity for it.

The smaller a spring OD, the greater the material stress in the spring for a given delivered force. Ultimately, there comes a time when the spring material will be overstressed. The way around this is to utilize larger diameter springs of greater wire thickness.

Valvetrain requirements outpace the stock-diameter spring's capability fairly early on in the development of a typical small-block Chevy. The standard spring pockets are simply too small to be able to house a mechanically reliable spring when significantly higher poundages are required.

The advantage of a barrel-wound spring is that it fits the stock spring pocket and retainer but its center di-

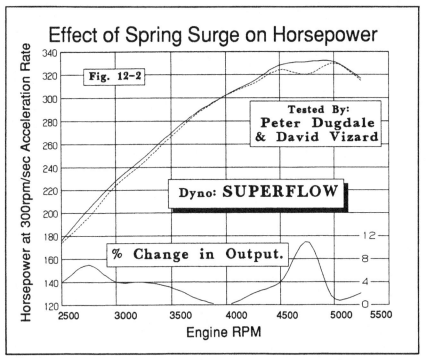

Figure 12-2: *Here is a classic case of spring surge causing loss of control of the valvetrain. Note that its effect comes in just after 4500rpm and is largely gone by 5000rpm. This is a relatively common characteristic of spring surge. However, increasing the seat load by 8-10lb not only eradicated the dip but also mar-* *ginally improved the output at low rpm, thus indicating that valve control was not all it could have been, even at relatively low rpm. In this instance Iskenderian recommended changing from a single to a dual spring to cure the problem without adding spring force.*

ameter is larger, thus reducing the amount of stress the spring sees. By making the spring barrel-wound, the stiffness of the spring varies from coil to coil. Assuming the same coil pitch, the smaller the spring diameter, the stiffer it is. This means the coils at either end of the spring are stiffer than those in the middle, producing a situation where the natural resonant frequency of the spring varies in a similar manner. As a result, no clearly defined natural resonant frequency exists for the spring as an overall unit. Consequently, it's more difficult for such a spring to develop surge.

The problem with this type of spring is that it falls foul to a limit that is imposed by the degree of barreling that the spring can accommodate. Although a barrel-wound spring may exhibit superior characteristics to a parallel-wound spring fitting the same spring seat, it may still fall short of what is required.

Variable-Rate Springs

A similar technique to defeat resonance can be applied by winding a parallel spring with a varying pitch of coil. This type of spring is known as a variable-rate spring. With a variable-rate spring the stiffness (not to be confused with its delivered force) increases with compression. With a normal spring the delivered force increases proportionally with compression.

In other words, the rate is constant. Figure 12-3 shows how the characteristics of these two types of springs differ. A progressive rate or variable-wound spring is easily recognized by the fact that its coils are close together at one end and widely spaced at the other. In operation the coils closest together collapse first, with the wider spaced ones progressively closing as more compression takes place.

This type of spring has a different vibration frequency, depending on where it is in the lift cycle. The beauty of it is that being parallel wound it can be damped by an inner spring, whereas a barrel spring cannot be easily damped with an inner spring or damper.

The variable-rate spring affords resistance to surging, plus a conventional means of damping it. Its design is greatly exploited in purpose-built race engines such as the Cosworth Indy and Formula One engines. But the design concept has not bled over to the small-block Chevrolet engine to any great extent and there are some intrinsic reasons for this. The primary reason is that for a very high rpm drag race engine there is a problem packaging an adequate spring of any sort into the space available.

Though a variable-rate spring is better on surge than a single-rate spring, it requires more room to deliver the same kind of spring force. However, the variable-rate spring is a potentially better design, except possibly for all-out drag race applications. For instance, if the engine utilizes a flat-tappet cam and spring forces for extended life are critical, less spring force is required for a given degree of valvetrain control with a variable-rate spring than a conventionally wound spring.

On a typical street application there is room to accommodate a dual variable-rate spring. This situation can also exist for a flat-tappet road-race engine.

Selecting Springs for an Application

An important point I want to make here is that it is not practical for a cam company to make a valve spring that is precisely correct for every application. In spite of this, there is a need to come as close as possible to the ideal spring setup.

Obviously the less demanding the situation, the less need for precise valve spring selection. For instance, if you're going to install a short-period RV-type camshaft that is likely to limit the engine to some 4750rpm maximum, then the need for sophisticated decisions as far as valve springs are concerned is largely eliminated.

One need only to look at spring selection from a realistic standpoint. The first step is to find the most suitable spring for the job. An easy solution to the problem is, go with the spring recommended by the cam grinder. It won't guarantee a spring that exactly fits your requirement, but it will ensure that it is fully functional.

When putting together catalogs, cam manufacturers assign a particular spring to as many cam applications as possible. After all, it is far from practical to hold hundreds of different types of springs in stock, so one spring will be utilized to cover several applications.

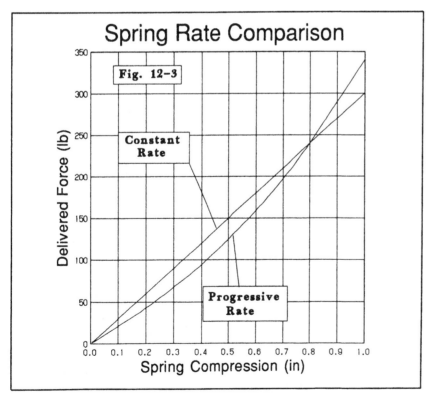

Figure 12-3: *The most common type of spring is a constant-rate spring. This is where the load increases proportionally with compression, and a graph of this produces a straight line. A progressive- or variable-rate spring gets stiffer as it's compressed and produces a curve typically as shown here.*

Since a particular cam profile can be used in a range of engine displacements from 283 up to 400-plus cubic inches, the rpm the engine is likely to produce will be *significantly* different from one extreme to the other. A cam that may peak at 6500 in a 283 may peak at only 5000 in a 400ci engine. This means that irrespective of the cam profile, the 400ci engine won't need as much spring force to control the valvetrain.

Common sense dictates there is little point in springing the engine to be able to turn 7000rpm when it will be all done at 5500rpm. So long as surge is held at bay, a spring that will allow about 5500rpm or so will be adequate for the 400ci engine.

By selecting a lighter spring, friction in the valvetrain will be cut allowing the engine to deliver just a bit more horsepower. Dropping 1000rpm out of the spring capability allows a substantial reduction in spring force. It proves enough to produce measurable differences on the dyno and certainly a measurable difference in fuel economy and oil temperature.

Another point to consider is that a cam may last indefinitely with a certain amount of spring force, but increasing it 10–15 percent can develop a situation that parallels the proverbial straw that breaks the camel's back. The seemingly minor increase in spring load may cause the cam life to drop from 100,000 to 25,000 miles. Most spring selections are made for the rpm range a cam will most likely produce in a 350ci motor because it's the most common.

However, if your engine's rpm range is likely to differ significantly from that quoted in the catalog, then consult the cam manufacturer as to the possibility of an alternate and more suitable spring. Sometimes it pays to go through several cam manufacturers catalogs. You may find a more applicable spring combination for your choice of cam. For instance, the particular manufacturer you're going with could recommend a single spring with a flat-wound damper whereas you may find another spring that is a dual and looks to be a better fit for your engine.

Of course, the ultimate technique for spring selection is by trial and error on the dyno or at the racetrack. The technique is simple enough: you choose a spring you think will get the job done, see how it works, then go stiffer or less stiff as the case may be. Use the minimum spring forces needed to get the job done.

When making adjustments to spring force, remember that seat bounce more often than not sets in before cam and follower separation over the nose. Because of this it is more important not to drop too much poundage out of the seat forces than it is to concern yourself with forces over the nose. Excessive over-the-nose loads with a flat-tappet cam usually wipe out the cam. But the seat loads are the most likely to present the first signs of trouble.

If you're attempting to drop overall spring forces, then drop them as a percentage rather than as a poundage. So, if you have a spring that is delivering 110lb on the seat and 300lb over the nose, don't be tempted to drop 20lb out of each because you've relieved the valve of almost 20 percent of its seat load, but only 6 percent of the over-the-nose load.

One factor we haven't looked at yet relates to the cam profile. A cam profile that is ground to set the valve down on the seat prolongs seat life. Some of the more radical camshafts of the past tended to have very high closing velocities and the heads therefore need to be sprung with high seat loads. This generates a problem in that it very quickly hammers out the seats. Although the seat may last significantly longer in terms of sealing ability, a hammered seat can cut the airflow.

It's rare that seat damage of any form enhances airflow so you can figure the more seat force a cam calls for, the quicker it is going to deform seats, thus necessitating a valve job. Each successive valve job is likely to depart from the optimum flow figures initially achieved by the head to a greater degree. Consequently, you can have a cylinder head that may seal up well, but the valve seats have been cut so many times that performance is lost.

Because of their more radical profiles, roller cams traditionally need much higher seat loads than flat-tappet cams. Such high seat loads are not mandatory, it's just that few cam grinders have chosen to design roller profiles that function with lesser seat loads.

Having made such a statement, I should make an allowance for a roller cam. Because a roller profile has virtual line contact with the cam profile, substantial surface stresses are seen. This is the primary reason a competition roller needs to be made from steel rather than cast iron. If the valves are floated and the roller separates from

the cam profile on return, it can hit the profile hard enough to put a minute dent in it. If and when this happens, it can produce some rather shattering shock loads.

Usually the first sign of trouble is the break-up of the needle roller bearings in the roller follower. The golden rule is that although you or your driver should avoid valve float with any type of cam and valvetrain, doing so with a roller setup is even more important. In an effort to minimize the changes of valve float under competitive conditions, the cam manufacturers tend to use much higher spring forces.

Spring Installation

From what we've discussed so far, it's pretty obvious that delivered spring force is of significant importance, and

---

Understanding Spring Rates

A spring's rate is the measure of its stiffness. This is normally quoted in pounds per square inch. For instance, if it takes 300lb to compress a spring 1in, then its rate is 300lb/in. If it was compressed 0.5in it would deliver a load of 150lb. The formula for rate is:

$$\frac{\text{increase in force}}{\text{amount of compression}}$$

Let's use an example out of the Competition Cam's catalog. Spring #980 has a delivered force of 84lb at 1.7in fitted height. When compressed to 1.250in the delivered force increases to 230lb. To calculate the rate we need first to determine how much force increase we are dealing with. In this instance it will be 230 − 84 = 146lb. The amount of compression the spring went through to achieve this force was 1.7in − 1.250in = 0.450in.

Now these two numbers are known, the rate can be calculated using the formula. Installing the numbers gives

$$\frac{146lb}{0.450in} = 324lb/in$$

For a variable spring rate it will be necessary to know the load/displacement figures for at least three points so that a curve of the changing spring rate can be drawn.

By looking through the cam manufacturers' spring catalogs you can check fitted length loads, solid heights, and so on, and calculate a spring package rate for comparative purposes to see if a better spring for your installation exists.

this becomes especially true as rpm and anticipated performance levels rise.

We've also seen how seat loads can be quite critical if spurious valve bounce at rpm below the maximum is to be avoided. Because of the importance of having the correct seat load, it's also obvious that the installed height, the spring length, and the rate are also important. If any of these factors vary too much, the correct seat loads will be off by more than an acceptable margin.

Manufacturing springs to tightly controlled tolerances is not easily accomplished. It takes only a small change in the wire diameter, the heat treatment, the shot-peening process, the overall length, and so on, to significantly alter the delivered load at a specified installed height. Quality springs from the well-known, reputable cam grinders are usually held to acceptable tolerances. However, if the

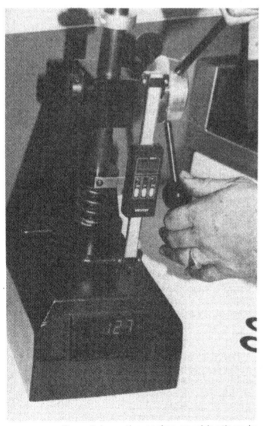

To match up the spring combinations in any given set, it's a good idea to strip down the spring, measure the delivered loads of each spring, and then package the springs together to achieve as near as possible to even overall delivering spring loads.

chances of a problem are to be reduced to a minimum it is necessary to try and eliminate as many variables as possible.

At this point consider that springs are not only subject to many manufacturing tolerances, but also to external influences that may alter their performance. For instance, when they've been in use for a while the delivered load inevitably decays. Just how much it drops depends again on numerous factors such as the heat treatment involved, whether or not the springs were hot spragged (a hot-compression process designed to reduce decay with use), the temperature the springs are run at in the engine, the shot-peening process, and so forth. All of these pre- and post-installational variables decree that we take all the necessary steps to install a spring with a known performance record.

Allowing that stock factory street cams can tolerate a relatively wide margin of error, let's deal with springs for a more serious application, involving an aftermarket cam. An important point here is that some of the largest cam companies claim that incorrect spring setup is close to being the number one culprit for cam failures. Thus, it is necessary to set up and shim spring heights to specification.

The starting point in setting valve springs to the correct specs is measuring each valve spring's capability rather than just reading it off the specification sheet. For this, a spring tester of one form or another is necessary. If you're a budget-conscientious do-it-yourselfer assembling your own cylinder heads, the least you should have available is a hydraulic spring tester that can be used in a vise. Used along with a calibration spring as sold by many of the leading cam manufacturers to cross-check results, these inexpensive spring testers can produce acceptable results. Using one of these testers, plus some care and patience, you can do a *passably* good job at setting up the springs.

A professional shop should use something a little more accurate. My current choice is the high-precision, electronic spring tester shown in the photos. It is produced by Steve Jennings Equipment in Santa Ana, California. Using professional-quality equipment makes it entirely practical to measure each spring and set up the valve spring height to a custom length in order to deliver the correct spring force.

In other words, we're setting the valve spring force to the correct specification rather than using the fitted length which only *implies* the correct delivered seat load if such things as free length and rate are correct. Using such equipment also detects any springs that may be deemed below par.

When sorting through a batch of springs, choosing those that are at middle limit on their stiffness tolerance is the best route to take unless evidence to the contrary exists. The reason is that the stiffer springs usually are the result of a heat treatment process that left them a little on the hard side. Such springs are more likely to crack from overstress if the material was close to its limit.

On the other hand, a spring that is at the bottom limit may have been over-tempered and may not deliver the seat load it should, or it may lose rate quicker.

Valve springs are, by necessity, mass-produced items and as such should be

Spring Prep Checklist
1. Strip spring assemblies.
2. Dress end faces flat on emery paper.
3. Radius all sharp edges on the spring tail.
4. Check and label developed force at fitted height of each spring. Discard and replace any spring significantly different.
5. Deburr all edges and radius tails of the flat-wound damper.
6. Pair off heavy outers and light inners or vice versa to even up delivered force of assemblies.
7. Assemble the springs and dampers.
8. With the spring retainer in place, check the spring poundage at the recommended fitted length and at the length produced at full valve lift. Again, look for assemblies significantly off the norm.
9. Select shims to place under those springs that have the lowest seat force to bring them within 5lb or so of the highest springs. From here on treat any spring and shim assembly as a single entity so that a certain spring always goes with a certain shim.
10. Using the spring tester, determine the fitted spring height required to develop the seat force called for by the cam spec. Install to this height rather than the recommended fitted height.

detailed before use. Preferably the detailing work should be done before you select the springs for delivered loads, especially when the ends are detailed.

The first operation would consist of smoothing the ends of the spring. To do this, put some 100–200 grit wet-and-dry sandpaper on a flat surface, stand the spring on the emery and moving it in a figure-eight pattern, flatten the ends of the spring. Next, using a coarse stone, deburr the tail of the spring. When using aluminum retainers it is especially important to put as generous a radius as possible on the very end of the tail.

With flat-wound dampers, make sure you deburr or better yet, radius all edges, as burrs along any interference edge can cause the springs to run significantly hotter. The very action of the springs generates a considerable amount of heat.

Remember, most spring packages use friction to damp surge. Intermittent friction levels due to burrs is not the way to do this. Steady friction levels need to be applied from the sides of the damper. Burrs on the corner will raise the temperature of the spring and possibly set up their own vibration. Once the flat-wound dampers have been deburred, check the fit of the damper in the spring.

You may have to do some juggling but what you're looking for is a snug fit between damper and spring, one where you can just push the damper in

with thumb pressure. If the damper is sloppy it is not doing its job. If a double or triple spring is being used and damping is by virtue of the spring fit, assemble as the "best pack." Again, you're looking for a snug fit of one spring inside the other.

For some applications, spring life becomes a major factor of success in competition. The quest for maximum power from a small-block Chevy often means the need for radical cams. This can put mechanical demands near, and sometimes over, the limit as far as valve spring stress levels are concerned.

When certain relatively well defined stress levels are exceeded, the spring breaks. Of course, springs rarely break instantly the first time the engine is turned over. It's usually fatigue that gets them. But for a spring near its stress limit, one pass down the strip can be sufficient for it to fail.

To get the best fatigue life from a spring it is important that both the heat treatment and shot peening be done to closely controlled specifications. This is why a quality spring for a Pro Stock-style application in a small-block Chevy needs to have a 100 percent inspection so only the best are used. However, if spring failure is still a problem there are a few steps that can be taken to reduce them.

For instance, ion nitriding appears to be able to extend the life of a highly stressed spring by at least a factor of 4.

This thermal electromagnetic process forms a hard, compressive layer in the first few thousandths inch of the material surface. Since most fatigue cracks

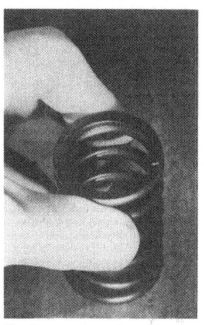

The first operation in detailing a valve spring is to polish the ends smooth on 400 grit wet-&-dry emery.

Some heavy-duty applications use rotator keepers as seen on the left. These will compress the spring about ⅛in more. You need to take this into account if you're changing from heavy-duty applications to this type of retainer.

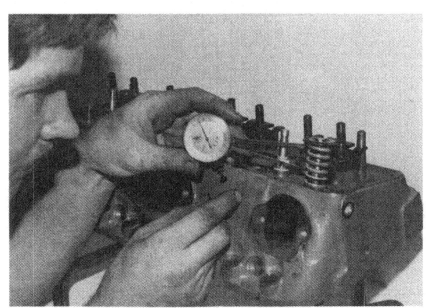

Until the installed height of a valve spring is set, delivered loads will not be consistent. This tool-room inside-dial caliper is being used for the job, but many companies market a less-expensive purpose-made height micrometer.

121

Spring seat diameters can vary dramatically depending on the springs required for the job.

start as a tensile overload, I find that the compressive stress in the surface may reduce surface stress below the critical level. This moves the spring into a more favorable fatigue life range. Ion nitriding is not a particularly common process in the United States so if you can't find a company locally, try Nitron Incorporated.

Apart from changing the metallurgical structure of the steel, there are other processes that supposedly help the fatigue life of the spring. Most of these are polymer coatings of some sort. Their function is to help spring life, not by changing any metallurgical factor, but their presence on the surface of the spring causes a reduction in spring vibrations. In other words, they act as a damper. Since a coating covers the spring, it will tend to damp vibrations occurring in any direction whereas frictional damping between the springs or a flat-wound damper tends only to damp vibrations in the vertical direction.

As a result, polymer coatings can add a little to the spring life so if you're looking for the last ounce from spring performance, then it's worthwhile doing. Companies that offer such services include Swain Technologies and Polydyne Coatings in Texas.

Spring Sizes

There comes a time when it's not practical to make a spring stiffer simply by making the helix angle steeper, the wire thicker, or the material harder. As hinted at before, there is a limit to the stresses a spring can take before breaking. If we're dealing with stock-size springs of 1.25in diameter, then limiting stresses can be reached way before the full mechanical potential of the valvetrain is reached. Therefore, it is entirely practical to produce cam profiles capable of outpacing the capability of a 1.25in diameter spring.

Two major points of concern exist here. The first is whether or not the spring can deliver the necessary forces

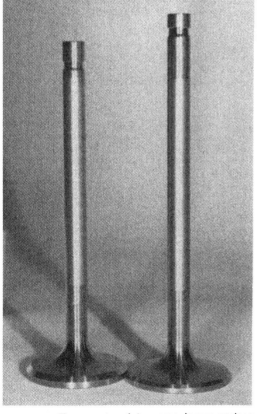

To accommodate some larger springs with the high lifts involved, it may be necessary to use a longer valve, as shown on the right.

The stock retainer is shown here in the foreground. Going clockwise we have an aluminum retainer, a steel retainer, and a titanium retainer. The titanium one weighs in at about 60 percent of the steel

one, yet has comparable strength. When it comes to cost effectiveness, however, a good aftermarket steel retainer is difficult to beat.

to control the valvetrain, and second, whether it can accommodate the lift. The necessity to increase spring pad diameter to install larger springs suitable for a high-performance camshaft has already been discussed, but another factor to consider is the spring height.

Normally the stiffer the spring, the greater the wire thickness involved. When wire thickness increases, the amount of lift possible to coil binding decreases if the package height remains unchanged. Utilizing double or triple springs allows a little more leeway in this area, but ultimately the spring package becomes difficult to install in the space available between the retainer and spring seat in the head. The only way around this is to use longer valves.

For a typical small-block Chevy head of the standard-type pattern, the use of 100–250 thousandths (0.100–0.250in) extra length valves is common. However, on specialty designed heads a custom-length valve is usually used so the problem of accommodating a spring suitable for a radical race cam is eliminated.

In spite of all the precautions that may be taken, springs can relax after a certain amount of use. When specifying spring requirements, cam designers make allowances for this in specing the original seat and over-the-nose loads delivered by the spring. Just how much the spring relaxes depends not only on its usage, but also on the quality of the spring. But even the tightest quality control can let a rogue spring slip through. In my experience, this happens more often than spring manufacturers care to admit.

For this reason it is a good idea, for very demanding applications, to check the delivered spring force with cylinder heads built up. Do this at the time of the build-up before the engine is run, and note the value of each spring. Hopefully, if the setup procedure has been done properly, each spring should be virtually identical to its neighbors. For what it's worth, Moroso Performance Products markets a tool to check installed spring forces.

Retainers

For a single spring and flat damper, the stock retainers do the job just fine and it's hard to conceive of any application that would justify an alternative. If using dual springs, however, the circumstances change. When an alternative spring means replacing the stock retainer, three material options are open to you: steel, aluminum, and titanium.

Steel is a proven material, of course, but it's always tempting to go with the lightest material possible. And while most people are budget conscious, an aluminum retainer looks like a pretty good bet. Although both materials can be used successfully, they have their limitations.

Aluminum is very soft and has only about half the strength of steel. It is also subject to a shorter fatigue life. If used with the flat-wound damper its life can be seriously shortened as the damper digs into the aluminum. Also, it

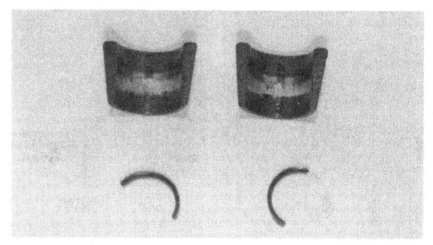

It loaded to an extreme, most keepers will fail by shearing of the key, as shown here.

The type of burst failure shown here is typical of that produced by a static press test on steel or aluminum retainers.

What you see here is the typical burst failure pattern of a Crane Posi-stop-type retainer. Instead of bursting at the bottom, where most retainers burst, it's separated at a much higher load around the top.

should not be used with excessively stiff springs.

If you consider something in the region of 300lb spring force maximum for an aluminum retainer, then reasonable reliability can be expected. However, be sure to prep the ends of the springs religiously. Otherwise, they will wear the retainer. If you can find a thin steel shim that will fit on the retainer to act as a wear cushion between the retainer and spring, do so; it will extend the life of the retainer dramatically.

For what it's worth, I rarely use aluminum retainers. They look good for fancy color photographs, but outside of this, my preference is for steel retainers. They are much stronger, less troublesome, and the extra weight involved just does not figure into the equation on an engine running at less than about 8000rpm.

If lightweight is needed, then titanium retainers are the way to go. Having said that, you should always question whether or not the expense of titanium retainers is justifiable. Potential gains from the small amount of weight saving are minimal and if you're working on a budget, chances are the money would have been better spent elsewhere.

When looking at titanium retainers, or any retainer, for an all-out race engine, the most important factor is the strength of the retainer. Heavy spring forces combined with high rpm and valve float can cause the valve and keeper assembly to pull through the retainer, unless you select one that's up to the job. Several manufacturers produce a 10 degree retainer and keeper set.

All other things being equal a 10 degree lock angle should have less tendency for the valve assembly to pull through the keeper. But there is also less grip on the valve stem, though this need not be a problem.

Unfortunately, "all things being equal" rarely applies. Both dimensions outside of the taper and the materials involved play a significant part in determining the strength of the retainer-keeper combination. The obvious constraints of high strength with minimum weight apply here as in many other areas of a high-performance engine. So the manufacturers must make what they feel are the most appropriate compromises.

The rising popularity of the 10 degree style keeper, such as produced by Competition Cams, forced Crane Cams to go the same route. But they did so along with a novel, yet simple high antiburst design. In this particular instance the retainer has a step at the bottom. This step is not, as is often thought (mainly due to the less than appropriate name of Posi-Stop), designed to stop the keepers from pulling through by bottoming out on the step. It is there simply to add radial reinforcement to the bottom of the keeper to prevent it from bursting outward from the load generated by the keepers.

This system seems to work very well and produces a high static load bearing capability, as shown on the test chart in figure 12-4. However, the static tests don't reproduce the same kind of failures as experienced by the engine.

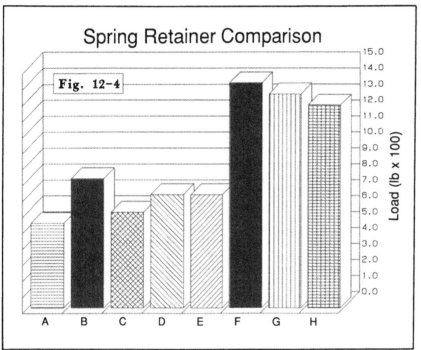

Figure 12-4: This chart shows the load to failure of some popular retainers. A is a typical aluminum retainer. It failed by bursting radially. B is a regular street-usage-brand retainer with regular stock or stock replacement keepers. In this test the keepers failed by stripping the notch that locates in the valve groove. C is a Competition Cams 10 degree steel retainer. It burst at some 6,000lb. D is an item similar to C but made from titanium. This went to 7,100lb before failure. E is a regular 7 degree Crane titanium retainer. Crane retainer F employed the anti-burst ring at the bottom of the taper. Its mode of failure was quite different from the others. It took more load to push the valve and hardened 7 degree keepers initially down the taper, but eventually they did bottom out on the antiburst ring. From this point on, the load required to deflect or fail them went up considerably. Ultimately it took twice as much load to fail these retainers as opposed to regular Crane titanium items. G is a Crane 10 degree retainer with an antiburst ring. This failed at some 12,700lb, but you should not take this as an implication that a 10 degree keeper isn't more effective at combating bursting. The 10 degree keeper's altogether bigger diameter means that the retainer itself has less material thickness. The last of the test pieces was a regular Crane 7 degree race retainer using, as in tests on F and G, hardened keepers. This shows that with the right keepers a steel retainer produces value-for-money results. So what do all these tests prove? A lot less than you would think! They are included here because a lot of magazine advertising was based on a similar test, so to see if they were for real some tests were run in our shop. However, the failures produced by a press in a static load condition do not reproduce the type of failures produced by the constant high-frequency hammering that retainers experience in service. On a press the centers tend to burst, but on an engine this type of failure is rare. Instead the outer edges move up, thus dishing the retainer. The moral here is to ignore press tests and go with what works in service—that means any top brand will work.

Incidentally, when you are prepping or checking 10 degree retainers it is worthwhile to set them up in the lathe and polish the bore. As the retainer angle increases, the effect friction has on reducing the clamping loads becomes more prominent. As a result, a 10 degree retainer is more sensitive to bore surface finish. Polishing this can increase its stem-clamping capability.

As far as my own choice in retainers is concerned, I tend to use 10 degree steel retainers on almost every application unless it's going to be a maximum-rpm unit. Also, if a heavy spring is to be used my preference is for the 10 degree retainers unless it's for a maximum spring-force-type application. The reason for the 10 degree choice is that they strip down easier than the 7 degree ones.

When assembling heads, smearing Crane Super Lube onto the retainers is a worthwhile habit to adopt as this cuts their tendency to stick and improves locking capability.

Having dealt with keepers and retainers, we're now at the tip of the valve. The end of any decent valve stem should be reasonably hard so that the action of the rocker bearing on it won't destroy the flat working surface.

Lash Caps

For certain applications, a lash cap figures into the equation. In some instances such as for titanium valves, some form of lash cap is almost mandatory as the titanium itself is not an adequate bearing material for a rocker, roller, or other component, to run on.

Depending upon the type of valve being used, a lash cap may either be built into the end of the valve or a separate hardened steel lash cap may

These heavy-duty Crane 7 degree keepers, made from a superior heat-treated material, prove to have more than twice the load-bearing capability of stock-type keepers.

be required as part of the valve-retainer-keeper assembly. Lash caps may also be needed to restore valvetrain geometry.

Decking the block and machining the head can easily drop the tip of the valve 50 thousandths (0.050in) closer to the crankshaft centerline. Using a typical 0.050in lash cap can sometimes help restore the original geometry, although pushrod length will almost certainly need attention to correct valvetrain geometry.

I've found with some brands of rockers if the rocker is too far down the stud, the radius at the end of the rocker stud fouls the underside of the aluminum rocker. It's quite a lengthy job pulling off all the rockers to machine or file them for clearance. Often, when things are this close, the inside radius of the rocker can get near or even foul the spring retainer.

Usually the quickest solution is to lengthen the valve slightly by use of a lash cap. Not only will this help rectify clearance problems, but also the lash cap distributes the load better over the end of the valve. The lash cap itself can

The difference in cross section between a 7 degree keeper and a 10 degree keeper is shown here. Note the 10 degree keeper is thicker at the bottom. If a spring limits the diameters that can be used on the retainer, the reduced thickness of the keepers tends to limit outright strength.

be made of very hard material to withstand even the most violent valve actions.

Camshaft Drives

13

Cam drives for a small-block Chevrolet are relatively problem free. Mostly what you need to know is how to select what is likely to work best for your particular application. In many respects the stock items are good, so let's deal with the stock cam drive first.

Stock Chevrolet Cam Drives

The stock Chevy cam drive crankshaft gear, usually made of sintered iron, drives through a Morse silent link chain to an aluminum cam sprocket having molded nylon teeth on it. Looking at this gear it's easy to conclude the molded teeth were for reasons of low production cost. Detroit being what they are for trying to save a cent, cost probably did have an influence, but this particular design is certainly not without virtues.

If your intention is to build a quiet-running engine, then the stock gear is almost certainly the best choice. The Morse silent link chain in combination with the nylon gears contributes greatly toward a quiet-running valvetrain. Also, the fact that nylon absorbs vibrations helps cut down the transmission of crank vibrations to the camshaft.

Evidence from various tests has strongly indicated that minimizing the transmission of harmonic vibrations from the crankshaft to the camshaft does indeed help the power output of the engine. If vibrations transmitted to the camshaft become too severe, all the cam designer's efforts toward calculating cam profiles that will supposedly run vibration free will be undone. If the valvetrain motion doesn't follow its intended path, then the probability that it will have a negative effect on power will be near 100 percent.

Tests indicate that on an all-out race small-block Chevy there's the potential to lose up to about 14hp by allowing too much torsional crank vibration to be transmitted to the cam. Though it may be a little on the delicate side, the stock-type sprocket can be used successfully even on an all-out drag race engine. You can also assume it's your number one choice if you're using a mild street cam.

However, something it doesn't take kindly to is excessive heat. Late-model smog motors tend to run much hotter than earlier model Chevys, and the only way to achieve a long life with a stock gear set is to make sure the oil is changed regularly, even if a stock cam is used. For less severe thermal conditions, the nylon gear and Morse silent chain setup can provide a useful life up to 100,000 miles, so long as the cam it's being used with isn't too radical.

The primary factor that seems to affect wear on the cam gear is the amount of tappet acceleration on the cams. Most modern hydraulic cams have, to coin a Harvey Crane phrase, a high degree of hydraulic intensity. The hydraulic intensity of a cam is, in a way, a measure of how fast it gets the hydraulic lifter moving in the initial phases of opening.

To determine the hydraulic intensity of a cam, subtract the 0.050in lift from the quoted seat timing figures; the number you are left with in degrees is the hydraulic intensity. Currently, most high-performance hydraulic street cams have a hydraulic intensity between 48 and 55 degrees—at least, all the modern designs do. Standard Chevrolet cams and some of the less radical aftermarket cams have hydraulic intensities just exceeding 70 degrees.

These types of cams are generally quieter running, and promote less wear on the stock nylon gears. However, they're also old profiles as a rule, and the technology used to design them may have been state of the art twenty years ago. Such a claim to fame can fall a long way short of what can be achieved these days.

Currently, several of the larger cam manufacturers have an ongoing program incorporating dynamic vibration analysis on their cams to produce higher hydraulic intensity cams that exhibit the same quiet-running characteristics as the earlier low-intensity cams. Generally speaking, modest valve spring loads and regular servicing will still allow the nylon gears to have a useful service life.

As far as very high output engines are concerned, more than just one or two successful Pro Stock-style engines have been built and set track records at

Don't sell short the stock timing gear and silent-link chain. It works well as long as the engine is never continually run too hot and oil changes are made regularly.

Fail to take these precautions, and you will change a perfectly good gear, as shown at the bottom, into scrap, as shown at the top.

the drag strip using modified stock gears.

If you're going to get a new set of gears for your particular engine, and you're looking at something with a relatively high rpm potential, then you need to select the sprocket type used pre-1967, along with the relevant chain. This sprocket is wider than the current ones. Since current sprockets are usable on early engines, the availability of the early sprocket will become increasingly difficult as time goes on; however, while they're still available, they should be considered your number one choice.

If the cam you intend using could be rated from the high-performance street specification upward, it's a good idea not to use the sintered bottom gear that normally comes with a stock Chevy timing set. The best bet here is to use a steel gear available from one of the high-performance gear sets. When you're buying the gear, make sure that you get one that's compatible with your chain, as there are several different types of chains.

If you need to acquire a sprocket separately, there are several sprockets on the market that are cut with advance and retard keyway slots in them. These are a help when it comes to setting the cam timing on your engine. They are usually marked either advance (+) and retard (−) or +4, −0, and −4°, depending on the manufacturer. Each alternate keyway represents a 4° (crankshaft) change of cam timing.

This type of sprocket is made both in the solid steel and the sintered variety. Although the sintered sprockets are generally adequate, your first choice should be the machined steel ones.

If you're using a fairly radical street cam in your motor, and you feel that the life expectancy of the nylon-faced sprocket may be questionable, then the next quietest setup to use is the steel or sintered steel cam sprocket together with the Morse silent chain. Most of the aftermarket speed equipment companies sell these at very affordable prices.

If you want to put together a high-output motor and you need an inexpensive cam drive, then probably the best off-the-shelf type to use is the truck-type true roller chain setup. Although these are available as a stock Chevrolet part, you can probably get the best deal from the aftermarket industry.

Most gear sets sold are of the Cloyes true roller chain type. This company also manufactures sprockets having a slightly oversize tooth pitch circle diameter. This provides the opportunity to resort proper chain tension on blocks that have had line bored or honed main bearings. The machining operation can move the crank center nearer to the cam center.

As for chain tightness, it's important to have a chain that initially runs with no slack in it. In fact, the chain must have an initial tension existing because as soon as the chain is used, wear takes place at each pivot and the chain is said to stretch. Actually, the chain does not stretch. What happens is that wear at each link, which during break-in may only be the odd thousandth inch or so, means that the chain can become longer by 0.001in at each link. With fifty or sixty links in it, you can understand how the chain can get 1/16in longer very quickly.

Many of the cam companies stick with the silent-link chain rather than going to the more exotic true-roller chain. This they normally use for the steel gear. The reason for this combination is that it's inexpensive and reliable.

This photo of a 383 dyno engine being built depicts many things you should note. First, the cam and sprocket are treated as one entity, and the lobe centerline angle of the cam—105 degrees—is marked on the sprocket. Second, note the aluminum bumper stop. Third, note the offset bush in the drilled-out dowel hole, and last, note the true roller chain. This was a combination together with a 280 street roller, which was known to work for a high-output street motor. The object of the exercise here was to test high-performance intake manifolds.

Once the chain has suffered its initial break-in wear, the apparent stretch that it undergoes decreases substantially. Some chains are broken in by the manufacturers, but either way it's best to use a chain with 100 miles or so on it, and size the sprocket with a BHJ gear set measuring fixture.

Sprocket Modifications

Unless horsepower isn't a criterion, in which case you wouldn't be reading this book, it's unlikely that you'll bolt a stock sprocket to your motor.

Probably the most important change that you will make to the sprocket is to drill out the existing dowel location hole to accommodate an offset bushing to allow cam timing adjustments. Normally this entails drilling the hole that takes the stock camshaft driving pin out to $^3/_8$in to accept an offset bushing.

The method I use entails drilling the hole *almost* all the way through, leaving a small lip on the outer edge of the hole so that the bushing cannot pass

The bolt holes in this timing sprocket have been ovalized to allow for movement of the cam relative to the sprocket. The next operation will be to drill out the dowel hole to accept the desired offset bushing.

through. Tightening the sprocket to the cam also clamps the bushing in place. This saves a lot of fiddling with it during assembly.

You will need to do a trial installation of the bushing in the sprocket to see that it doesn't stand too proud of the cam sprocket surface. Consider 0.005in maximum; if there's any more clearance, file a chamfer on the outer edge of the bushing until the required fit is achieved.

Because of the taper on the flat-tappet cam and the way the oil pump thrusts the camshaft into the block thrust face, I find that end float on a small-block Chevy cam is not usually of any real consequence. However, this doesn't mean that it's zero. Various vibrations and clearances can cause the cam to float backward and forward a certain amount. When this happens it introduces unwanted ignition timing scatter.

To eliminate this problem a cam bumper stop should be installed. Most cam bumper stops are made from a simple aluminum billet with a rounded nose. It's best to put a saw-cut oiling groove in the end of the billet prior to installing it into the cam sprocket. Once positioned, the bumper stop is held in place by the sprocket-securing bolt lock washer.

Next, using a file adjust the length of the cam button to give about a 0.002in interference fit between the timing cover (with gasket installed) and the button itself. When the timing cover is tightened down, it will exert a small pre-load toward the cam thrust face. By making a saw cut in the radiused end, the button initially wears quickly because of the high-point loading.

After a short period of running, it establishes a sufficiently large contact area to act as a bearing. The slot allows

the oil to completely wipe the bearing surface so once broken in, wear becomes minimal. In practice the bumper stop keeps the end float down to the odd few thousandth inch or so.

As an alternative to an aluminum bumper stop, you can make your own out of nylon or a nylon derivative such as Teflon. Neither of these materials are lubrication sensitive, and as a result you don't have to be quite so finicky about getting the precise clearance, although too much pre-load should be avoided since it will cause wear on the cam thrust face.

For most street cams, simply bearing against the cam cover proves adequate, but for a high-output engine it's preferable to go a step further.

Rather than relying on the front cover, which is flexible, I recommend using a water-pump-mounted cam bumper stop support. Water pumps with an adjustable bumper stop bolt already built in are available from Howard Stewart or Edelbrock Corporation. Or, you can make your own by installing a support plate on the back of the pump. The idea is to have the bumper stop press on the cover in a position centered on the cam.

If you want a really fancy setup for a bumper stop, some cam companies market needle roller items. These should be set up with about 0.002in clearance between the cover and stop rather than an interference fit.

To simplify clearance setting it's best to trial assemble the cam and sprocket without the timing chain or pan. This allows you to reach into the block with one hand and push on the back of the

If you want to time a cam the hard way, you're going to need a selection of these offset dowels. They come in 1 degree increments.

If you don't consider a plain aluminum cam bumper stop high-tech enough for your motor, you can always pay a little more money and get a fully rollerized one like this. All of the major cam manufacturers have them.

cam with the other to check the end float.

Big cams and higher-than-stock oil pressures often go hand in hand. Under such circumstances, the block thrust face can suffer excessive wear.

One of the easiest ways to counter this is to add lubricant via a drilled hole in the cam thrust face to the relevant oil galley. This provides a pressure feed to that area. When a corresponding groove to distribute the oil is cut in the face of the sprocket, it will go a long way toward preventing wear.

However, an even better method is to machine the sprocket face to allow a brass or bronze shim bearing to be positioned between the block face and the cam sprocket. If the block face is pressure fed with oil, you'll need to put a couple of holes in the shim to transmit oil to both sides of it.

Another route to go, although a little more costly, is to use a Torrington needle roller thrust bearing between the cam sprocket and the block. The needle roller needs very little lubrication, though, so it will make the necessity of a pressure feed redundant.

Adjustable Timing

Earlier, we discussed sprocket modifications to allow cam timing adjust-

ment. Timing adjustments made by changing the offset bushings can be time consuming, and even professional engine builders used to doing the job can take ½ to ¾ hour to time in a cam. Thus, you have to ask the question that even if the cam is timed in to the

manufacturer's spec, is that spec guaranteed to be exactly what your engine needs to make maximum power?

A more ideal situation, especially for a competition engine that is to be dynoed, is to have adjustable cam timing. This avoids hassles and allows cam timing to be explored by simply advancing or retarding as necessary.

Two systems are available to do this. APT makes adjustable sprockets that considerably reduce the time it takes to install a cam to spec. Adjusting the cam timing entails no more than loosening some Allen screws, advancing or retarding the sprocket, and retightening the Allen screws. That's all there is

If you want precision timing gears in steel rather than cast iron, as well as the ability to simply adjust the timing rather than fool around with offset dowels and a roller

chain, this APT setup is what you need. At a quarter of the cost it will do almost everything a belt drive will do.

If a split cover is used with the APT adjustable timing gear, quick changes in cam timing can be made, as it will allow the timing cover to be removed independently, rather than forcing you to drop the pan in order to remove the timing cover.

to it; no worrying about whether you have installed the bushing or sprocket the right way, or finding you've just made an adjustment the opposite way to what you intended.

The APT vernier sprocket represents the simplest system. The other system I am familiar with is the Jessel belt drive. This method allows cam timing to be altered *externally*, making for sixty-second cam timing changes.

Each system has its own merits. The APT vernier sprocket is a direct replacement for the stock-type sprocket. It employs a roller chain and, unlike many gear sets, also uses a hob-cut steel gear for both the crank and sprocket, thus ensuring good concentricity and tooth-to-tooth accuracy. To maximize the convenience of this gear, it's necessary to use a timing cover that can either have a section removed, or can be removed in its entirety without dropping the sump.

Check out a stock cam cover and you will see that it has the location for the front pan oil seal on it. This prevents the stock cover from being removed until the pan is dropped. The most cost-effective way around this problem is to get a split timing cover, such as those sold by RHS, Speedomotive, Summit Racing, and others. The split cover is comprised of a section that holds the front oil seal and also a completely independent cam cover.

These covers are relatively inexpensive, chromed to look good, and come with the necessary extra gaskets.

By employing a split timing cover, the cam becomes quickly accessible for timing changes. If you want to go a little more upscale, there are several cast cam covers available that ultimately permit easy access to the sprocket without necessarily removing the crank damper. Probably the simplest way to access the cam sprocket is to use one of the timing covers from Competition Cams or Manley. They have a cast perimeter section with a relatively thick cast-aluminum flat front cover that bolts onto it.

The front cover can be horizontally split in two at some point immediately accessible to and above the crank damper. Obviously, to reach the cam sprocket will require the removal of the water pump. With the top half of the timing cover independently removable, access directly to the sprocket is

Shown here are the parts for the Jessel belt drive for a small-block Chevy. This is a high-quality item, and the quality is reflected in the price.

The first step toward assembling a Jessel belt-drive setup is to install the back plate.

Next, the snout is located on the camshaft, and the end-thrust bearings and the end-thrust retaining plate positioned and installed around the cam. On the end of the crankshaft, the bottom-tooth belt pulley is installed.

easily gained to make quick cam timing changes. To seal up the cover when assembling, I use a piece of L-section sealing strip and silicone sealer.

Belt Drive

Although much more costly, the Jessel belt drive is a worthy alternative to the APT vernier sprocket. Although on the expensive side, this quality setup from Jessel Engineering offers the most versatile and speedy means of adjusting cam timing. One of these belt drives is used on virtually all of my development engines, as it allows easy cam timing exploration as well as the other normally adjusted variables such as ignition and fuel.

On the dyno, the Jessel belt drive allows cam timing adjustments without the need to remove any other parts. Changing the cam timing in a vehicle without removing the water pump may be another issue, and would depend on accessibility at the front of the motor.

The belt drive aspect of the Jessel unit has several advantages over a chain. It runs very quietly, and there is no backlash in the system. Also, probably the most important point, the belt drive has the tendency to damp out high-frequency vibrations. However, the lower frequency vibrations that a crank can develop are still very much present, and therefore the Jessel belt drive is best when used with a damper that adequately damps out any critical vibrations within the rpm range most used.

Though no back-to-back tests have been done, there are indications that the Jessel belt drive is worth a little extra horsepower on high-rpm engines. This is presumably because it runs more efficiently than a chain drive. Although I have no figures to back up claims of extra power, they do not sound unreasonable. One aspect of the Jessel belt drive that is of interest is that it is made to clear the standard cam timing cover. Although development work can be done with the cover off, it is best run with a cover on.

One of the problems with any belt drive is that they are very intolerant of foreign bodies becoming trapped between the belt and the gears. Although the belts are tough, they will break if a stone or other object becomes trapped between it and the gear, resulting in at least a minimum number of bent valves, and at worst maybe some holed pistons. Therefore in service, run the setup with adequate shielding for the belt.

Gear Drives

My gear drive experience is limited to one or two sprint car engines and the use of a Summers Brothers gear drive. For the most part, the use of gear drives can be equated with two factors: durability and convenience. In many instances, the gear drive is a convenient way to go because some applications demand certain accessories to be mounted on the cover. A sprint car fuel-injection pump drive is a good example.

Several companies manufacture gear drives together with an appropriate timing cover setup to perform

Initial timing is done by aligning the dots during assembly of the Jessel belt-drive system.

After installation, the cam timing can either be set where you want it, based on previous experience, or it can be set while the engine is on the dyno, by slackening off the four bolts and adjusting the timing—in either the advance or retard position—a set number of degrees as measured by the gear scale as shown here.

these additional functions. For instance, the Keith Black gear drive and cover incorporates all the features required in a chain drive plus a fuel pump drive.

My only concern with gear drives is that they present a solid coupling between the crank and the cam, and on the face of it this may sound like a good feature. Unfortunately, it makes them good crank-to-cam vibration transmitters. The gear drives, for the most part, have a tendency to transmit greater vibration amplitudes than a chain or belt.

Although I've not measured crank-to-cam vibrations on such setups, I can pass along some suggestions based on educated guesses which can minimize any possible negative effects from gear-transmitted vibrations.

First, use as large a damper on the crankshaft snout as is practical. Remember, the effect of the mass of a damper on reducing acceleration power can be a lot less than the effect of crank vibrations reducing power, so it is the lesser of the two evils. Apart from that, the worst it can do is make the crankshaft live longer. Also, the spurious vibrations caused by the crankshaft could be a factor accounting for some broken valve springs. It's safe to assume that unwanted vibrations are far more likely to harm a system than benefit it.

Next, let's consider gear accuracy. If any cyclic error in gear accuracy is present, a vibration may be developed by the gears, and transmitted by the cam. If the gears are running eccentrically or the tooth pitch varies in a cyclic way, then even if the crankshaft did rotate at a perfectly uniform speed, the cam would be accelerated back and forth due to the inaccuracy of transmitting that motion from crank to cam.

This phenomenon is not peculiar to gear drives. Such inaccuracies also affect other types of cam drives, though to a lesser extent because of the averaging effect.

Regardless, it's worth checking for gear or sprocket truth; some sprockets are so bad they have a visible error. For this reason, you need to be sure that you're buying a gear drive from a company that prides itself on precision engineering. The Summers Brothers drive proved to be totally functional.

Gear drives typically employ an idler gear so camshaft rotation remains the same direction as the crankshaft. Without an idler gear, the cam rotation is reversed, requiring a suitably ground camshaft. Still, the employment of an idler gear means one more part in the system.

If you feel that a reverse drive cam is of no problem, then Isky offers a two-gear setup that is about as simple as you can get. This system replaces the stock chain drive and with the reverse cam gives the desired valve timing.

Although it looks to be a bulky item, the Jessel belt drive will actually fit under a stock timing cover.

This 350 circle track engine had some pretty good parts in it, but nothing really exotic. It was still on iron heads, and with a moderately radical 300 degree roller race cam, it cranked out some 585hp at 7200 rpm.

Camshaft and Valvetrain Installation *14*

Essentially, three cam-design criteria determine whether your engine will produce a strong and reliable power output. These are the design of the profile, the timing figure selected, and the installation procedure used. A typical end user has little or no influence over the first factor. The quality of design is in the hands of the cam designer and the computer.

On the other hand, considerable influence can be wielded over the second factor if you know how to determine suitable timing figures for the application you have in mind. If you have absorbed the contents of earlier chapters, you should have a good idea of how to select cam timing for your engine's needs. However, irrespective of how well the cam is designed, if it's installed incorrectly its full power potential simply won't be realized.

Another point to consider is that the more precisely the cam fits the needs of the engine in terms of total torque and power output, the more sensitive it is likely to be as far as its setting in the engine is concerned. Thus, a cam having mismatched timing figures is less likely to lose a significant amount of horsepower due to mistiming because the valve events are already adrift of optimal.

Conversely, if you're installing a cam with valve events close to optimal for the particular rpm range involved, having the cam off will lose a bigger percentage of power, so cam timing then becomes all important.

Cam Timing

There are many methods available to time a cam in to produce the intended timing figures, but before delving into these, let me clarify one point. The whole argument for timing a cam in hinges on the fact that when the cam is set right, it will make the best power curve. Anything less than optimal means the engine produces less than its best.

The largest obstacle here is that almost every engine hot rodded is unique by virtue of the parts combination used. When setting a cam to the manufacturer's spec, what you're doing is installing it at a figure most likely to work for a typical spec of engine like yours. There is almost no point in worrying abut the last degree of accuracy simply because you do not know whether having that 1 degree of error will be better or worse for the engine.

The only real way to set a cam into a motor is to do it on the dynamometer. The only exception would be building a replica engine of a previously optimized spec. Only when a combination of components and timing has already been optimized can this step be omitted without a potential loss in output. The timing figure cam grinders specify are those most likely to work for the speed equipment parts most commonly used. Fortunately, most aftermarket cam manufacturers' timing figures are, based on years of experience, close to what is needed. Unless you know better, by virtue of your own dyno or drag strip testing, set the cam in to these figures.

Timing Techniques

Given a full set of timing figures, there are several techniques that you can use to time a cam in, some more complex than others.

The first method, which is probably the most commonly used, is to set the full-lift point of the intake valve to a specified position of crank rotation after top dead center on the intake stroke. What you will be doing is setting the cam so that the intake valve reaches full lift at a specific crank angle from TDC. Most small-block Chevy cams are timed in between the 102–110 degrees after TDC on number one intake.

The exact position required is influenced mostly by the cam's lobe centerline angle. We've already described how to figure out a cam's lobe centerline angle if it's not quoted on the cam spec card. Once the lobe centerline angle is known it's simply a question of deciding how much advance the cam is going to need to get the job done. Most small-block Chevy cams run best with 4 degrees of advance.

Another cam timing technique is the split overlap method. Here the cam is set so that it produces an equal amount of lift on intake and exhaust when the piston is at TDC during the overlap period. This technique tends to work quite well on twin-cam engines where the cam advance required will often be close to zero, but anytime a significant amount of advance is needed or a cam other than a symmetrically patterned one is used, this method becomes ineffective.

For dual-pattern cams, complex corrections are required that can't be done unless the incremental lift profile of the cam is known. The method is seldom used for small-block Chevys because Chevy cams are usually dual pattern and rarely run at zero degrees advance.

A closely related method to the split overlap technique is to set the intake valve a certain number of thousandths inch open at TDC on the beginning of the intake stroke. This spec calls for the cam manufacturers to know precisely what timing your engine will need. It can achieve an accurately timed cam but the figure will be different for every profile, rocker, and pushrod combination.

The problem is that unless this figure is known there's little chance of you determining it, short of running your own tests. If you've a mind to use this technique, any subsequent loss of cam paperwork will mean reverting to technique number one.

The next method, at one time quite common, is to physically measure the cam timing at the 0.050in lift point. Of course, if you're going to do this on the number one cylinder you may as well go through and do it on all the other cylinders. This will check the accuracy of your camshaft, block, and valvetrain as a working combination.

Remember, if a cam timing error exists it may not be just the cam at fault, it may be block errors. Only an inspection on a cam checking machine such as a Cam Doctor is going to reveal the existence of significant grinding errors in the cam.

The last technique of any consequence involves measuring valve opening difference at TDC. This technique allows the cam to be advanced the required amount to produce the correct timing. For instance, on a small-block Chevrolet the valve opening events at TDC would be set so that the intake valve has somewhere between 0.008 and 0.030in more lift than the exhaust. This, of course, presumes that we're dealing with a single-pattern or a cam not having significantly different intake-to-exhaust duration.

Again, this technique requires you to know something about the cam profile other than just its timing figures. It also tells you little about the relationship of the cam timing to the crankshaft events, but because it's not set in a conventional method, you won't actually know what the cam advance is for future reference.

When considering the pros and cons of all these techniques for setting the cam, it appears that setting the cam to a specified full-open figure after TDC is the best way to go simply because it allows the setting of a known advance. This can then be used as a reference point for future cam settings, whether or not the same cam grind is being used.

Technique #1

Setting a cam to reach its full-open point a given number of degrees after top dead center on the number one inlet looks easy enough to achieve, but one major stumbling block occurs which proves to be the principal point of confusion for most novices.

The problem is that as a cam profile reaches its full-lift point, the movement of the follower in relation to the angular movement of the cam becomes very small. On some cams the lift may actually dwell over a certain period, which makes finding the center of the dwell period difficult and therefore a more practical technique must be used to get around the problem. Such a technique involves averaging out two points, one prior to and one after the full-lift point.

As an example, assume that a cam generated 0.350in full lift, and the dwell over the nose of the cam was such that it made it impossible to distinguish which was the center of the full lift. To determine where that point is, we would find the angle necessary to raise the follower to say, 0.340in lift (0.010in short of full lift), and the angle taken to go over peak lift and back down to 0.340in follower lift. At both these points the lifter is moving relatively quickly compared with the angular motion of the cam, so each point can be defined fairly accurately.

Let's assume that the two figures turn out to be 94 degrees to get to 0.010in before full lift, and 122 degrees to go past full lift and back down to 0.010in less than full-lift point. So, here we have 94 and 122, and we know that full lift should occur between those two points. By averaging it, we can see that full lift would occur at 108 degrees after TDC. This, then, is the technique that this timing method hinges on.

There are some cam manufacturers that argue that if a symmetrical profile is used, this is a perfectly acceptable way to time the cam, but if an asymmetrical cam is used, it will introduce an error. This is true, but in practice I find that the amount of error introduced is very small, and usually amounts to little more than 0.5 to 1 degree.

However, the real criterion here is whether or not the engine builder has timed the cam to within 1 degree of what the engine wants. So ultimately, no technique for setting a cam is actually correct other than dyno setting.

Quibbling about an amount as small as 1 degree when the engine's needs could be a significantly greater difference than the 1 degree error, should not be considered an issue. Having highlighted the technique, let us now go through it step by step.

The first step is to gather the tools needed for the job. They will include a dial indicator reading in at least thousandths inch, a magnetic base, and a large protractor (you can usually get one from any of the cam companies).

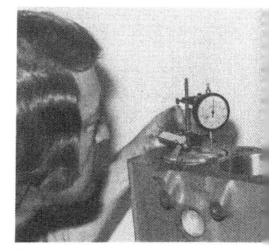

If the center of the piston is not a convenient place to check for TDC, then take the rock out of the piston by sliding the appropriate feeler gauge down the side of the piston to the skirt. This technique assumes, of course, that there are no rings on the piston at this stage. However, it's worth remembering that you only need one piston installed to do the cam timing on the short block.

This is the proper way to check where TDC is occurring: by putting the dial gauge in the center of the piston, the effect of rock is eliminated.

The last item you'll need will be a follower of the type intended for use with your cam.

The most common cam installation is the flat-tappet type, and this being the case it's easy to make up a follower that will eliminate the need for a long dial gauge extension, thereby killing two birds with one stone. All you need to do is take two old hydraulic followers, so long as the bases are still in reasonably good condition, and disassemble them, take out the valve body of one, turn it around, reinstall the circlip, and then slide the valve body on so that you now have two followers back to back.

After thorough cleaning, they can be Loctited together to make a single assembly. Thus, you now have a tall cam follower with a good surface on which the end of the dial gauge can rest. If a roller cam is being installed, it's best to have a spare pair of rollers, modified with a flat-faced extension of some 3–4in, for a dial gauge to measure from. To adjust the cam timing you will either need a Jessel belt drive, and APT adjustable sprocket set, or offset bushings.

If you're going with offset dowels, you will need a selection on hand, and you will have previously needed to drill the timing sprocket to accept them and elongated the bolt holes.

The ideal time to do cam timing is near the completion of the short-block assembly. In other words, it should be close to the last operation on the short-block.

The next step is to establish the TDC position to close limits. To do this, set the magnetic dial indicator on top of the block, and locate the dial gauge on the piston centerline. It's important to measure on the centerline because moderate to wide clearance pistons will have a considerable rock as they go over TDC. Measuring at the edge of the piston will produce a false reading and hamper efforts to get a true TDC position. Turn the crank until the dial gauge indicates the piston is at the top of the stroke, then locate the protractor on the crankshaft and tighten up the crank bolt to hold it in place.

Using an adjustable pointer—it can be made of welding rod—set the pointer to indicate zero. Now rotate the engine away from zero in either direction, and check to see that when a piston reaches TDC as indicated by the dial indicator, the zero point still occurs at the protractor.

Any technique that relies on finding the limit of travel is also likely to have a certain amount of definition problem due to the fact that the piston may

Some timing wheels, such as this Isky one and the smaller one from Competition Cams, are the same size as a large damper. Therefore it's convenient to use a timing cover pointer as seen here, rather than a bent piece of welding wire.

Having established TDC, the next move is to mount the timing gears with the dots aligned.

Once the protractor is mounted on the crankshaft, be sure the pointer indicates exactly TDC, as all measurements are referenced from this.

appear to dwell slightly at TDC. If you feel it necessary to check the zero precisely, bring the piston up exactly 0.010in short of the top of the block and then check the angular position indicated on the protractor. Next, rotate it through TDC until it's once again 0.010in down the lobe.

The two figures obtained should be an even amount either side of TDC if the pointer position is correct. This averaging technique is, in essence, the same as the one used to determine the full-lift point on the cam. However, with most crank, rod, and piston assemblies you'll find that the piston dwells for a short enough time at TDC that, for the most part, you'll be able to establish TDC within half a degree by simply noting where the exact peak piston position is.

At this point, the cam should be installed in the block. The timing chain and sprocket should have a zero bushing installed, and the timing dots should be aligned. This will be your starting point for any subsequent adjustments.

Next, locate the extended cam follower on the number one inlet lobe, and position the dial indicator on the top face of the extended cam follower. Now rotate the engine in the correct direction until full lift is established from the dial indicator reading. At this point set the dial gauge to zero, and then rotate the engine backward until the follower is at about half lift.

Now slowly rotate the engine forward until it's exactly 0.010in shy of full lift. Note the angle on the protractor, then continue to rotate the engine very carefully until the follower reaches full lift, and drops back down to 0.010in exactly. Again, note the reading on the protractor. Add this reading to the first reading and divide by 2. The answer

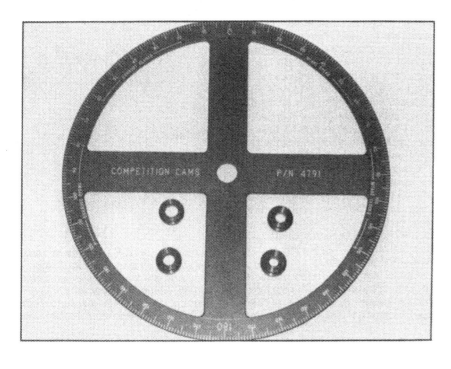

For convenience and accuracy of setting, the big Competition Cams protractor along with its crankshaft snout adaptor, which allows zeroing of the protractor

and the ability to turn the crank on this keyed location, makes it a snap to use. Precision and convenience in one package.

If you're timing in flat-tappet cams you don't need anything fancy in the way of dial gauges. Just a fancy lifter, like this one made out of two discarded hydraulic lifters, will do.

you're left with is the centerline position of the cam in relation to the crank.

If the cam is advanced, the number of degrees shown by your calculations will be smaller than the required one; if the cam's retarded, they will be bigger. For instance, let's say the target is to time the cam so that it reaches full-lift 104 degrees after TDC. If your calculations indicate it's at 102, then the cam is advanced; if it shows 106, then it's retarded.

Now it's time to select your offset bushing. Most offset bushings are stamped with the amount of offset they provide, however, it doesn't hurt to check this since they are mass produced and often their accuracy leaves a little to be desired. Basically, you can figure that about 0.005in offset will change the cam timing 1 degree. If you use a pair of vernier calipers to check this, remember if there is 0.005in offset, there will be 0.010in difference between the thick side and the thin side.

Now comes the question of which way the bushing should be installed to advance or retard the cam. Let's assume you are looking at the front of the motor, which means everything is going around clockwise. If you need to advance the cam, the bushing hole needs to be offset to the right; if you

need to retard the cam, it needs to be offset to the left.

If a brand-new timing chain is being used, it's a good idea to put the cam in slightly more advanced than you want, say 0.5 to 1 degree, because wear on the links of the timing chain will cause the cam to retard slightly.

If you're just making a cam change, and you're using a timing chain that is already broken in, but in perfect condition, then go ahead and time the cam exactly where you want it.

Very often you'll find that it takes two or three tries to get the desired cam timing. Each time it's necessary to disassemble the sprocket gear from the cam and rebuild it to make your new timing check. As was stated in the cam drive chapter, the quickest way to obviate this is to use an APT adjustable cam timing sprocket.

Advancing or retarding the timing becomes as simple as undoing some Allen bolts and either rotating the cam in the correct direction to put it where you want it, or rotating the crank in the opposite direction, and then retightening the bolts.

Setting Up the Valvetrain

Two important features of cam timing that are affected by the valvetrain on a small-block Chevrolet are the rate at which the valve opens from the TDC point, and the amount of lift that is

available when the piston is at peak velocity. Depending on the bore-stroke-rod combination used, this will occur somewhere between 73 and 78 degrees after TDC.

You may be forgiven for assuming that the characteristics of these two points are totally dependent on the camshaft, but this proves not to be the case. The ratio delivered by the rocker varies as it goes through its lift curve. To understand how this is so, study the basic drawing of a rocker in figure 14-1.

Here, we see the simplest geometry possible; that is, the pivot point and the location of the pushrod and valve contact points are all on the same plane. With such a rocker, the ratio is highest at the point where the rocker is horizontal. As it travels through its arc, its ability to transfer motion from the pushrod end to the valve stem lessens and the wiping action of the tip of the rocker across the end of the valve increases.

This action puts more side load on the valve. If roller rockers are used, this is not necessarily a major problem. If regular nonroller tip rockers are used, then the amount of side load applied to the guide can have a significant effect on guide wear.

To offset side loading, rockers are designed so that the position between the pushrod contact point, valve tip, and ball pivot are in fact not aligned.

To find where the intake valve is fully open, engine builders use the technique of taking degree readings an even point before and after full lift, usually 10 thousandths, and then averaging out the result.

Having determined in which direction the cam is out, you can either make adjustments the easy way or the hard way. The hard way is to fool around with offset dowels; the easy way, if you're using the APT adjustable gears, is to simply undo the socket-head locking bolts.

Figure 14-2 shows the kind of geometry normally seen. By moving the pivot down in relation to the pushrod and valve tip, we find that as the valve goes through its lift cycle, the tip of the rocker tends to swing forward. Its rotation about the center point of the ball pivot moves it back, and the two have a tendency to cancel each other out. This doesn't mean that there is no rubbing between the tip of the valve and the rocker, but relocating the centers as described cuts this unwanted motion, and reduces side load.

With a plain nonrollerized rocker the accepted longer wear life is usually produced when the rocker travels through an arc that is ⅓ above the horizontal point to ⅔ below it. Over this range the sweep of the pad across the valve tip is minimized, while the most effective use is normally made of the available rocker ratio.

With a stud-mounted rocker, as used by the small-block Chevy, the position of the rocker in the valvetrain is dictated by the pushrod length.

To set up the valvetrain for best output, it's a matter of selecting the right pushrod length to give the best valve accelerations at TDC consistent with the best lift point at about 75 degrees after TDC. To be able to determine the correct pushrod length you will need an adjustable pushrod. They are sold by most of the larger cam manufacturers, so you should have no difficulty in obtaining them.

Once you've obtained an adjustable pushrod, you will need to assemble the valves in one cylinder of a cylinder head. It's best to use the inner springs only, at this point. Then using a dial gauge suitably mounted to measure the lift, continue to adjust the pushrod until you find the maximum valve lift generated at 75 degrees after TDC. Depending on the type of rocker geometry existing, this figure does not always correspond to the same pushrod length that will produce maximum valve lift, but the length of pushrod required at 75 degrees valve lift does, for most practical purposes, produce the fastest opening at TDC.

If roller rockers are used, then ideally we need to be looking at a rocker angle whereby the rocker is just approaching the horizontal point as the piston reaches TDC. At the horizontal point the rocker ratio is usually the greatest, and that leads to the fastest acceleration at the valve compared with lifter acceleration at the cam profile.

It shouldn't come as a surprise that it takes quite a while to go through the process of adjusting pushrods and continually checking the results. There is a shorter method to correctly measure pushrod length.

Manley manufactures a plastic pushrod setting gauge that appears to set the pushrod length correctly for a cam that generates around 0.600in lift. If

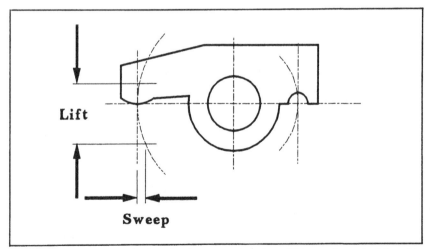

Next, move the cam gear in the appropriate direction and retighten. If you look through the lightening holes of this gear, you'll see how much the cam had to be moved to get the timing correct. This is a typical amount of error. In this photo, the tabs on the cam to sprocket lock washer are being bent over. I normally only use these lock washers when a bumper stop is used. I've never experienced a problem with cam bolts coming undone when correctly torqued.

Figure 14-1: *Seen here is the simplest geometry that a rocker can have. Notice that the center of the pushrod cup, the rocker pivot, and the point at which the rocker makes contact on the valve, are all on a common horizontal centerline. Starting from one third above to two thirds below on the lift curve results in a fairly large sweep across the top of the valve stem. Worse yet, most of the side load occurs at the end of the valve lift where spring loads are highest, so this type of rocker tends to increase wear, both on the tip of the rocker and in the guide. Another strike against such geometry is that as the rocker reaches its full lift point, so the ratio delivered drops off.*

the lift is significantly less than this, or significantly more, you may have to compensate for it, and again it could well depend on the type of rocker you are using. Of course, this method will only work with a ball-pivot-type rocker.

If the valve lift is higher than 0.600in, take the difference between 0.600 and whatever lift is generated. Let's say the cam gives 0.700in lift nominally, so there's 0.100in discrepancy. Multiply this number by 0.22 and shorten the pushrod by that amount.

If, in this case, the lift was 0.700in net when the tappet ramp is subtracted, then the pushrod would have to be made 0.022in shorter than the Manley valve pushrod measuring tool indicated. If the valve lift is less than 0.600in, subtract the lift from 600 and divide your answer by 3. Now put a feeler gauge of this size on the end of the valve stem, and check to see what pushrod length is required by the setting tool.

Using this technique should give you a close starting point at which to set your adjustable pushrod. If you want to check, go ahead and do so because geometry changes in the rocker will affect this technique, and you may want to try a pushrod length just a little shorter and a little longer to see whether a better result is obtained. But for most practical purposes, this technique will put your pushrod length very close to what is needed.

The most important aspect affecting pushrod length, though, is not necessarily getting the maximum from the valvetrain, but compensating for any positional change of the rocker pivot point due to decking the block and milling the head. If the pushrod turns

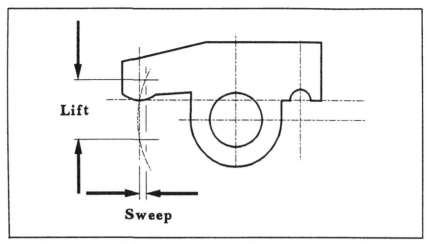

Figure 14-2: *By repositioning the pivot point most of the sliding action across the top of the valve takes place at the beginning of the lift, when spring loads and the resulting side loads are minimum. During the most heavily loaded part of the rockers travel, i.e., the upper two thirds of the* lift, *the motion of the tip across the valve stem is minimal. This increases the guide life substantially, and the ratio delivered toward the top end of the valve lift is better than the previous design, shown in Figure 14-1.*

out to be about 0.100in too long—a figure that could easily be exceeded if you're looking for high compression—then we find that with a regular-type lifter the arc described does not start with the rocker at the right angle.

Consequently, most of the lift takes place after the horizontal line rather than ⅓ before and ⅔ after. The result is that right at the end of the lift phase, the valve stem is subjected to the highest side loads by the rocker, which unfortunately also happens when the spring loads are highest. This maximizes rather than minimizes the force transmitted to the guide, and leads to accelerated wear.

If you're using a relatively high lift cam with stock-style rockers, such as a nonroller tip rocker, then if good guide life is to be achieved it is necessary to set up the pushrod length so that the lift is more evenly distributed about the horizontal.

The ⅓ before to ⅔ after guideline is a good ratio to go by, but if valve guide wear proves to be a problem, then you need to set it up so that more lift takes place prior to the horizontal point, or the engine needs to be converted to roller rockers. Once you've established the correct length you can then order the appropriate-length item from your favorite cam company.

Cures for Engine Block Inaccuracies

15

If you've never prepped a block for a high-performance engine, you may assume that boring and honing the cylinders, decking, align boring, and doing a few other jobs covers the subject. This is far from the case. Indeed, you may be wondering why we are talking blocks in a cam book. Prepping for a maximum-output unit goes many steps further, and the accuracy of the block can greatly influence the effectiveness of the valvetrain.

Block Inaccuracies

Is it worth asking what block inaccuracies can exist and what causes them? It's a fair question, since all the blocks are cast from essentially the same pattern design and are machined on similar production lines. If this is the case, why should they differ? The answer is simple: they aren't all cast at the same location or from the same patterns, nor are they machined on the same production line. So apparently, small variations can occur on a finished block.

When blocks are cast, the process involved can bring about its own random variations. Pouring near white hot molten iron into a mold made mostly of sand and resin is something of a thermal and mechanical shock. Three things happen: particles of sand can break away from the mold and be carried into certain areas, the resins release gases, and the cores themselves—at least those that are installed into the mold—tend to try and float in the much heavier liquid cast iron. The result is inconsistency in the casting process.

Core shifts and such may be bad enough in themselves, but adding production line inconsistencies compounds the problem. Though usually minor, they are nonetheless relevant.

One machining chip in the wrong place can cause a block location error when transferring from one machining operation to another. The result is a less than satisfactory piece, even though the blocks before and after may have been acceptable.

Datum Centerline

From the point of view of valvetrain effectiveness the crankshaft centerline is the most important reference axis in the block. Virtually every valvetrain modification involving the block extract more power hinges on the accuracy of the surfaces and bearing centerlines in relation to the crankshaft centerline.

Align boring and/or honing of the main bearings for size is the starting point for blueprinting the block. If the existing caps are to be used, the technique is to let down the caps by machining a little material from the cap faces, install them, and then align hone the housing bores to correct any misalignment. Align honing usually results in the crank centerline moving nearer

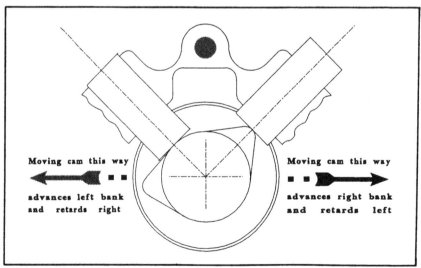

This end view of the cam and lifters indicates how an inaccuracy in the cam location can affect the timing; however, this is just a simple case. The alignment of the cam may not be perfect, and it could be off at an angle relative to the crank. This causes an advanced error at one end of the block and a retarded error at the other.

The first step toward accurizing the block is to make sure there's a good datum to work on. This means line boring or line honing the mains as a starter.

to the cam centerline. This must be allowed for when it comes time to install the cam timing gears.

As mentioned previously, Cloyes produces cam sprockets with the necessary larger pitch circle diameter to take up any additional chain slack produced. By measuring the new center-to-center distance and selecting an appropriate gear set, the correct chain tension can be achieved.

Installing a chain-sprocket setup that is either too tight or too loose is undesirable. The problem is knowing exactly what center-to-center distance a particular chain and sprocket set will deliver. An easy answer is to use a BHJ gear set measuring fixture. The gear set is installed on the fixture and an air cylinder applies the necessary tension. The installed center distance is then read out on a dial gauge. By testing a few gear sets it is possible to arrive at a suitable one which, within close limits, matches the measured cam-to-crank centerline of the block.

If steel caps are installed there is usually too much material to be honed out of the now-stepped bore. This means that align boring must be done. In many instances, a good machinist can set the tooling up so that it barely kisses the main bearing housings in the block while taking the requisite amount from the caps. Realigning the housings in this way means that the crank-to-cam center distance is unaltered and the likelihood of a stock gear set giving the correct installed tension, though not ensured, is increased.

Deck Heights
The small-block Chevy's deck height is important for a number of reasons. First, the piston's approach to the cylinder head quench area is critical if detonation is to be suppressed for maximum power. If crank throws, rod lengths, and piston heights are accurately controlled, then the last remaining ingredient for accurate piston-to-quench-area clearance without individually fitting each assembly to its cylinder is to precisely machine the block height. Both decks must obviously be parallel to the crank centerline and each deck must be 90 degrees to the other and 45 degrees to the cam-crank centerline.

Again, BHJ makes a special fixture to facilitate machining of the deck and position it properly in relation to the crank. When the decks are machined together with any machining of the

heads, the rocker assembly moves nearer to the crankshaft centerline. This means selecting the correct pushrod length to suit the now shorter distance between crank centerline and the fulcrum on the rocker. If block decks aren't parallel and consistent the required pushrod length may vary from cylinder to cylinder, so deck accuracy needs to be controlled within about 0.002in.

A sloppy timing chain is not good for power. If the block has been line-honed, the center distance between the cam and the crank may have closed up. The

Once the center-to-center distance is known, this BHJ fixture can be used to

Bores
After the deck is machined another BHJ fixture, the Bore-True, can be used to position the bores precisely in relation to the crank centerline and the correct distance from the front face of the block. This ensures every piston and rod assembly is in the correct position over its relevant crank throw to minimize any side loading. Displacement of the bore across the block will

first step toward compensating for this is to measure the center-to-center distance as seen here.

select a timing chain to give the correct tension.

cause a change in the cam timing relative to the piston position. Although there may be justification for offsetting the bores, the key to success is to ensure that they are all the same.

The BHJ Bore-True also affords the user an opportunity to relocate the cylinder head dowel holes. Prior to decking the block, the cylinder head dowel holes are tapped and a threaded cast-iron plug inserted. This gets machined flush with the block deck during the decking operation. With the Bore-True fixture in place, the boring machine locates from the fixture bores rather than the block bores.

Whether bores should be centered over the crank or not has, in the past, been the subject of some controversy. Certain engines, such as the flat-head Ford V-8, actually used a substantial cylinder-to-crank centerline offset. What this did was to increase the proportion of the crankshaft revolution that took part on the power stroke.

On some long-stroke engines, offsets as large as a $\frac{1}{4}$in were used. Of course, offsets such as this are impractical on a small-block Chevy and with its modern big-bore, short-stroke design it is debatable whether any significant advantage would be gained.

The indications are that small offsets can provide some benefit. When offsetting a bore, the intention is to relocate the position of the wrist pin in relation to the crank centerline. Again pros and cons exist, but small offsets can be readily accomplished by offsetting the pin in the piston.

Lifter Bores

Once the caps are aligned and sized, everything done to the block needs to be referenced to this centerline. Potentially one of the most power-robbing errors is produced by inaccuracies of the camshaft and lifter bores in relation to the crank centerline.

If the lifter bores or cam centerline are displaced in the block from their intended position, a change in cam timing will result. Though the main bearing bores are align bored at the factory, the cam bearing bores are not. It would seem these are done in three operations.

First, the two end cam bearing housings are machined, then the two intermediate ones, and finally the center

Assuming the pistons, rods, and crank are dimensionally accurate, to get the minimum piston-to-deck clearance, it's necessary to have the block decked parallel with the main bearings. This BHJ fixture ensures that the block will be parallel with the mains, and the decks square with each other.

Here's the BHJ Block Tru setup ready to start machining. For the most part, it's convenient to deck small-block Chevies to 9.00in crank center to deck height.

This BHJ Bore Tru fixture is designed to locate the bores directly over the crank's centerline.

one. After this machining is done, cam bearings are installed and align bored.

When a block is stripped and hot tanked, the first items to be removed are the cam bearings. Replacing them with pre-sized bearings can mean that the original alignment, however good or bad it was, is now lost. Though whatever error that occurs is unlikely to cause a cam to physically bind up, those errors that do exist are just the beginning of a trail of small misalignments that can lead to a substantial reduction in power.

In the first place, it is possible to have the cam bearings skewed out of alignment with the crankshaft centerline when viewed from above the block. This axis error can cause cam timing to vary on each cylinder. Take a look at the drawing in figure 15-1 and you can see that moving the camshaft centerline from one side of the crank centerline to the other will produce timing changes.

If we were dealing with an inline engine such errors could be adjusted out, but with a V-8, displacing the cam to one side causes one bank to advance and the other to retard. When the cam is timed in on #1 cylinder any error that may have been split between each bank is now applied solely to the other bank. This can drop output more than if the error was split evenly between each bank. Still, errors at this point are normally small and can be partially compensated for by checking the cam timing on #1 and #2 cylinders and splitting the error.

Positional displacement of the lifter bores is more difficult to deal with and cannot be significantly compensated for by cam timing adjustment. This is because the lifter bores may not exhibit the same errors down the length of the engine.

To true up the lifter bores, this BHJ Lifter Tru fixture is used. The first move is to install this bar with accurately positioned holes into the cam bearings.

Once the top plate of the Bore Tru fixture is located, it is possible not only to accurately position the bores, but also to reposition the cylinder-head-locating dowel holes in relation to the bores.

Next, the end plates are installed. This puts the cam bar in the correct angular orientation.

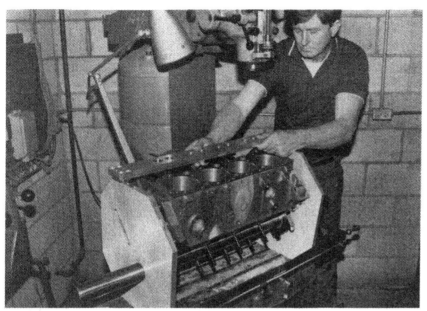

This allows location of the top plate. The accurate holes in this plate and the cam bar now provide an accurate reference for the cutter to true up the cam follower holes.

Essentially all that's left to do now is to run the special reaming tool through the fixture, and machine the lifter bores accurately in position.

Some lifter bores may be producing advanced timing and others retarded, depending on the angle they make with the cam. Others may be displaced such that the cam and lifter centerlines don't intersect, which means that as far as the cam is concerned the lifter diameter is effectively reduced. If edge riding of the lifter on the cam lobe is to be avoided, then the cam profile must be ground with less velocity. That's not good for a maximum-output engine. The only sure way of correcting the problem is to ensure accuracy of the crank-cam-lifter system.

Correction of any cam-lifter centerline errors are normally started by align boring the cam bearing housings and installing the Sealed Power cam bearings with the oversize OD. During this operation, some engine builders increase the size of the oil groove in the cam bearing housing in an effort to improve oil flow to the mains. With the crank and cam as reference points, lifter bores can be positionally corrected in relation to the cam centerline.

There was a time when this had to be done on a milling machine and was a lengthy operation, but BHJ, among the many other specialty automotive tools

they produce, has a fixture that greatly simplifies accurizing the lifter bores in relation to the cam on a small-block Chevy.

This fixture uses two special end plates which locate off mandrels situated in the cam and main bearings. The cam location mandrel has pilot holes corresponding to the lifter centerlines. This, in conjunction with an accurately located plate above the lifter valley, which also has pilot holes, allows a cutter to reposition the lifter bores with far more precision than the original factory-produced bores.

It is not uncommon for the lifter bores to be displaced as much as 0.020in. Accumulated errors can alter valve events by as much as 7 degrees. If you consider that lifter bores can have at-random errors, then it's not hard to see that any timing precision on the cam is lost as the motion is transmitted to the valve.

Precision machining the lifter bores remedies the situation, but boring them now means they are oversize. The standard diameter for resizing a small-block Chevy lifter bore is usually 0.875in, this being the stock size of a Ford lifter. Some racing rules call for

stock 0.842in diameter lifters and to accommodate this BHJ produces sleeves that can be used to resize a lifter back to stock Chevrolet dimensions.

At first you may wonder why some sanctioning bodies limit lifter size. The bottom line is that bigger lifter diameters mean higher maximum lifter velocities. If there is no reason to limit the size of the lifter, then it's a good idea to leave it at 0.875in diameter as this typically allows lifter velocity to be increased from 0.007525in per degree to 0.007612in per degree.

Correcting the position of the lifter bores is just about the most difficult precision job to do on a small-block Chevy and, aside from obvious blueprinting exercises to minimize friction, on average produces the best returns for the effort involved.

Camshaft Selection

16

Cams for street application probably span a wider range of duration and timing figures than any other area. Changing a cam can satisfy requirements ranging from additional low-end torque and more mileage for a recreational vehicle, right through to good top-end horsepower for a street-driven bracket racer. To the novice engine tuner it seems a bit of a mystery as to how the cam manufacturer gets more torque from a cam whose specifications seem less capable of allowing the engine to breathe than does the stock cam.

The main ingredient that the cam grinder uses is faster opening rates. If we're considering low-end horsepower to pull a big camper or other heavy cargo, then it's pounds-feet of torque in the 1000–3500rpm range that matter most, especially if the vehicle has a manual transmission. With an automatic transmission it is unlikely that the stall speed will ever be much below about 1200–1300rpm, so power immediately below that is not critical.

On the other hand, a manual-transmission vehicle will require good engine control for steep-grade starts. This means being able to pull away without having to turn the engine at 5000rpm and slip the clutch. Under these conditions, low-end torque counts for everything and the nearer to steam engine-like performance your small-block Chevy exhibits, the better it will handle heavy-duty low-speed work.

A key factor concerns the acceleration rates imparted by the cam to the lifter as well as the opening and closing points of the valves. Although increased overlap is responsible for lack of vacuum and bad low-speed running, there comes a point at which reducing overlap any further serves no useful purpose in terms of low-end power.

Once overlap drops below about 40 degrees, the amount of improvement in the engine's manners becomes insignificant with any further reduction. Thus if short-period cams are used, the lobe centerline need not take into account the need to improve idle quality simply because the overlap

is already insufficient to cause any problems.

The cam can now be ground with a more optimum lobe centerline angle. For short-period cams it is not uncommon to use 108–110 degrees, whereas many of the longer period cams are using lobe centerline angles of 112–114. But, this often varies from one manufacturer to another.

By tightening up the lobe centerline angle on a short-period rapid-acceleration cam, we find that the intake valve accelerations may produce more valve lift at TDC than a slightly longer period, slower opening OEM-type cam.

Although the aftermarket profile may have less duration, it may produce as much or maybe slightly more lift than the OEM cam it replaced. The amount of opening area it delivers during the induction stroke may be at least equal, sometimes more than, that delivered by the original cam. However, because the valve closes sooner after BDC, at low rpm it traps more charge, which means more torque.

Since the opening area of this shorter cam during the induction stroke may still be about the same as the stock cam, it will generate at least the same top-end horsepower. Al-

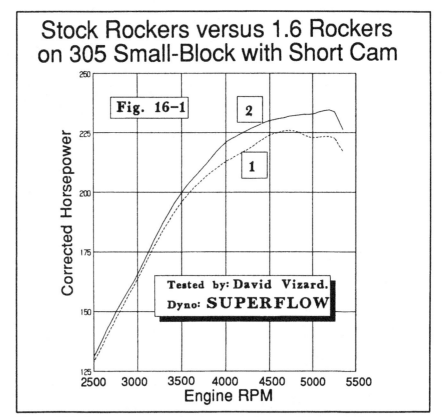

Figure 16-1: *Because of the 305's reduced bore size it cannot accommodate valves as large as the 350. As a result, even though cubic inches are down, the engine has a harder time breathing, and therefore responds well to a high-lift rocker. This particular engine was equipped with a stock Chevrolet cam typical of most smog-era engines. Retaining the original factory timing, 1.6 rockers boosted the power as seen here, after suitable attention had been given to the exhaust to reduce backpressure.*

though in the case of very short cams, peak power is often at a lower rpm than the original equipment cams. With cams under about 260 degrees duration, the difficulty is getting the cams to breathe much past 4500–4750rpm. The short period precludes the use of any high-lift figures at the cam, making the use of high-lift rockers more desirable to try and recover some of the much needed valve lift.

High-lift rockers usually perform well on 350s, but if you're running one of the popular displacement engines of 383 or even a 400ci engine, the high-lift rockers can pay off handsomely. Changing stock rockers to a 1.6:1 Competition Cams Magnum rocker on a 400ci engine with pocket-ported heads can often deliver in excess of 20hp.

increase, which makes the amount of power per dollar spent a pretty good deal.

The more common application of high-lift rockers on a 350 is usually good for 15–17hp on a typical street-cammed engine. Figure 16-1 shows the result of a test on a 305ci engine.

Cams and Compression

With short cams the earlier closing of the intake valve, as opposed to that delivered by an OEM cam, often helps increase the dynamic low-speed compression.

By closing the intake valve earlier, more air is trapped above the piston so the effective compression ratio is increased. This contributes to some of the cam's effectiveness; however, when the cam starts to get much longer than about 270 degrees, it is necessary to consider the effect of the valve closure point on the dynamic compression ratio. Relating compression to closure point was dealt with in an earlier chapter, and for the bigger

street cams, it's time to put those recommendations into practice.

At about this point we can run into difficulties, especially with some of the later model cars employing thin-wall cylinder head castings.

General Motors started this practice in the late 1970s, and although they opted to move away from the very thin lightweight castings since they caused service problems, the castings on 1985–1991 305s or 350s do not have much material on the deck face to allow them to be milled for increased compression. Therefore, if you are putting together, or hopping up, a motor utilizing as many stock parts as possible, the cam you choose must be related to the compression that you're able to generate from the components being used.

If you intend to install a cam into a late-model emission car, then consider that increasing the overlap is not only likely to be detrimental to low-speed power, idle quality, cruise vacuum, and economy, but it is also likely

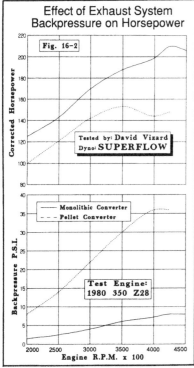

Figure 16-2: Late-model emission motors utilizing a pellet-type catalytic converter suffer from a great deal of backpressure. In this chart here you can see the effect of changing the converter from a pellet-type unit, which flowed around 200cfm, to a monolithic-type of converter, which flowed about 450cfm. See how the backpressure dropped from over 35psi down to about 6.5psi at 4000rpm. On the other hand, horsepower rose from 142hp at 4000rpm to no less than 200hp at 4000rpm. The moral here is before you make a cam change, make sure that excessive exhaust system backpressure is not going to be working against you.

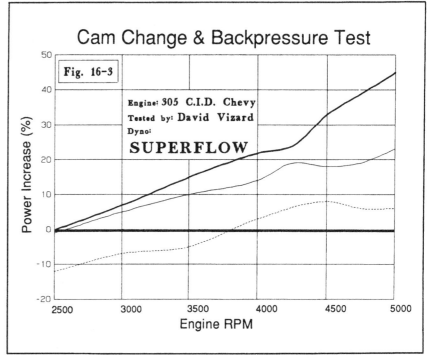

Figure 16-3: This test demonstrates how the effectiveness of a cam is largely negated by excessive backpressure. The lower dotted line indicates the power change with no changes to the exhaust system. In this particular case, the exhaust system utilized a pellet-type converter, and backpressure was around the 30psi mark. Notice the cam produced no increase, and actually reduced power up

until 3750rpm. Above that less than 10hp increase was seen. By changing to a high-flow converter, the amount of power gained by the cam went from 8hp to 23hp. Lastly, installing some emission-legal headers feeding into a high-flow catalytic converter and muffling system showed that the cam change produced some 45hp increase at 5000rpm.

146

to affect the match of the calibration between the computer and the engine's delivered advance and fueling characteristics.

For the most part, if you expect to make a cam change without a complementary change to the computer, then the overlap figures at least must not be too dissimilar from stock. Also, the point at which the intake valve closes should be relatively similar to the stock cam.

Within these constraints, the valve needs to be lifted as much as possible. On the other hand, opening of the exhaust valve can be changed quite significantly without necessarily upsetting the match between computer and engine characteristics. As a result, a dual-pattern cam proves to be a good choice, where computer reprogramming is something to avoid.

With many GM vehicles, but especially those with the pellet-type converter, much of the advantage of a cam can be invalidated by the fact that the pellet converters cause a great deal of exhaust pressure (see figure 16-2).

Installing a cam that allows better engine breathing, which many do, causes backpressure to reach even higher values. Although an increase in power is usually seen, the full advantage of the cam's potential is never achieved. The best advice I can give is that if you intend to install a cam into a late-model computer-type car, then you need to install a low-backpressure converter.

If you look at figure 16-3, you'll see just how much of a negative effect a restrictive exhaust can have on a higher performance cam. In this particular instance, the 305 test engine utilized all the emission exhaust of a late-model car; the only difference was that an electronic Holley was used to calibrate the mixture manually instead of using a computer control. The reason is that this test is to investigate backpressure versus a cam change, rather than the overall effect the computer may have on the engine.

As you can see, with the stock exhaust system, the cam made little difference to the engine output. By changing the restrictive stock converter to a higher flowing type, not only was a big chunk of power released from the exhaust, but also a substantially bigger gain was made from the change of cam.

Installing a cam as part of a package can be very effective. If we take a stock 350, it's possible to add more than 100hp at the top end of the engine's output with absolutely no loss in low-end output compared to the original power curve. Sure, the bigger cam may have less low-end torque than the cam it replaced, but all of the other modifications, including the exhaust and intake manifold, can help step up the low-end torque. If this means losing a little low-end because of a bigger cam, the overall trade-off is still very favorable.

The bottom line is that selecting the right combination of parts has allowed the engine to make more horsepower everywhere in the rev range compared with the stock power curve, more than a 50 percent increase in top-end horsepower, and over 1000rpm additional rev range. All of this adds up to quite an increase in performance. Running the numbers through a computer-simulated test on a typical Z28 Camaro gave the performance figures shown in figure 16-4. The program used was developed in the test shop, however, excellent programs that do the same

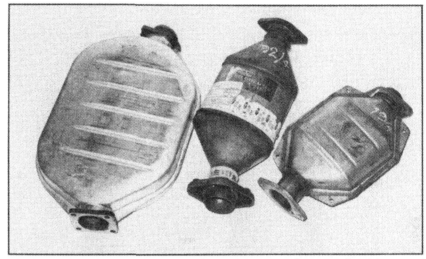

The GM pellet converter, as shown on the left, spells death to any real power output from the engine. They're so restrictive in flow they cause massive back pressure. The monolithic type of converters, which are a honeycombed core of the type shown on the right and of which there are many variances, flow considerably more, and are usually worth 15hp or more hp just by making a straight swap. This figure can be doubled if a hot cam has been installed in the engine.

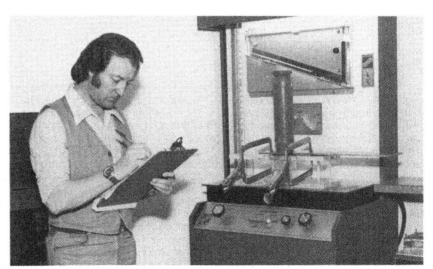

Many straight-through glasspack mufflers look like they should flow well; however, my tests indicate that a large proportion of them either don't muffle, don't flow, or don't do either.

147

thing are available from Racing Systems Analyst and Performance Trends Incorporated.

If your intention is to stick with the stock torque converter, then for a 350 or larger engine, about a 275 degree duration cam is the longest you should consider installing. On smaller displacement engines, still having the 4in bore, you may find that even 275 degrees is a little too much. On the long-stroke engines, such as the 305, a 275 degree cam will react more or less the same as it does in a 350.

In a 400ci engine, you can probably get away with as much as 280 degrees

of cam timing before the engine gets too cammy to give satisfactory low-end output. But again, these figures all depend on the basic specification of the engine, and to make a cam work properly, we need to consider low backpressure, good induction system, and a compatible compression. Even though we've covered those subjects before, it won't hurt to illustrate a point here.

Assuming you have a 350ci engine, let's see exactly what a 270-plus degree cam can do. In this particular test I used an Isky 270 Mega Cam. The Mega Cam actually measured out at 274

degrees of duration at 6 thousandths (0.006in) tappet lift. A difference between these figures and Isky's occurs because they use 0.006in on the opening ramp and 9 thousandths (0.009in) on the closing ramp. I selected the Isky Mega Cam for the test because it's an off-the-shelf cam ground at 108 degree lobe centerline. Whereas this may not be the best for idle quality and vacuum, it certainly is good for torque and horsepower.

In this particular test, the stock 929 Chevrolet cam was optimized, something that most of you won't be doing. As you can see from the power figures in figure 16-5, the Mega Cam picked up considerable torque and horsepower. The horsepower was up by some 62 over the optimized stock cam, while peak torque was up 10–12lb-ft.

Now, at this point I should comment on the tests. First, it is difficult to know whether or not your stock cam is optimized. Chances are it isn't, however, with production tolerances floating as much as they do, it is possible that somebody out there has a motor with a stock cam set to produce near optimum timing figures. For these tests, the Jessel belt drive used was adjusted until the stock cam delivered the best torque and power figures.

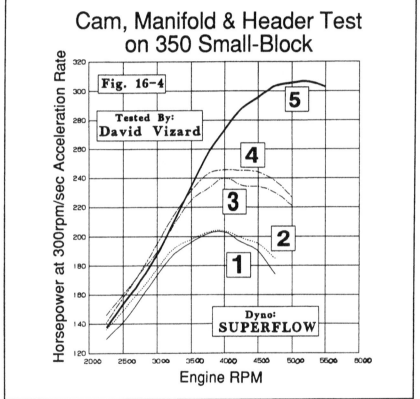

Figure 16-4: From these figures you can see just how effective a camshaft can be in the overall picture when modifying a small-block Chevy engine. Curve 1 is a stock Chevy 350 with all of its emission gear on. The exhaust system used in this test was a high-flow monolithic converter along with a stock Z28 muffler system. By advancing the cam some 4 degrees, power curve 2 was produced. Power curve 3 was produced by installing 1⅝in headers dumping through two high-flow catalytic converters and two Sonic Turbos. Curve 4 was produced by adding a Weiand Street Ram manifold to the engine, and curve 5 was produced by plugging in the appropriate cam that

Weiand market to accompany this manifold. Looking at power figures is one thing, but what actually matters is what it can do in the car. The original car on street tires and with zero rollout at the start line of the dragstrip, was good for 16.12sec at 86.2mph. 0-60 came up in 8sec flat, with the car covering 430ft to make that speed. After the cam, headers and intake manifold were bolted on, the car's potential changed to 14.42sec for the quarter at 100.1mph. 0-60 came up in 6sec with the car covering 290ft to get there. These times would have been better had more traction been available, as wheelspin at the higher output became a problem.

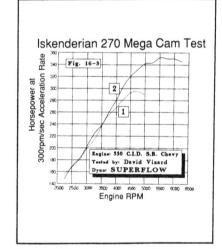

Figure 16-5: Here's what a Megacam will typically do to a 350 utilizing pocket-ported closed-chamber heads. Power climbed from 295hp to 355hp—a solid 60hp increase. The Megacam comes normally ground on a 108 LCA, tighter than most cams. It's worth noting that similar results can be achieved with Competition Cams' 270 HE Cam and the Crane 272 cam, all in single-pattern form when they are also ground on a 108 degree LCA.

On the other hand, the Isky Mega Cam was simply installed at the figures recommended by Isky and run. It was done this way because this is how a typical enthusiast would approach the situation—most people don't have their own $250,000 dyno. The numbers you see in figure 16-5 represent the minimum gain that you can expect the Isky cam to put out over the stock cam. These numbers assume that the exhaust backpressure in your engine is no more than the low level experienced in the Power Pro test.

Once duration figures reach the 275–280 degree mark, it becomes necessary to consider that transmission modifications may be needed to retain compatibility with the type of power curve produced by the longer cam. This is not so critical if your vehicle has a manual transmission, but with an automatic transmission, a reduction of bottom-end torque can seriously slow the vehicle's launch. The result is usually a bad elapsed time for the quarter mile because it will not leave hard, although top speeds may be higher (see figure 16-5).

Thus it's virtually mandatory to use a higher stall torque converter. This may seem like no problem other than having to buy a higher stall converter and install it. But a closer look at the overall picture shows that it's not quite that cut and dried.

A few facts about high-stall torque converters will allow you to appreciate the greater intricacies of making a correct choice at this point in the game. First, many types of high-stall converters are much less efficient at transmitting power at part-throttle due to increased slippage. The end result is that some of the horsepower that is developed at the crankshaft is turned back into heat in the converter, and never gets to the road.

Consider the situation where a change of converter is just barely necessary. You could find that the usually greater inefficiency of the high-stall converter offsets any gains a slightly hotter cam may have made.

This being the case at the transition point between being able to use a stock converter and needing a higher stall converter, much attention must be paid to the working specification of the engine. Let's say you opt for a 280 degree cam instead of a 270. Sure, the 280 degree cam will give more horsepower, but, if the additional horsepower it produces is simply used up in

the converter, the whole point of the exercise will be lost.

When contemplating a 280 degree cam, you should consider maximizing the compression of the engine to make the absolute best of the 280 degree cam. The reason for advocating the highest possible compression with a big cam is that it considerably improves the low-end power.

The motor will also come on the cam sooner, which means that your engine-transmission combination will only need a minimal amount of extra stall speed to get the job done. In other words, it will allow the tightest possible converter consistent with the cam's requirement for a slightly higher stall.

If you intend to build a weekend warrior for some seriously quick trips

The genuine turbo muffler is on the left. On the right is a muffler which simply uses the name "turbo" and little of the technology involved in its original counterpart. The original turbo was large, had only a reasonable through-flow of air, and did not do much muffling. It only made it on the production car because a turbo takes out half the noise before it even gets to a muffler. There are effective turbo mufflers on the market, and there are a lot of ineffective ones.

To ensure a reasonable cam and manifold compatibility, some manifold companies, such as Weiand and Edelbrock, are offering camshafts that are known to be functional with their particular manifold designs.

149

down the drag strip, then a cam in the 290–305 degree bracket will probably be required. When using cams of this duration, serious consideration must be given to just how streetable the end result will be. Sure, anything is drivable on the street, but the convenience of doing so diminishes rapidly with cams this big.

As a starter, a converter with a stall speed of 3000–4000rpm will be needed. The compression ratio will

Without necessarily going big on the cam, a well-prepped small-block can put excessive demands on the stock torque converter. This unit from Art Carr has improved torque multiplication at stall.

have to be raised significantly; there's almost no point in using less than about 10.5:1 and at 11:1 the compression with iron heads is going to be borderline in terms of detonation on service station fuel.

If cams as long as 300 degrees are used in conjunction with well-ported cylinder heads, good exhaust systems, and adequate carburetion, I find that the engine's rpm potential can be high enough to require valve spring forces a little stronger than is reliably handled with a flat-tappet cam. In essence, a long-period cam like this can be a relatively cheap way of getting a lot of horsepower, but spring loads should not exceed about 350lb over the nose. If they do, cam and lifter life will be relatively short. Using a 305 degree hydraulic cam does not in itself provide any problems other than it's necessary to get the combination right.

If you've put a lot of effort into obtaining high flow from the heads, intake manifolds, and so on, then the cam capability with such components may simply outpace the springs' capability to hold valve float in check. Either that or the heads may warrant more lift than a flat-tappet hydraulic cam produces. If you think you've reached this stage, the next step is to consider going to a street-roller-type cam. The advantage of a street roller is

that higher lifter velocities can be achieved, thus greater valve lift can be developed at the valve. Also, the roller does not cause the cam profile to wipe out as would a flat-tappet cam when spring loads are of a suitable magnitude for the rpm capability used.

Let's compare a street roller cam to say, a race roller cam. A street roller cam is one that has lower acceleration rates; in other words, the profile is less aggressive. It's not commonly realized that a roller lifter experiences a great deal of side load when rapid lifter acceleration rates are employed. Excessive side load could lead to the breakup of the roller follower, or rapid wear of the follower bores in the block.

A street roller is one that has acceptable side loads for good follower reliability and block life, yet enjoys many of the attributes of a cam capable of higher peak velocities. Also, a street roller cam is often ground on a high-grade cast-iron blank to avoid surface fatigue, yet such a cam retains compatibility with the distributor gear and so promises a long service life.

If you're electing to go the roller cam route, keeping your engine on a tight budget is not necessarily a major priority, in which case you'll probably want to run roller rockers on the engine. In this situation, it makes sense almost without exception to use at least a 1.6 rocker on the intake.

As for what is needed on the exhaust, this will depend on whether a single- or dual-pattern cam is used. The effects of high-ratio rockers on the exhausts were discussed at length in chapter 11, so if you need to clarify any

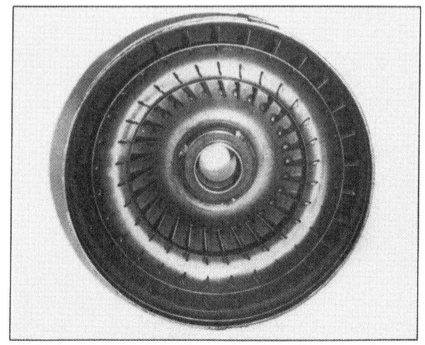

This Art Carr unit also has braised fins within to prevent the converter from physically breaking up due to the torque input.

If a moderately large street cam is used, a change in vacuum modulator may be required so that light throttle shifts are made at a more appropriate point.

points in this area, refer to that chapter.

You may have wanted to stick with the hydraulic cam because of the convenience of low maintenance with this type of lifter. In the mid 1980s, hydraulic roller followers hit the scene and are gradually taking over as a more popular option today. The hydraulic roller follower has all of the attributes of low maintenance that a regular flat-tappet lifter has, along with the low friction and wear characteristics of a roller.

As to the power advantages of a hydraulic roller over a comparable timing hydraulic flat-tappet cam, we see a measurable difference on cams of 260 degrees or more duration (see figure 16-6). As duration figures increase the hydraulic roller, if suitably designed, will start to outpace the equivalent hydraulic flat-tappet cam by an ever-increasing amount. But the roller really comes into its own when cams of 275–280 degrees or more duration are considered. Under these circumstances you can figure that a good hydraulic roller cam will, depending on the engine's capacity, release 15-20hp more.

Alternatively, you could select a shorter period cam that would produce the same top-end horsepower as a flat-tappet cam, but produce better low-end power. In other words, the roller cam has the ability to extend top-end horsepower without making such a great sacrifice in bottom-end power.

The main advantage of a roller, beside reduced friction, is that it can take the valvetrain to higher velocities than a flat-tappet. That is, the positive acceleration level used continues for longer up the flank of the cam. This allows more lift to be achieved by the intake valve in the critical part of the stroke from TDC to about halfway down the bore.

We can sum up what's been said so far under three headings: duration, lift, and cost. Given enough cash, you can buy anything that modern-day technology can produce. But few of us are in that situation, so the problem is how to get the best value for the dollar. In this context, it is necessary to look at torque output as well as horsepower.

Anytime a performance cam is installed in an engine it can produce a high-horsepower output, representing a good horsepower per dollar ratio, yet the engine's peak torque or torque curve in the lower part may have suffered to the extent that it's necessary to spend a lot of money in other areas to make that big cam work.

A good example of what can be achieved is shown in the test results in figure 16-7. Here, a Crane cam was used in a relatively well prepped motor to see how much horsepower could be derived just by making a cam change. A 350 motor with pocket-ported 186 heads was used, with the compression ratio set at 10:1, not unbelievably high for a stock cam, and not uselessly low for a long-period cam. Carburetion was by a 650 Holley on an Edelbrock Victor Junior manifold. The manifold favors mid- and top-end horsepower, while the carburetor with small venturis more than likely would assist the low-end power. Certainly for the kind of rpm expected of a big-cammed motor, a 650cfm Holley was probably a little on the small side.

In spite of this you can see that changing from a stock cam to a high-output Crane cam resulted in an increase of 100hp. To be able to use such a radical cam on the street, though, is going to require some good combinations planning on your part. First, the amount of vacuum available with a cam of this duration is far less than the stock cam, so any vacuum-operated ancillaries on the engine are going to function much less effectively. More than likely, a vacuum reservoir will be needed.

Calibration Changes

Just installing a cam and doing little else is unlikely to give the kind of

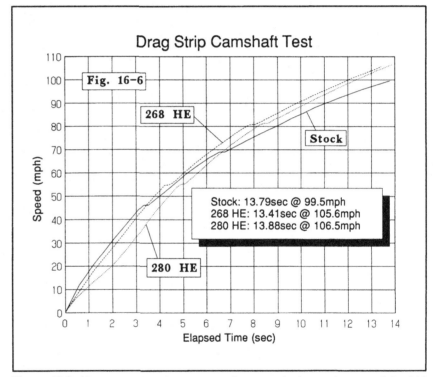

Figure 16-6: *Horsepower numbers are one thing, but I have a saying that "Horsepower sells engines, Torque wins races." If an engine is not operating in the torque band, then many of the advantages of a high-performance cam will be lost. Here is a classic example. A 350 Z28 equipped with headers and a blueprinted engine, but with the stock cam and converter, reached the end of the strip in 13.79sec with a terminal speed of 99.5mph. Substituting a 280 HE Competition Cams' cam actually resulted in the car slowing to 13.88 for the quarter, but the mph was up to 106.5. If you look at the speed versus time curve you will see that* because the low-end torque of the 280 degree cam was much less, the car was lazy off the line. Using a smaller 268 HE cam resulted in a 13.41 second quarter at 105.6mph. These tests show that performance is all about combinations. Just for the record, with a 280 degree cam, performance made a really dramatic increase when it was used with a compatible high stall torque converter. With a 3200rpm stall, the same car ran a 12.6 for the quarter with 106.8mph in the lights. However, that high-stall converter cost some 3mpg for regular street driving.*

results seen from some of the tests shown. Changes to the engine's ignition and carburetion settings will almost certainly be required. Installing a cam with a greater amount of overlap and delayed valve closure typically needs a radical change in the ignition system's advance curve.

Any cam whose characteristics are likely to reduce the low-end output will reduce it even more if the ignition advance curve is not properly set up. A long-period cam requires the ignition timing to come on much sooner because cylinder filling at low rpm is less, hence the combustion process occurs at a slower rate. It's only by lighting up the charge sooner that the combustion process produces peak cylinder pressures at the optimum crank angle.

The most effective use of a small-block Chevy's induced charge is achieved when most of the charge is burnt by the time the crank is 50 degrees past TDC on the power stroke. Because the lower pressure charge burns more slowly, valuable low-end output can be lost. Having the ignition timing too far retarded by 4 or 5 degrees does not mean that the end of the combustion cycle is 4 or 5 degrees late.

Realistically, any error in the timing is magnified by the time the combustion nears the end of the burning phase. If you're installing a cam of 275 or more degrees, then it's almost certain that some kind of change to the ignition advance curve will be required.

By the time we're looking at 290 degree cams, most stock ignition advance curves are way off optimum. This means that installing a big cam is going to warrant recalibration of the distributor advance curve. Most engines will, of course, be using the HEI distributor, and for this there are advance curve kits on the market; however, be warned. Advance curve kits do not provide an accurate change in the advance curve. You could install one of these kits and find that your ignition advance curve is still as far off as it was when you started.

Figure 16-9 shows the effect of simply installing some proprietary brands of advance kits, which are all purported to do roughly the same thing— notice how much error there is in the advance curves.

The only real way to get your distributor right is to take it to a competent distributor shop and have them set the advance curve up with more initial advance. Most good distributor technicians can, from experience, put the advance curve fairly close to what is needed at the low-end.

If a relatively large cam is used, then it could be that your stock HEI is going to run out of spark before the cam runs

To make the best of a moderately large cam and a fairly well-prepared engine, you may want to go to the extent of installing a shift kit. Beware of shift kits that hit too hard in the shifts, however. If you have a strong motor in front of a 350 Turbo Hydramatic transmission, hard shifts can lead to breakages in parts.

Hard shifts are uncomfortable to the passengers and driver, detrimental to the transmission, and serve no useful purpose in terms of added performance. A softer shift may well wear out clutches quicker, but at least your transmission will last a lot longer.

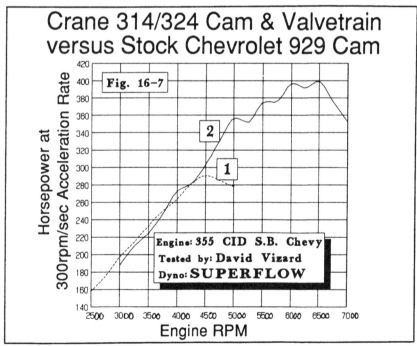

Figure 16-7: *Just how much power can be achieved with cam and valvetrain modifications? Well, I'm not saying that this is the ultimate that can be achieved by a long shot, but changing the camshaft and rockers on my test engine resulted in 105hp increase. As you can see from the graph, that is a pretty healthy amount of additional power. If the compression ratio had been optimized for the bigger cam, even more power would have been realized.*

out of breathing. The stock HEI is very good at delivering high-output sparks at low rpm, but the spark is definitely on the way out at 5500rpm. The only way to preserve the spark at rpm higher than this is to run closer gaps, or get yourself the components necessary to hop up your HEI distributor.

If you have to make changes to the distributor to allow it to spark to 7000rpm, then some fairly major changes are needed. With this in mind it's worthwhile to consider getting a distributor custom-built for the job.

I recommend Performance Distributors in Memphis. This company works closely with Competition Cams, and has a great deal of experience in matching distributor curves to cam specs. Every distributor is bench tested prior to shipping, and you can order various options including high-output coils and special modules. With these changes the Performance Distributors' HEI can put a healthy spark into a relatively large gap at rpm exceeding 7000.

If you're pushing for more rpm than that, with an external coil it can be made to fire up to 9000rpm, which should be plenty for most street applications.

Once the ignition timing is as required, it's necessary to look at the calibration of the carburetor. Usually, the most obvious problem when installing a big cam is that the engine is more reluctant to idle smoothly. It may be partly due to the carburetor because the amount of vacuum involved with a long-period cam is less than with a short-period cam.

A reduction in vacuum also means a reduced signal for idle circuit operation, which usually means bigger idle jets and an increase in the idle butterfly opening. Because the manifold vacuum is less, the amount of fuel that is properly atomized at idle is now less. Add to this the fact that the exhaust pollution from the extra overlap is likely to be greater, and we can see that there exists all the ingredients for a rough-idling engine. Because of this, all the carburetor settings become that much more critical.

The carburetor will probably require larger idle jets, but the most noticeable aspect likely to cause problems will be the transition circuit. To get the engine to idle it may be necessary to set the butterflies open a relatively large amount. On a Holley carburetor these butterflies may be well past most of the transition slot.

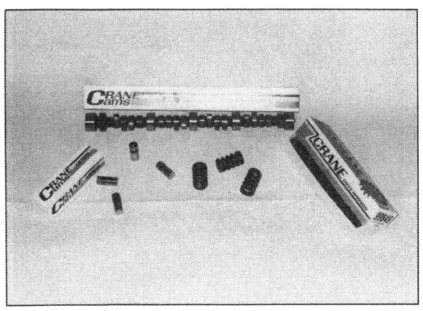

Many of the cam manufacturers complain that one of the biggest problems they encounter with simple cam changes is the fact that the end users are reluctant to buy lifters and springs because they feel their own are in good enough condition. But without new lifters, the cam will wipe itself out, and without the correct springs, the extra lift could bring about coil binding on the originals, and the cam will wipe itself out. Unless you know exactly what you're doing, take advice from the cam manufacturers as to what you will need to make your cam work.

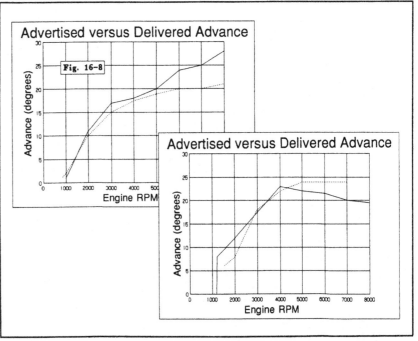

Figure 16-8: *Watch out for those off-the-shelf curve kits that are supposed to do all sorts of wonderful things for your ignition timing. They rarely deliver what they're supposed to—the only effective way (other than luck) of getting the ignition curve right on your particular distributor, assuming you know what's needed, is to have it re-curved in a distributor shop that specializes in such things. As you can see from these graphs, what you buy over the counter in your speed shop could be just as far off, if not further. If you are stuck for a source, I use distributors built by Performance Distributors of Memphis.*

This Gill Mink-built 350 small-block cranked out some 365hp on the dyno. A lot of attention went into the engine, such as fully ported 186 iron heads, matching the compression to the cam, and porting the intake manifold (notice the intake manifold is a stock iron one). The cam selected was a relatively short cam; the engine could pull from as little as 400 in high gear with a manual transmission, and on the dragstrip it could eat a 1992 Corvette alive. All this in a 1970½ Camaro.

With cams over 280 degrees, the power-band is likely to move up into an rpm range where the stock HEI ignition cannot really deliver the goods in terms of spark out. However, the convenience of an HEI has much to commend it, so it's worthwhile hopping it up. Competition Distributors offers special modules and high output coils.

Trying to move away in traffic by giving the carburetor some throttle will move the butterfly completely past the transition slot, yet its airflow requirement won't be enough to start pulling on the main jet. This means that the engine will suffer a severe lean spot, and may even completely cut out.

If this problem exists, the solution is to drill a small hole in the butterfly, to allow a portion of the idle air through. This allows the butterfly to be closed much further, so that it can now operate over a greater portion of the transition slot. Of course, putting a hole in the butterfly is going to mean a substantial increase in the idle jet size because the communicated signal to the jet is now reduced.

Another aspect you need to consider is that the pump jets will probably be inadequate, and so may the power valve restriction channel and the main jets. Bear in mind when calibrating a Holley carburetor that the main jet is supposed to calibrate the high-speed cruise, not the full power circuit. The full power circuit is controlled mostly by the power valve restriction channel. Many cams fail to deliver what they are supposed to by virtue of the fact that the carbs they are used with are never dialed in properly.

If you're having difficulty calibrating your Holley carburetor, then I thoroughly recommend using Edelbrock's Weber Power Plate Conversion. It allows all of the circuits to be altered much easier by using Weber jets, emulsion tubes, and air correctors. All circuits, including the idle circuit, transition circuit, high-speed cruise, and main circuit can be calibrated very closely with a lot less hassle than on a regular Holley.

If a big cam is to be used, it's tempting to install a big carburetor. The only problem is that large carburetors can exaggerate the lack of low-end power. The worst offender in the Holley range is the 850cfm unit. Not necessarily because it is 850cfm, but because it has the worst booster-signal to cfm passed ratio of any Holley carburetor. If you suspect your engine needs a carburetor as big as 850cfm, yet you still want to maintain as much low-end horsepower as possible, then I suggest that you use one of the smaller carburetors as a basis, and modify it.

Alternatively, you may want to get a professional job done by one of the more competent carburetor modifying companies. I thoroughly recommend Braswell Carburetion in Tucson, Arizona, for the job. However, this company does most of its work for professional racers. It produces a top-quality product, so you must expect to pay accordingly. If you call them, do not expect free advice.

The cost of a custom-modified carburetor is almost as much as that of a Holley fuel-injection kit. When it comes to optimizing part-throttle requirements, the Holley fuel-injection kit can produce better results more simply and speedily in terms of idle, part-throttle fuel economy, and response than a stock Holley carburetor. It is easy to set up since it's just a question of adjusting knobs until the best performance is obtained. This being the case, it's a good idea to look at fuel injection if you intend using a long-period cam.

Competition Distributors also offers a range of vacuum cans to tailor your distributor. Or better yet, send them your distributor and they'll rebuild it to the required specification. They're usually good, and they work in close conjunction with Competition Cams, so they have a lot of experience in tailoring centrifugal and vacuum advance curves to suit particular cams.

If you're trying to make your engine have as broad a power band as possible, then don't go too big on your carburetor. Use a K&N Stubstack, and it will add cfm to the carburetor without losing its low-end tractability. This gives you the opportunity to have an engine making good torque output at both ends of the rpm range.

Buying a Camshaft and Valvetrain 17

This is going to be a short chapter, but even so it will be important. If you've read and absorbed even 50 percent of what's in this book, you'll be in a much better position to choose the type of cam and timing figures required for your engine.

My basic advice is to choose your cam company carefully. Ask yourself if they have adequate research and development facilities of their own to develop their camshafts. Are they working with enough successful racers to be right on the cutting edge of what is needed? Can they produce the quality? And last of all, can you afford their prices?

In the past, many magazine article features have advocated buying both your cam and valvetrain from one manufacturer. This is certainly good advice, especially if you are inexperienced in this area. By buying all of your parts from one manufacturer you will be drawing on their experience. Once you know what you're doing with your cam and valvetrain, and have worked with various combinations, there's nothing precluding a mix-and-match type deal.

Of course, you may want something special in the way of a camshaft. Many cam companies are prepared to work with their customers to produce set-ups to suit their needs. Such services carry an appropriate price, though. There are many other cam companies that provide satisfactory service.

I've worked successfully with Crane, Competition Cams, Elgin Cams, Iskenderian, and Ultradyne Racing. To the best of my knowledge, all of these companies use advanced computer programs to generate profiles, and if they don't have a profile in stock to do the job you want, they can work one up, although going that route may be expensive.

On occasion, I've also used Harvey Crane's services as a consultant. Having left Crane Cams, Harvey now acts as an independent consultant and is a source that I recommend to serious race teams that have a valvetrain problem. However, be warned—Harvey's services do not come cheap. His charges per hour are similar to that of a good attorney. But paying out that kind of money ensures that you are getting the advice of a top professional who is recognized the world over as an expert in cam technology.

Computers are making great strides in cam design and production and achieving some amazingly fast turnaround rates. For instance, Bob Glidden phoned Competition Cams with a requirement for a special camshaft at about two o'clock one afternoon. The requirement entailed designing a new profile, making a master, then grinding the cam. From conceptual discussions to the shipping of the cam, finished and ready to install, took six hours. Twenty years ago, it may have taken six days of round-the-clock work.

Apart from the actual production of the cam lobe, there may be other engineering services that you require. For instance, if you need the cam to survive under arduous conditions, you might consider having it hard faced. This process involves grinding the surface of the cam down somewhat, and then building it up with a hard-facing alloy, and then regrinding the cam on the hard facing. It's an expensive process, but it does produce a near bullet-proof flat-tappet cam. I've had limited experience with this process, and the only cam company I've used for hard-face cams is Elgin Cams. But as of this writing, the cams are still being used in race engines and have been for some six years.

Sources

Allan Lockheed & Associates
PO Box 10828
Golden, CO 80401-0600

Andrews Products Inc.
5212 N. Shapland Avenue
Rosemont, IL 60018

APT
561 Iowa Avenue
Annex E
Riverside, CA 92507

Audie Technology
RD2, Box 201-D
Verona, NY 13478

B&M Automotive Products
9152 Independence Avenue
Chatsworth, CA 91311

BHJ Products
37530 Enterprise Court
Newark, CA 94560

Braswell Carburetion
1650 E. 18th Street
Tucson, AZ 85719

Brzezinski Racing Products
W229, N5087 Duplainville Road
Pewaukee, WI 53072

C&G Porting
2712 N. Columbus Boulevard
Tucson, AZ 85712

Cloyes Gear & Products
4520 Beidler Road
Willoughby, OH 44094

Competition Cams
3406 Democrat Road
Memphis, TN 38118

Cosworth Engineering Inc. (USA)
23205 Early Avenue
Torrance, CA 90505

Cosworth Engineering Inc. (UK)
St. James Mill Road
Northampton
NN5 5JJ England

Crane Cams
530 Fentress Boulevard
Daytona Beach, FL 32014

Crower Cam & Equipment
3333 Main Street
Chula Vista, CA 92011

Edelbrock Corporation
411 Coral Circle
El Segundo, CA 90245

Elgin Cams
55 Perry Street
Redwood City, CA 94063

Erson Cams
550 Mallory Way
Carson City, NV 89701

Garret Automotive
3201 N. Lomita Boulevard
Torrance, CA 90505

Holley Replacement Parts Division
11955 E. Nine Mile Road
Warren, MI 48090

Howard Stewart Engine Components
108 N. Main Street
High Point, NC 27262

Iskenderian Racing Cams
16020 S. Broadway
Gardena, CA 90248

Jessel Engineering
1720 Route 34 North
Wall, NJ 07719

Keith Black Systems Inc.
5630 Imperial Highway
South Gate, CA 90280

Latham Supercharger Co.
31166 Via Colinas
West Lake Village, CA 91362

Lazer Cams
2895 Sanderwood Drive
Memphis, TN 38118

Manley Performance
13 Race Street
Bloomfield, NJ 07003

Moroso Performance Sales
80 Carter Drive
Guildford, CT 06437

Motor Machine & Supply
2643 N. 1st Avenue
Tucson, AZ 85719

Nitron Inc.
300 Canal Street
Lawrence, MA 01840

Paxton Superchargers
929 Olympic Boulevard
Santa Monica, CA 90404

Performance Distributors
2699 Barris Drive
Memphis, TN 38132

Performance Techniques
346 South "I" Street
Unit 3
San Bernardino, CA 92410

Performance Trends Inc.
PO Box 573
Dearborn Heights, MI 48127

Polydyne Coatings
Polymer Dynamics Inc.
4116 Siegal
Houston, TX 77009

Quadrant Scientific
639 W. Dahlia Street
Louisville, CO 80027

Racing Systems Analysis (RSA)
PO Box 7676
Phoenix, AZ 85011

Rhoads Lifters
PO Box 830
Taylor, AZ 85939

Sealed Power Corporation
100 Terrace Plaza
Muskegon, MI 49443

Steve Jennings Equipment
1401 E. Bochard Street
Santa Ana, CA 92705

Summers Bros. Inc.
530 S. Mountain Avenue
Ontario, CA 91762

SuperFlow Corporation
3512 N. Tejon
Colorado Springs, CO 80907

Swain Tech Coatings
35 Main Street
Scottsville, NY 14546

T&D Machine Products
5734 Bankfield Avenue
Culver City, CA 90230

TRW Inc.
8001 E. Pleasant Valley
Cleveland, OH 44131

Ultradyne Racing Cams
8678 Whitworth
Southaven, MS 38671

Vortech Engineering Inc.
5351 Bonsai Avenue
Moorpark, CA 93021

Weiand Automotive Industries
2316 San Fernando Road
Los Angeles, CA 90065

Whipple Industries
3292½ N. Weber
Fresno, CA 93722

Index

CPSIA information can be obtained
at www.ICGtesting.com
Printed in the USA
BVOW04s0744101117

PP8262900001B/1/P